Satiric TV in the Americas

SATIRIC TV IN THE AMERICAS

Critical Metatainment as Negotiated Dissent

Paul Alonso

OXFORD
UNIVERSITY PRESS

Oxford University Press is a department of the University of Oxford. It furthers
the University's objective of excellence in research, scholarship, and education
by publishing worldwide. Oxford is a registered trade mark of Oxford University
Press in the UK and certain other countries.

Published in the United States of America by Oxford University Press
198 Madison Avenue, New York, NY 10016, United States of America.

© Oxford University Press 2018

First issued as an Oxford University Press paperback, 2020

CIP data is on file at the Library of Congress
ISBN 978-0-19-063650-0 (hardcover) | ISBN 978-0-19-753749-7 (paperback)

To Nina and Solange

CONTENTS

ACKNOWLEDGMENTS

I want to thank Rosental Alves, Mercedes Lynn de Uriarte, Bob Jensen, Dustin Harp, and Henry Dietz for their encouragement of my academic and professional path at the University of Texas at Austin. I also want to acknowledge the contributions and comments of the following colleagues and friends: Pablo Lapegna, Alejandro Martínez, Ingrid Bachmann, Teresa Correa, Laura Dixon, and Amber Day. Finally, I'm grateful to the Ivan Allen College of Liberal Arts, at Georgia Tech, for all the support in the completion of this book.

CHAPTER 1

Introduction

TV Satire and Critical Metatainment in the Americas

In times of global infotainment, the crisis of modern journalism, the omnipresence of celebrity culture and reality TV, and the colonization of public discourse by media spectacle and entertainment, new satiric media have emerged as prominent critical voices on social, cultural, and political issues. In the United States, comedians like Jon Stewart and Stephen Colbert were considered two of the most influential "journalists" of the country, the fake news magazine *The Onion* has played a critical role in reframing the news agenda in the post 9/11 era, and President Obama plugged sociopolitical information on the online satiric show *Between Two Ferns*. In France, the most outrageous terrorist attack on freedom of expression was directed toward the satiric magazine *Charlie Hebdo* on January 7, 2015, causing the deaths of 12 people and highlighting the role that satire plays in today's sociopolitical discourse. In the Trump era, the emblematic *Saturday Night Live (SNL)* and many other (global) satirists have taken an aggressive role in ridiculing an administration that accuses the media of disseminating "fake news."

The increasing importance of satire has overlapped with significant changes in the relation between news reporting, entertainment media, and politics during the past decades. Boundaries between journalism and entertainment and between public affairs and pop culture have become difficult to discern. Journalism mingles with show business. Celebrities make the news and become politicians. Politicians entertain people and become celebrities. Political journalists embrace entertainment formats.

Comedians mimic reporters covering politics. Infotainment arose as a global phenomenon, highly encouraged since the start of commercial TV. The "reality" portrayed in the media often resembles a 24-hour spectacle covered and broadcast live with a tabloid approach. Paparazzi, talk shows, and reality shows rank among the most popular TV genres.

Increasingly, the public is dissatisfied with news, and press credibility is diminishing in the United States (Mitchell & Rosenstiel, 2012). This overall dissatisfaction, coupled with the rise of the Internet and declining print advertising revenues, has helped lead the journalism industry into an economic and institutional crisis (Bennett, 2001; Kovach & Rosenstiel, 2001; Mitchell & Rosenstiel, 2012). Surveys show that newspapers' primary audience is over 40 years old and that most young people (ages 18–29) turn to late-night television and comedy shows, rather than traditional news media, for news ("Americans Spending More Time Following the News," 2010). Likewise, media producers now consider it essential to include the E-factor (the need to make it entertaining) in the majority of cultural products. Online media, the most vibrant communication venue, continues its search for a profitable business model when an overload of information makes it difficult to discern its legitimacy and value. This occurs in the midst of concerns about the public's ignorance of the political process and civic disengagement (Buckingham, 2000; Delli Carpini & Keeter, 1996; Entman, 1989; Putman, 2001), the consolidation of a society of spectacle (Debord, 1977; Kellner, 2003, 2005), and contemporary society's obsession with celebrity culture (Gamson, 1994; Marshall, 1997, 2006; Turner, 2004) and reality TV (Escoffery, 2006; Turner, 2010).

In this context, new satiric TV shows have gained increasing political, social, and cultural influence and power in today's societies. In *Satiric TV in the Americas*, I analyze some of the most representative and influential satiric TV shows in the Americas, focusing on cases in Argentina, Peru, Ecuador, Mexico, and the United States. The programs adopted a critical role in their respective countries, challenging the status quo, traditional journalism, and/or the prevalent local media culture. They not only responded to their specific national, cultural, social, and political contexts but also demonstrated important similarities: They parody journalistic/ entertainment genres questioning their authority and values, use humor to develop sociopolitical and cultural critiques, and engage in a discursive struggle over the notion of "truth" in the media. Besides the obvious difference of platforms (national or cable TV for most of the cases, and online TV for the cases analyzed in Chapter 6), the case studies also bifurcate into two subgroups: on the one hand, the shows that overtly parody the news agenda or develop a news reporting function (*Last Week Tonight*

With John Oliver and its predecessors *The Daily Show With Jon Stewart* and *The Colbert Report* in the United States, Brozo's *El Mañanero* and *El Pulso de La República* in Mexico, and Bayly's *El Francotirador* in Peru) and on the other hand, the shows that develop a critique on today's society of media spectacle, the entertainment industry, and celebrity culture and their role in the reproduction of social prejudices (Capusotto's *Peter Capusotto y sus videos* and Malena Pichot's *Cualca* in Argentina, and *Enchufe TV* in Ecuador).

    Satiric TV in the Americas seeks to illuminate the phenomenon of satire as resistance and negotiation in public discourse, the role of entertainment media as a site where sociopolitical tensions are played out, and the changing notions of journalism in today's democratic societies. In this book I argue that new forms of postmodern satire have played an unprecedented role at the heart of public debate and political communication, filling the gaps left not only by traditional journalism and commercial media but also by weak social institutions and discredited political elites. I do not contend that these new types of postmodern satire replace journalism or other nonfiction genres, but rather that they constitute radically new forms of negotiated dissent that respond, at the national and global level, to the relation between power and media, the evolution of media spectacle and infotainment as a primary form of political communication, and the connection between national traumas, social tensions, and popular culture. In order to demonstrate these ideas, I address the following questions: What is the critical dialogue that contemporary satiric TV establishes with mainstream journalism and media in the context of an economic and institutional crisis of journalism and the overwhelming presence of spectacle and infotainment in public discourse? What has been the main role of satiric TV in today's political communication and national democracies? How are satiric discourses constructed in order to develop criticism and transgression? What are the carnivalesque elements of satiric TV and what role do they play in satire's discursive struggle to question "truth" in today's media? Does satiric TV have any impact on the reality it criticizes? If so, how does it intervene in reality? Through a methodological approach based on discourse and textual analysis of the shows, the hosts' personas, and representative media contents, I answer these questions by offering three insights: First, after presenting a theoretical framework on global infotainment, spectacle, celebrity culture, media hybridity, satire, and carnival, I contextualize, describe, and connect the cases in relation to the national contexts to which they react.[1] Second, I analyze the discourse

---

1. In contrasting these satiric cases, I pay attention to the relation between media and political systems, because "one cannot understand the news media without

and specific critiques developed by the satirists and their critical dialogue with the local media culture, evaluating the cases' particularities and evolution. Third, I briefly explore the links between the cases and their national satiric traditions as well as their influence on the emergence of new local satiric experiments on the Web. Lastly, I scrutinize the cultural role they have played in their societies, drawing conclusions based on their specific platforms and national contexts while interpreting the similarities and differences among the cases. From a broader scope, I evaluate what we can learn about today's democracies and their contradictions through the analysis of symptomatic satiric media while extending and refining the literature on contemporary satire. While there is significant academic research on recent U.S. satiric infotainment, the phenomenon in Latin America remains unexplored. This book is the first to map, contextualize, and analyze relevant cases to understand the relation between political information, social and cultural dissent, critical humor, and entertainment in the region. It also shows that, as satiric formats travel to a particular national context, they are appropriated in different ways and adapted to local circumstances, thus having distinctive implications.

MEDIA SPECTACLE AND GLOBAL INFOTAINMENT

Spectacle has always been a key component of power. Emperors, kings, and later presidents and dictators have cultivated spectacles as part of their practices of social control. While the term "spectacle" refers to an event or image that is particularly striking in its visual display to the point of instigating awe in spectators, the idea of spectacle has come to mean an empty, media-obsessed, image-saturated world that numbs viewers with an attack of spectacular images (Sturken, 2008). All the cases analyzed in this book exist within the context of today's societies of spectacle, a concept first developed by French theorist Guy Debord in the 1960s. It describes a media and consumer society organized around the production and consumption of images, commodities, and staged events. For Debord (1977), the spectacle is a tool of pacification and depoliticization; it is a permanent

---

understanding the nature of the state, the system of political parties, the pattern of relations between economic and political interests, and the development of civil society, among other elements of social structure" (Hallin & Mancini, 2004, p. 8). As Hallin and Mancini (2004) argued, while we can assume that a media system "reflects" other aspects of social structure, there is evidence that media institutions have an impact of their own on the other social structures. It is in the intersection between these spheres that journalism and satire operate.

"opium war" that stupefies social subjects and distracts them from other tasks of social life.

Since classical Greece and ancient Rome, spectacle has been used for political purposes in diverse historical periods (such as imperial Spain during the counterreformation, Nazi Germany, or Latin American populism). More recently, telepopulists from the Right (Fujimori in Peru, Menem in Argentina, Collor de Melo in Brazil, and Donald Trump in the United States) or the Left (mainly Hugo Chávez in Venezuela, who even hosted his own TV show, *Aló Presidente*) have used spectacle and infotainment to connect with the masses. In the 1930s, the Frankfurt School theorists analyzed cultural industries and mass culture in organized capitalism (both in its fascist and democratic forms) as new types of ideological control that lead to a totally administered or "one-dimensional" society (Horkheimer & Adorno, 1972; Marcuse, 1964). For Baudrillard (1983b) the triumph of spectacle over meaning gave rise to an era of simulation, a process that replaces the "real" with the "virtual," generating simulacra, representations of the real. Žižek (2002), for example, has interpreted the 9/11 terrorist attacks as a spectacle of terrorism that connected with Hollywood films' questioning of audiences' notions of reality as their ultimate spectacular experience. In this scenario, the mass media has been one of the main channels of spectacle. Kellner (2003, 2005) has posited that in today's world, media spectacle has colonized most aspects of social life:

> Media spectacles are those phenomena of media culture that embody contemporary society's basic values, serve to initiate individuals into its ways of life, and dramatize its controversies and struggles, as well as its modes of conflict resolution. They include media extravaganzas, sporting events, political happenings and those attention-grabbing occurrences that we call news—a phenomenon that itself has been subjected to the logic of spectacle and tabloidization in the era of the media sensationalism, political scandal and contestation. (Kellner, 2003, p. 2)

At the same time, the move toward a society of spectacle has paralleled a global trend toward infotainment and tabloidization in media content. Infotainment refers to a "cluster of program types that blur traditional distinctions between information-oriented and entertainment-based genres of television programming" (Baym, 2008, p. 2276). Global infotainment also means "the globalization of a U.S.-style ratings-driven television journalism which privileges privatized soft news—about celebrities, crime, corruption and violence—and presents it as a form of spectacle, at the expense of news about political, civic and public affairs" (Thussu, 2007a, p. 8).

According to Altheide (2004), today news and politics must conform to an entertainment-driven media logic. This process was intensified during the 1990s, a period of unprecedented decay in international broadcast journalism. In the United States, a 1997 study by the Project for Excellence in Journalism noted: "There has been a shift toward lifestyle, celebrity, entertainment and celebrity crime/scandal in the news, and away from government and foreign affairs ("Changing Definitions of News," 1998). Kovach and Rosenstiel (2001) argued that profit-oriented journalism and the combination of infotainment and political spin affected news agendas. They suggested four main reasons for this: the 24/7 cycle with its appetite for live news; the proliferation of news networks; increasingly sophisticated methods of news management and the growing importance of "spin"; and a ratings-driven news industry that promotes a "blockbuster mentality," privileging dramatic and entertainment reports over other forms of political news. Interestingly, *The Daily Show* (the predecessor of *Last Week Tonight With John Oliver*) began during the 1990s. Jaime Bayly, one the most representative Peruvian fiction writers of the 1990s, hosted popular late-night shows during that decade (when he became popular nationally and internationally), before inaugurating *El Francotirador* in 2001. Brozo, the subversive clown created by comedian Victor Trujillo, also made his debut on Mexican TV in the 1990s before hosting *El Mañanero*. Diego Capusotto was one of the most notable comedians who participated in *De la Cabeza, Todo por Dos Pesos,* and *ChaChaCha*, the most iconic comedy shows of the last decade of the 20th century on Argentinean TV.

CELEBRITY CULTURE AND IDENTITY

One of the products consolidated by media spectacle and global infotainment is celebrity culture, now not only the subject of entertainment media, but also increasingly an integral element of much hard news and current affairs coverage. For Daniel Boorstin, a "celebrity is a person who is well-known for their well-knownness" (Turner, 2004, p. 5). Celebrities are anyone the public is interested in for whatever reason. They are especially remarkable not because they possess a particular level of economic, political, or religious power or wisdom, but because what they do and their way of life arouse considerable interest. Although they enjoy some of the social privileges of an elite, they are a powerless elite, objects of an interest over which they have no control (Turner, Bonner, & Marshall, 2000). In practice, however, the distinction between celebrity and other kinds of social and political elite status becomes less clear. Even those who do possess institutional power—like high-profile politicians—frequently choose to represent themselves through the modes used for celebrities. According to Langer (1998), today virtually any construction of elites depicts the individuals concerned as remarkable simply by featuring them in terms of "doings and ways of life." This implies that celebrity is not a property of specific individuals. Rather, it is constituted discursively by the way the individual is represented by image-makers. In this sense, celebrity is constructed by others rather than inherent (Marshall, 1997).

Today's media culture encourages everyone to think of themselves as potential celebrities possessing unique gifts (Hedges, 2009). In this culture of narcissism, the subject feels special, entitled, and unique. In a society of spectacle, the culture of personality demands of all the role of a performer: Life itself is like a movie in which we are "at once performance artists in, and audiences for, a grand ongoing show" (Gabler, 1998, p. 4). This fabricated and theatrical culture becomes, as Boorstin (1961) noted, more real than reality, and the public can no longer distinguish between truth and fiction. People then interpret reality through illusion:

> When opinions cannot be distinguished from facts, when there is no universal standard to determine truth in law, in science, in scholarship, or in reporting the events of the day, when the most valued skill is the ability to entertain, the world becomes a place where lies become true . . . Creators, who make massive profits selling illusions, have a vested interest in maintaining the power structures they control. The fantasy of celebrity culture is not designed simply to entertain. It is designed to keep us from fighting back. (Hedges, 2009, p. 51)

As Turner et al. (2000) highlight, the interest in celebrities today can be seen as another symptom of the media's decreasing role as an entity that prioritizes the dissemination of information and that instead increasingly aligns with a model that more directly participates in constructing, circulating, and questioning identities. In a postmodern culture characterized by the overwhelming change and reproduction of images where the spectacle of reality becomes a "hyperreality of imploded meaning" (Baudrillard, 1983b, 1994), the media becomes essential in the relation between identity and the postmodern individual. The philosophical proclamation of "the death of the subject" implied the discursive disintegration of the modern individual (the project of the Enlightenment and Rationalism informed with ego, causality and agency) as a fictitious construction (Derrida, 1978). Consequently, the postmodern individual has embarked on a personal quest for meaning, constructing social reality based on his particular needs in terms of "fantasy, humor, the culture of desire, and immediate gratification" (Rosenau, 1992, p. 53). Thus, the postmodern individual, without a solid or particular identity, is characterized by fragmentation. In a world of circulating fictions with no reference to reality, the production of cultural identities ("selves") actually seduces the individual himself (Baudrillard, 1983a, 1994). In this sense, identity is constructed and reconstructed through the constant negotiation of the self within a context, making it a malleable narrative that is situated and contingent (Edley & Wetherell, 1997; Stapleton, 2000). In order to attain a coherent and acceptable version of the self, the postmodern subject exists within a struggle to give meaning to his life by giving meaning to meaningless representations. For Caldwell (2009), the postmodern individual creates an unfixed pseudo-identity through the act of consumption. It becomes a continuous cultural performance of an unattainable identity because of the endless possibilities of consumption. In postmodern culture, as noted by Caldwell, what are being consumed are images and culturally available representations, where celebrity culture becomes a vast and renewable source. The relationship between media spectacle, celebrity culture, and identity is, therefore, especially relevant for this book. Not only are all the satiric TV hosts celebrities in their countries and main (sometimes, ironic) players of local show business, but some of them also question local and global identities by developing a systematic critique on the role that media and celebrity culture play in their discursive construction.

TABLOIDIZATION, HYBRIDITY, AND DISCURSIVE INTEGRATION IN THE POST-NETWORK ERA

The evolution of global infotainment and media spectacle is closely related to the process of tabloidization in the media. While the term "tabloid" was initially used to describe smaller sized newspapers, it has also come to refer to the idea of sensational news coverage (Grabe, 2008). Stories dealing with celebrities, crime, sex, disasters, accidents, and public fears have been labeled tabloid topics. While the tabloidization of television has been perceived as a process of declining standards of content within an increasingly consumerist environment (Bourdieu, 1998; Dahlgren, 1995; Langer, 1998), it has also been interpreted as a democratizing tool by its capacity to engage audiences and its frequent inclusion of non-elite people, issues, and values (Biressi & Nunn, 2008; Sparks & Tulloch, 2000). At the same time, it has been argued that sensationalism plays an important role in maintaining a society's commonly shared notions of decency and morality by publicly showcasing what is unacceptable (Stevens, 1985). Stories about family conflicts, substance abuse, violence, disaster, and other disorders of everyday life are regarded by media producers as more significant to the lives of ordinary people than the traditional political and economic issues discussed by the elites.

In a historic period defined by media spectacles and tabloid culture, debates have become polarized: Is humanity becoming more stupid or has culture been democratized? Since the advent of mass media, there has been a tension between "dumbing down" the public or raising them up, between educating or entertaining the crowd, between the will of the people or the good of the people, and between the market and the ethical. Nevertheless, scholars like Thussu (2007b) argue that debates about how infotainment and tabloidization "dumb down" audiences mask their dimension as part of a wider process of corporate colonization with political, economic, military, and cultural vectors of neoliberal imperialism.

While neither journalists nor critics agree precisely on the definition of tabloidization, Bird (2008) summarizes some key areas of the phenomenon that can be discussed as issues of style (a movement away from longer, complex, analytical modes into shorter, punchier narratives; an increasing emphasis on the personal tone; and greater use of visual images) or content (usually framed in terms of trivialization). These previous characteristics of tabloidization are similar to what Brants (1998) called the "infotainment scale," which also takes into account the topical focus of a given program as well as its format and style. On one end of the scale are those programs that contain factual content about policy matters packaged within a serious format. On the opposite end are shows that emphasize dramatic, personalized content within an informal format. Those two extremes, however, are idealized types, with various infotainment programs occupying a wide range of positions in between. Similarly, Delli Carpini and Williams (1994, 2001) suggested that infotainment is best understood as a phenomenon of border-crossing that problematizes the common assumptions that news is necessarily serious and that entertainment shows contain little in the way of sociopolitical significance. In this sense, media content and public discourse have been shaped by hybridization: the thorough melding of news, politics, show business, and marketing. Baym (2005) called this process "discursive integration," in which these once differentiated discourses "have lost their distinctiveness and are being melded into previously unimagined combinations" (262). The consequential hybrid programming also results from globalization and has a potentially wide range of implications for public information, political communication, and democratic discourse. Scholars have argued that globalization produces the emergence of a variety of "hybrid," "creolized," or "glocal" phenomena, in which local elements are incorporated within globalized forms and other combinations (Robertson, 1995). While hybridy and *mestizaje* are intrinsic characteristics of postcolonial societies, the production and consumption of cultural products represent a struggle for meanings between classes within countries, between high and popular cultures, and between local, national, and imported cultural traditions (Garcia Canclini, 1995; Kraidy, 2005). For Martin-Barbero (1993), it reveals the syncretic nature of popular culture that both adopts and resists the dominant culture and also transforms it. In this sense, hybridization describes a process in which elements of different cultures are synthesized together into new forms that reflect elements of the original cultures, but constitute distinct new ones (Garcia Canclini, 1995).

In this scenario, global formats must connect with local culture to reach audiences at new locations (Moran, 2009; Straubhaar, 2007). According to the notion of "cultural proximity," audiences tend "to prefer and select local or national cultural content that is more proximate and relevant to them" (Straubhaar, 1991, p. 43). The consequential process of hybridization then becomes a negotiation about how the global allows space for the local (Kraidy, 2005; Pieterse, 2009; Straubhaar, 2007). While audience preference still largely depends on cultural proximity of the local and the national (Straubhaar, 1991), regional programming also holds significance, highlighting the relevance of Latin America as a geo-linguistic market (Sinclair, 2004). Nevertheless, the national and the regional are far from being natural and homogeneous categories but rather are televisually manufactured and market-tailored products (Piñón, 2014). The satiric shows analyzed in this book are prevalent examples of hybrid products shaped by globalization and the phenomenon of discursive integration in media contents. As such, they reflect the permanent tensions within local/global cultures and power melees. Their willingness to transgress positions them in a particularly revealing space of glocal discursive struggles.

Today's hybrid, discursively integrated media contents exist within an unstable media environment. While TV remains the primary medium of mass communication (and the main source of news) in the Americas, technological developments have generated changes in the production, control, financing, and distribution of contents leading to a post-network or post-TV era, in which media content has increasingly become nonlinear data circulating across diverse platforms (Lotz, 2007; Spigel & Olsson, 2004). Traditional media producers have progressively lost control over where and when the audience, whose attention is spread over a variety of platforms, watches particular content. Jenkins (2006) explains this "paradigm shift" as a move from "medium-specific content toward content that flows across multiple media channels, toward the increased interdependence of communication systems, toward multiple ways of accessing media content, and toward ever more complex relations between top-down corporate media and bottom-up participatory culture" (Jenkins, 2006, p. 243). The resulting "convergence culture" can then also be seen as a complementary phenomenon that has paralleled the complex, hybrid process of discursive integration exemplified in today's satiric contents. In other words, not only is today's satire more hybrid than ever in terms of content, but it is also created and disseminated through a multiplatform and "convergence" mentality.

SATIRE, CARNIVAL, AND CRITICAL METATAINMENT

Infotainment and spectacle have usually been framed in negative ways for democracy and political communication (Bourdieu, 1998; Garcia Canclini, 2001; Postman, 1985). However, satirists have also used them to negotiate an appealing and critical voice. Popular TV shows like *The Daily Show With Jon Stewart* and *The Colbert Report* have proven to be influential in U.S. political communication and even political action (Baym, 2010; Day, 2011; Jones, 2010). Some critics have called these shows "neo-modern" journalism (Baym, 2005) or new types of public journalism (Faina, 2012), whereas others accuse them of promoting cynicism instead of civic engagement (Hart & Hartelius, 2007). This debate, however, is not new. Contemporary political satire, combined with infotainment in today's society of media spectacle, comes from an old literary tradition traced to Juvenal and Horace, and later, Swift and Twain. While there has been much debate about the definition of satire (Condren, 2012), it is frequently and imprecisely considered a subgenre of comedy because of its humorous component. But satire is a particular type of humor that ridicules human vices and follies through the use of parody, irony, travesty, and grotesquery, holding people accountable for their actions. Characterized by exaggeration and use of wit, satire is "an attack on or criticism of any stupidity or vice in the form of scathing humor," and it is also a critique to "dangerous religious, political, moral, or social standards" (Cuddon, 1991, p. 202). The satiric attack becomes then a "verbal aggression in which one aspect of historical reality is exposed to ridicule" (Fletcher, 1987, p. ix).

From the psychoanalysis perspective, Freud (1960) saw humor as a way to channel our aggression toward power. For Freud, "tendentious jokes" functioned similarly to dreams, giving voice to our unconscious feelings and repressed desires. This humorous pleasure is produced by "a disjunction between the way things are and the way they are represented in a joke, between expectation and actuality. Humor defeats our expectations by producing a novel actuality, by changing the situation in which we find ourselves" (Critchley, 2002, p. 1). In other words, satirical humor offers a lens for realizing that a certain accepted "reality" is not the only possible one. This humorous operation (and the consequential act of laughter) tends to be aggressive. Satire is a verbal attack that "passes judgment on the object of that attack, thereby enunciating a perceived breach in societal norms or values" (Gray, Jones, & Thompson, 2009, p. 12), while transforming human emotions and chaotic impulses (such as anger, indignation, or shame) into "a useful and artistic expression" (Test, 1991, p. 4).

Since ancient Greece, however, the nature and intentions of satiric humor have been ambivalent between cynicism and kynicism, the latter one associated more closely with contemporary political satire (ranging from Jon Stewart to *South Park*). While cynicism is the belief that there is no hope for change, that truth is dead, kynicism (a non-nihilistic form of cynicism) maintains that truth does exist and is worth saving from political and media manipulations (Higgie, 2014). Derived from the ancient Greek "kynismos," which encompasses a philosophy that seeks truth through subversive challenge rather than reasoned argument, kynicism originated with the philosopher Diogenes of Sinope, whom Plato is said to have called "Socrates gone mad" (Sloterdijk, 1988, p. 104). Labeled a "kyon," or dog, Diogenes chose to live poor and homeless, regularly defecating and masturbating in public spaces, thereby resembling an abandoned animal (Chaloupka, 1999). In contrast to the idealistic and civilized philosophies of his era, Diogenes' behavior was part of a "satirical resistance" to bring about "uncivil enlightment" (Sloterdijk, 1988, p. 102). His animal-like behavior was a way to expose the artificiality of social conventions, and to perform the ancient Cynic credo of "defacing the currency," a metaphor for kynical practice, which encouraged him to test and challenge "all usages and laws to see whether or not they had any genuine validity" (Cutler, 2005, p. 28). This practice is essentially connected with the kynic's exercise of free speech, or "parrehsia," which translates broadly as "saying everything" and "telling the truth as one sees it" (Monoson, 2000, pp. 52–53). As part of the performative nature of kynicism, audience participation is crucial; this is probably why Diogenes chose to live his life as a kynic in the busiest public spaces of Athens, and used spectacle to gather and then "confront its attracted audience with their own distorted values" (Bosman, 2006, p. 97). In order to achieve this, humor and satire were key to Diogenes' performances, allowing him to subvert social conventions and engage in outrageous behavior without alienating his audience entirely. Nevertheless, kynic satiric resistance should not be considered necessarily funny or comedic.

While comedy evokes laughter as an end in itself, satire uses laughter as a weapon and "against a butt existing outside the work itself" (Abrams, 1985, p. 166). Furthermore, laughter is certainly an important outcome for satire to have its full effect, but it is not a necessary feature of the genre: "Laughter is ultimately something satire may or may not produce within the audience; it is not something that resides in the artistic expression itself . . . Satire need not be funny" (Gray et al., 2009, p. 13). In today's global mediascape, saturated with television humor based on the constant repetition of jokes and prejudiced stereotypes (Mulkay, 1988), satire frequently runs the risk of not being funny or of being misunderstood. This is probably why satire has found its way onto television difficult, because producers and TV executives have always been reluctant to alienate audiences. In contrast to most television content, satire does not offer easily digestible meanings. It requires a level of sophistication that places difficult demands on audiences, such as a sharp state of awareness, mental participation, and shared knowledge. Nevertheless, satire performs the important function of saying what is otherwise unsaid, especially in certain sociopolitical contexts:

> When historical reality presents periods of social and political rupture (such as culture wars, hot wars, and unpopular leaders) or mind-numbing manufactured realities (such as celebrity culture, media spin, and news management), satire becomes a potent means for enunciating critiques and asserting unsettling truths that audiences may need or want to hear. (Gray et al., 2009, p. 15)

In this sense, as Test (1991) notes, "satire is mainly about a time and a place and people" (p. 35). It helps individuals to create connections to others, an imagined community based on the audience's moral commonality (Schutz, 1977, p. 332). Along these lines, satire connects at many levels with Bakhtin's conceptualizations of carnival, based on his analysis of the popular culture of 16th-century France, situating Rabelais's comic, satirical, and grotesque writing in the context of diversion, rituals, and spectacle. According to Bakhtin (1984), carnival—a prevailing spirit of fun mixed with social criticism—captures and rearticulates the sharp and cruel humor of ordinary people expressed in the unofficial spaces of popular culture where they can mock authority. Carnival, then, is marked by "the suspension of hierarchic distinctions and barriers among men and of certain norms and prohibitions of usual life" (Bakhtin, 1984, p. 15). Carnival behavior was transgressive (and for some critics, even revolutionary) because it overturned conventional oppositions (high and low, mind and body, the spiritual and the profane, culture and nature, male and female) and created no division between spectators and performers. It was a space of freedom through laughter embodied in the figure of the court jester, the one who is able to speak truth to power without getting his head cut off.

Critics of carnival maintain that it is not politically potent because, in the end, it can serve the purposes of the powerful—people have fun, reverse the hierarchies to mock the power, and then go back to an unreflective daily life. Thus, there ends the potential for transgression (Eco, 1984). The modern turn degraded the carnival spirit and its radical utopian character, gradually declining into a less challenging, more conservative "holiday mood" (Bakhtin, 1984, p. 33). Likewise, some characteristics of carnival culture (its embracing of bad taste, offensive and vulgar language, ritualistic degradation, and parody and its emphasis upon excess) are typical of tabloid media, which is energized by its relationship to "popular tastes for melodrama, scandal and sexual intrigue" (Glynn, 2000, p. 115). In fact, tabloid media tend to adopt a carnivalesque tone and idioms to hold on to their authoritative status as the voice of the people while mimicking carnival's tone of transgression (Convoy, 2002). They maintain the stance of being on the side of common sense and the little man against the powerful, even if, as media institutions, they belong to structures of the capitalist elite. In this sense, the tabloids' superficial carnivalesque language can be detrimental to the very constituency they claim to serve. The tabloid media redirect carnivalesque impulses into a circle of consumption and commodification (Convoy, 2002). They never attack the central ideologies of the status quo in regard to gender, nation, or the capitalist system. While medieval carnival conceived laughter as a transformative act, postmodern forms of entertainment tend to develop parody without a final target (Colletta, 2009).

As part of this tension between revolutionary and domesticated humor, the satiric cases analyzed in this book are inserted in an irreverent carnivalesque tradition, but they also negotiate their limits of transgression within commercial TV systems. They mock authority and traditional journalism and nonfiction genres. They parody officialdom with their spirit of fun mixed with social criticism while exposing the ubiquitousness of spectacle with a self-referential and metatextual approach, especially in relation to the entertainment industry and celebrity culture to which they belong and which they criticize. They target the powerful or challenge some aspects of the status quo (especially on issues of culture, politics, race, sexuality, or class). At the same time, they are part of the commercial media and their capitalist structure. Within this organization, these cases have been commercially successful, as they reveal fissures for sociopolitical criticism within a mediascape saturated with the conservative rhetoric of tabloid content. The previous characteristics configure my notion of "critical metatainment"—a postmodern-carnivalesque result of and a transgressive, self-referential reaction to the process of tabloidization and the cult of celebrity in the media spectacle era. This book, then, is an attempt to understand contemporary satiric media as distinctively postmodern, multilayered, and complex discursive objects that emerge from the collapse of modernity and its arbitrary dichotomies.

STRUCTURE OF THE BOOK

Chapter 2 analyzes *Last Week Tonight With John Oliver*, the political news satire show aired on HBO since 2014, and the latest development of the political infotainment trend in the United States that gained enormous influence with the popularity of Comedy Central's *The Daily Show With Jon Stewart* and then *The Colbert Report*. While *The Daily Show* satirized TV journalism's coverage of news and *The Colbert Report* parodied the conservative rhetoric in the media, *Last Week Tonight* presents investigations, generating in-depth coverage of national and international public interest issues. Chapter 2 analyzes *Last Week Tonight* in relation to the academic debates and scholarly work generated by its successful predecessors. By contextualizing and examining the show in relation to the evolution of political infotainment in the United States, I show how *Last Week Tonight* not only fills gaps left by mainstream media, but also takes satire to a more international, activist, and investigative level. Because U.S. political infotainment has been internationally influential, this chapter also serves to illuminate the debates about the genre to be applied to the Latin American cases, which have remained academically unexplored.

Chapter 3 takes the debate to Peru. In 2009, Jaime Bayly, one of the most influential TV journalists of the country, announced that he wanted to be the first bisexual, impotent, and agnostic president of Peru. He launched an atypical and unofficial electoral campaign, fueled by his irreverent and popular TV show *El Francotirador* (The Sniper). Bayly's yearlong virtual campaign increasingly gained importance and local and international media coverage. He even polled at 10% in Lima, the capital city, but ultimately dropped out of the race a few months before the elections. This chapter analyzes how Bayly constructed his ambiguous and contradictory media persona during his 30-year media career and how he capitalized on its political appeal in his electoral run while revealing social tensions in contemporary Peru. His intense, controversial, and sometimes transgressive life in the media is read as a symbol of how entertainment replaces other argumentative and informative forms of political communication in Peru, a deeply divided society with fragile social institutions, precarious democracy, and a discredited political class. Bayly's life in the media also illuminates how massive media spectacle became a contested arena to negotiate political power both during and since President Fujimori's authoritarian regime (1990–2000).

Similar to Bayly regarding his court jester role, *Brozo, el payaso tenebroso* (the shady clown)—a misogynistic, alcoholic, coarse, and marginal character—is one of the most popular and influential "journalists" in Mexico. His show, *El Mañanero*, has been broadcast on Mexican TV since 2000, when the 71-year regime of the Partido Revolucionario Institucional (PRI) ended. Chapter 4 analyzes the carnivalesque role of Brozo as a subversive and profane court jester able to confront with impunity the elites from the heart of the Mexican power de facto: Televisa, one of the biggest media conglomerates of the world with a problematic adhesion to political power. Connecting with the Mexican tradition of clowns and satiric underdogs, this chapter also examines Brozo's media performance and discursive configuration in relation to the history of institutionalized corruption and violence against journalists in Mexico.

From a different perspective and through sketches, *Peter Capusotto y sus videos* is an Argentinean satirical show that criticizes the entertainment industry in social and political terms. Hosted by actor and comedian Diego Capusotto, the popular show is broadcast on TV Pública (the state channel) in Argentina. Videos of the show are available online and have become popular throughout the region. Through fictional characters and a documentary/journalistic style, Capusotto ridicules celebrity culture and targets stereotypes exposing the inconsistencies of Argentinean devotion to popular culture icons, revealing their absurdities but also their influence and power. Chapter 5 analyzes the role of the show in deconstructing and questioning key aspects of the local urban identity reflected in popular culture, more specifically in rock music (*rock nacional*), a genre with a particular evolution and relevance in the country. Through the analysis of Bombita Rodríguez, Violencia Rivas, and Micky Vainilla, some of Capusotto's most famous characters, this chapter illustrates how the show's satirical approach demystifies Argentinean identities that exist within the realm of media spectacle while exposing sociopolitical tensions after the 2001 socioeconomic crisis and during the Kirchner governments. In this context, the show not only questions the contradictions of *rock nacional* but also develops a structural critique on identity and Argentinean politics and media culture.

Chapter 6 focuses on Latin American digital satire, analyzing first the case of *Enchufe.tv*, an online comedy series that satirizes Ecuadorian idiosyncrasies and local urban culture. *Enchufe.tv* has become the most popular online TV series in the country (also broadcast in national TV) and a regional phenomenon in Latin America. The show questions cultural stereotypes and social norms while adapting and parodying transnational audiovisual formats and entertainment genres. In the context of President Correa's attacks on the private media and freedom of expression, *Enchufe.tv* developed irreverent and commercially successful satiric content for local and international audiences. Through interviews with the producers and an analysis of *Enchufe.tv*'s content, this case illuminates how satiric transgression is negotiated in repressive media environments and how they adopt glocal strategies to connect with regional audiences. Second, I describe the cases of *El Pulso de La República*, an independent Mexican online satiric news show created in 2012 by comedian Chumel Torres; and *Cualca*, an Argentinean satiric sketch show focused on gender issues, created by feminist YouTube star Malena Pichot. These cases not only reveal successful models for the development of Latin American independent digital media but also exemplify how cultural globalization and hybridity operate in today's transnational entertainment and commercial critical humor.

Finally, in chapter 7, I detail my conclusions, returning to the questions posed earlier in this introduction. Summarizing the analysis of the cases in light of those questions, I contrast and compare the cases in order to illuminate similarities and differences. The final analysis also highlights the local implications of the global trend toward infotainment and spectacle, locating satire at a privileged intersection between transgression and media norms. Using the notion of "critical metatainment," I finally argue that the global trend toward political satire television should be understood as a space of "negotiated dissent," where sociopolitical and cultural tensions are played out.

REFERENCES

Abrams, M. (1985). *A glossary of literary terms* (5th ed.). Orlando, FL: Holt, Rinehart, and Winston.

Altheide, D. (2004). Media logic and political communication. *Political Communication, 21,* 293–296.

Americans spending more time following the news. (2010). *Pew Research Center.* Retrieved from http://www.people-press.org/2010/09/12/americans-spending-more-time-following-the-news/

Bakhtin, M. (1984). *Rabelais and his world.* Bloomington, IN: Indiana University Press.

Baudrillard, J. (1983a). On seduction. In M. Poster (Ed.), *Jean Baudrillard: Selected writings*. Stanford, CA: Stanford University Press.

Baudrillard, J. (1983b). *Simulations*. New York, NY: Semiotext(e).

Baudrillard, J. (1994). *Simulacra and simulation*. Ann Arbor, MI: University of Michigan Press.

Baym, G. (2005). The Daily Show: Discursive integration and the reinvention of political journalism. *Political Communication, 22*(3), 259–276.

Baym, G. (2008). Infotainment. In W. Donsbach (Ed.), *The International Encyclopedia of Communication* (pp. 2276–2280). Hoboken, NJ: Wiley-Blackwell.

Baym, G. (2010). *From Cronkite to Colbert: The evolution of broadcast news*. Boulder, CO: Paradigm.

Bennett, W. L. (2001). *News: The politics of illusion* (4th ed.). New York, NY: Longman.

Bird, S. E. (2008). Tabloidization. In W. Donsbach (Ed.), *The International Encyclopedia of Communication* (pp. 4947–4952). Hoboken, NJ: Wiley-Blackwell.

Biressi, A., & Nunn, H. (Eds.). (2008). *The tabloid culture reader*. New York, NY: Open University Press.

Boorstin, D. (1961). *The image: A guide to pseudo-events in America*. New York, NY: Atheneum.

Bosman, P. (2006). Selling cynicism: The pragmatics of Diogenes' comic performances. *The Classical Quarterly, 56*(1), 93–104.

Bourdieu, P. (1998). *On television*. New York, NY: New Press.

Brants, K. (1998). Who's afraid of infotainment? *European Journal of Communication, 13*(3), 315.

Buckingham, D. (2000). *The making of citizens: Young people, news, and politics*. London, U.K.: Routledge.

Caldwell, R. A. (2009). The unicorn is dead: Postmodernism, consumption, and the production of the "self." In B. G. Harden & R. Carley (Eds.), *Co-opting culture* (pp. 43–61). Lanham, MD: Lexington Books.

Chaloupka, W. (1999). *Everybody knows: Cynicism in America*. Minneapolis, MN: University of Minnesota Press.

Changing definitions of news. (1998). *Pew Research Center*. Retrieved from http://www.journalism.org/1998/03/06/changing-definitions-of-news/

Colletta, L. (2009). Political satire and postmodern irony in the age of Stephen Colbert and Jon Stewart. *Journal of Popular Culture, 42*(5), 856–874.

Condren, C. (2012). Satire and definition. *Humor: International Journal of Humor Research, 25*(4), 375–399. http://dx.doi.org/10.1515/humor-2012-0019

Conboy, M. (2002). *The press and popular culture*. London, U.K.: SAGE.

Critchley, S. (2002). *On humour*. New York, NY: Routledge.

Cuddon, J. A. (1991). *The Penguin dictionary of literary terms and literary theory*. London, U.K.: Penguin.

Cutler, I. (2005). *Cynicism from Diogenes to Dilbert*. Jefferson, NC: McFarland.

Dahlgren, P. (1995). *Television and the public sphere*. London, U.K.: SAGE.

Day, A. (2011). *Satire and dissent*. Bloomington, IN: Indiana University Press.

Debord, G. (1977). *The society of spectacle*. Detroit, MI: Red and Black.

Delli Carpini, M. X., & Keeter, S. (1996). *What Americans know about politics and why it matters*. New Haven, CT: Yale University Press.

Delli Carpini, M. X., & Williams, B. A. (1994). "Fictional" and "non-fictional" television celebrates Earth Day: Or, politics is comedy plus pretense. *Cultural Studies, 8*(1), 74–98.

Delli Carpini, M. X., & Williams, B. A. (2001). Let us infotain you: Politics in the new media environment. In W. L. Bennett & R. M. Entman (Eds.), *Mediated politics: Communication in the future of democracy* (pp. 160–181). New York, NY: Cambridge University Press.

Derrida, J. (1978). *Writing and difference*. Chicago, IL: University of Chicago Press.

Eco, U. (1984). The frames of comic freedom. In T. Sebeok (Ed.), *Carnival!* Berlin, Germany: Mouton.

Edley, N., & Wetherell, M. (1997). Jockeying for position: The construction of masculine identities. *Discourse & Society, 8*(2), 203–217.

Entman, R. (1989). *Democracy without citizens: Media and the decay of American politics*. New York, NY: Oxford University Press.

Escoffery, D. S. (Ed.). (2006). *How real is reality TV? Essays on representation and truth*. Jefferson, NC: McFarland.

Faina, J. (2012). Public journalism is a joke: The case of Jon Stewart and Stephen Colbert. *Journalism, 14*(4), 541–555.

Fletcher, M. D. (1987). *Contemporary political satire: Narrative strategies in the post-modern context*. Lanham, MD: University Press of America.

Freud, S. (1960). *Jokes and their relation to the unconscious*. London, U.K.: Hogarth.

Gabler, N. (1998). *Life the movie: How entertainment conquered reality*. New York, NY: Knopf.

Gamson, J. (1994). *Claims to fame: Celebrity in contemporary America*. Berkeley, CA: University of California Press.

Garcia Canclini, N. (1995). *Hybrid culture: Strategies for entering and leaving modernity*. Minneapolis, MN: University of Minnesota Press.

Garcia Canclini, N. (2001). *Citizens and consumers*. Minneapolis, MN: University of Minnesota Press.

Glynn, G. (2000). *Tabloid culture: Trash taste, popular power, and the transformation of American television*. Durham, NC: Duke University Press.

Grabe, M. (2008). Tabloid press. In W. Donsbach (Ed.), *The International Encyclopedia of Communication* (pp. 4945–4947). Hoboken, NJ: Wiley-Blackwell.

Gray, J., Jones, J., & Thompson, E. (Eds.). (2009). *Satire TV: Politics and comedy in the post-network era*. New York, NY: NYU Press.

Hallin, D. C., & Mancini, P. (2004). *Comparing media systems: Three models of media and politics*. Cambridge, U.K.: Cambridge University Press.

Hart, R. P., & Hartelius, E. J. (2007). The political sins of Jon Stewart. *Critical Studies in Media Communication, 24*(3), 263–272. http://dx.doi.org/10.1080/07393180701520991

Hedges, C. (2009). *The empire of illusion: The end of literacy and the triumph of spectacle*. New York, NY: Nation Books.

Higgie, R. (2014). Kynical dogs and cynical masters: Contemporary satire, politics, and truth-telling. *Humor: International Journal of Humor Research, 27*(2), 183–201.

Horkheimer, M., & Adorno, T. (1972). *Dialectic of enlightenment*. New York, NY: Continuum.

Jenkins, H. (2006). *Convergence culture: Where old and new media collide*. New York, NY: NYU Press.

Jones, J. (2010). *Entertaining politics: Satiric television and political engagement*. Lanham, MD: Rowman & Littlefield.

Kellner, D. (2003). *Media spectacle*. New York, NY: Routledge.

Kellner, D. (2005). *Media spectacle and the crisis of democracy: Terrorism, war, and election battles*. Boulder, CO: Paradigm.

Kovach, B., & Rosenstiel, T. (2001). *The elements of journalism: What newspeople should know and the public should expect*. New York, NY: Crown.

Kraidy, M. (2005). *Hybridity or the cultural logic of globalization*. Philadelphia, PA: Temple University Press.

Langer, J. (1998). *Tabloid television: Popular journalism and the "other news."* London, U.K.: Routledge.

Lotz, A. D. (2007). *The television will be revolutionized*. New York, NY: NYU Press.

Marcuse, H. (1964). *One-dimensional man*. Boston, MA: Beacon.

Marshall, P. D. (1997). *Celebrity and power: Fame in contemporary context*. Minneapolis, MN: University of Minnesota Press.

Marshall, P. D. (Ed.). (2006). *The celebrity culture reader*. New York, NY: Routledge.

Martin-Barbero, J. (1993). *Communications, culture and hegemony: From the media to mediations*. Newbury Park, CA: SAGE.

Mazella, D. (2007). *The making of modern cynicism*. Charlottesville, VA: University of Virginia Press.

Mitchell, A., & Rosenstiel, T. (2012). *The state of the news media 2012: An annual report on American journalism*. Washington, DC: Pew Research Center's Project for Excellence in Journalism.

Monoson, S. S. (2000). *Plato's democratic entanglements: Athenian politics and the practice of philosophy*. Princeton, NJ: Princeton University Press.

Moran, A. (2009). Global franchising, local customizing: The cultural economy of TV program formats. *Continuum: Journal of Media & Cultural Studies, 23*(2), 115–125.

Mulkay, M. (1988). *On humor: Its nature and its place in modern society*. New York, NY: Basil Blackwell.

Pieterse, J. N. (2009). *Globalization and culture: Global melange*. Lanham, MD: Rowman & Littlefield.

Piñón, J. (2014). Corporate transnationalism: The U.S. Hispanic and Latin American television industries. In A. Dávida & Y. Rivero (Eds.), *Contemporary latina/o media* (pp. 21–43). New York, NY: NYU Press.

Postman, N. (1985). *Amusing ourselves to death: Public discourse in the age of show business*. New York, NY: Penguin.

Putman, R. (2001). The strange disappearance of civic America. *The American Prospect*. Retrieved from http://prospect.org/article/strange-disappearance-civic-america

Robertson, R. (1995). Glocalization: Time-space and homogeneity-heterogeneity. In M. Featherstone, S. Lash, & R. Robertson (Eds.), *Global modernities* (pp. 25–44). Thousand Oaks, CA: SAGE.

Rosenau, P. M. (1992). *Post-modernism and the social sciences*. Princeton, NJ: Princeton University Press.

Schutz, C. (1977). *Political humor: From Aristophanes to Sam Ervin*. London, U.K.: Associated University Press.

Sinclair, J. (2004). Geo-linguistic region as global space: The case of Latin America. In R. Allen & A. Hill (Eds.), *The television studies reader* (pp. 130–138). London, U.K.: Routledge.

Sloterdijk, P. (1988). *Critique of cynical reason*. (M. Eldred, Trans.). London, U.K.: Verso.

Sparks, C., & Tulloch, J. (Eds.). (2000). *Tabloid tales: Global debates about media standards*. Lanham, MD: Rowman & Littlefield.

Spigel, L., & Olsson, J. (Eds.). (2004). *Television after TV: Essays of a medium in transition*. Durham, NC: Duke University Press.

Stapleton, K. (2000). In search of the self: Feminism, postmodernity, and identity. *Feminism and Psychology, 10*(4), 463–469.

Stevens, J. D. (1985). Sensationalism in perspective. *Journalism History, 12*(3/4), 78–79.

Straubhaar, J. (1991). Beyond media imperialism: Asymmetrical interdependence and cultural proximity. *Critical Studies in Mass Communication, 8*, 39–59.

Straubhaar, J. (2007). *World television: From global to local*. Los Angeles, CA: SAGE.

Sturken, M. (2008). Spectacle. In W. Donsbach (Ed.), *The International Encyclopedia of Communication* (pp. 4964–4965). Hoboken, NJ: Wiley-Blackwell.

Test, G. (1991). *Satire: Spirit and art*. Tampa, FL: University of South Florida Press.

Thussu, D. K. (2007a). The "Murdochization" of news? The case of Star TV in India. *Media, Culture & Society, 29*(4), 593–611. http://dx.doi.org/10.1177/0163443707076191

Thussu, D. K. (2007b). *News as entertainment: The rise of global infotainment*. Thousand Oaks, CA: SAGE.

Turner, G. (2004). *Understanding celebrity*. London, U.K.: SAGE.

Turner, G. (2010). *Ordinary people and the media: The demotic turn*. London, U.K.: SAGE.

Turner, G., Bonner, F., & Marshall, P. D. (2000). *Fame games: The production of celebrity in Australia*. Cambridge, U.K.: Cambridge University Press.

Žižek, S. (2002). *Welcome to the desert of the real*. London, U.K.: Verso.

CHAPTER 2

Last Week Tonight With John Oliver and the Stewart/Colbert Impact on U.S. Political Communication in the Post-Network Era

In June 2014, *Last Week Tonight With John Oliver (LWT)* devoted a 13-minute in-depth segment to the issue of net neutrality,[1] a topic that the British host introduced as more boring than "featuring Sting" and "even boring by C-SPAN standards." After humorously and comprehensively explaining the technological complexities, the social implications, the economic practices, and the power dynamics behind an unregulated market, Oliver asked his viewers (potential online commentators) to manifest their opposition to an internet system that would allow enhanced speed for certain users to the detriment of others. He asked them to urge the Federal Communications Commission (FCC) to maintain the Web's status as a level playing field. Pointing at the FCC's website, Oliver said, looking at the camera, "We need you to get out there and for once in your lives, focus your indiscriminate rage in a useful direction! Seize your moment, my lovely trolls. Turn on caps lock and fly, my pretties! Fly, fly, fly!" The next day, the commission's site collapsed and displayed a message that read, "We've been experiencing technical difficulties with our comment system due to heavy traffic." The *LWT* segment, which has garnered more than 10 million

---

1. Net Neutrality (*LWT*, June 1, 2014): https://www.youtube.com/watch?v=fpbOEo RrHyU

views on YouTube, was widely cited and prompted attention and public debate about the issue. Oliver's coverage generated so much attention that Tom Wheeler, chairman of the FCC, felt compelled to "state for the record" that he was "not a dingo,"[2] answering to Oliver. For many observers, it significantly contributed to the FCC's approval of strong net neutrality rules a few months later and had a wider reach than many expensive advocacy campaigns. This is an example of how *Last Week Tonight With John Oliver*, the satirical show which has aired on HBO since 2014, has tackled complex and controversial issues of the public agenda while promoting social agitation and debate. It has been the latest development of the political infotainment trend in the United States that gained enormous influence with the popularity of Comedy Central's *The Daily Show With Jon Stewart (TDS)* and, subsequently, *The Colbert Report (TCR)*. While *TDS* satirized TV journalism's coverage of news and *TCR* parodied the conservative rhetoric in the media, *LWT* presents investigations and in-depth coverage of national and international public interest issues.

Reacting to the "Foxification" of news and the ideological polarization in the media after 9/11, *The Daily Show* became a media phenomenon in the United States and an essential force in American political communication. Its host until 2015 and identified by *The New York Times* as "the most trusted name in fake news" (Kakutani, 2008), comedian Jon Stewart has been one of the most admired "journalists" in the country ("Today's Journalists Less Prominent," 2007). For almost 20 years, the show has offered a satiric interpretation of politics and current events, mocking both those who make and report the news. It features a cast of "correspondents" (Oliver and Colbert were correspondents at *TDS* before hosting their own spin-off shows) and includes interviews with celebrities, politicians, and media personalities. Stewart's interviews with prominent personalities soon became, as described by *Rolling Stone* magazine, the "hot destination for anyone who wants to sell books or seem hip, from presidential candidates to military dictators" (Dowd, 2006). The show has received many distinctions and awards (including 18 Primetime Emmy Awards, and two Peabody Awards for its coverage of the 2000 and 2004 presidential elections), while also generating global impact: Not only has an edited version of the show aired outside the United States, but its format has inspired international versions unaffiliated with Comedy Central, such as the Persian-language satire program *Parazit*, Germany's *Heute Show*, and *Al Bernameg*

---

2. Tom Wheeler Is Not a Dingo (*LWT*, June 15, 2014): https://www.youtube.com/watch?v=hkjkQ-wCZ5A

in Egypt.[3] On the other hand, in *The Colbert Report* (2005–2014), comedian Stephen Colbert parodied right-wing pundits (with a special focus on Fox News's Bill O'Reilly). Described by Colbert as a "well intentioned, poorly informed, high status idiot," the character takes conservative positions and spins them out to their extreme, evidencing their inconsistencies and absurdity. *TCR* not only satirized the right-wing pundits by exposing their irrational argumentations but also became a precedent of authentic satiric activism with his interventions in the real world of politics such as Colbert's super PAC, which was highly discussed and covered in the news and entertainment media.

The success of these satirical shows has taken place in times when the institution of journalism is in a state of crisis (Fuller, 2012; Hachten, 2005; Kovach & Rosenstiel, 2001). Increasingly, the public is dissatisfied with news, and press credibility is diminishing. In 2011, 66% of Americans surveyed said that news stories often are inaccurate, 77% said that news organizations tend to favor one side, and 80% said that the powerful often influence news organizations, according to the Pew Research Center (2011). This overall dissatisfaction, coupled with the rise of the internet and declining print advertising revenues, helped usher the journalism industry into an economic crisis (Edmonds, Guskin, Mitchell, & Jurkowitz, 2013; Edmonds, Guskin, Rosenstiel, & Mitchell, 2012; Holcomb, 2014; Mitchell & Matsa, 2015; Mitchell & Rosenstiel, 2012). Surveys showed that newspapers' primary audience is over 45 years old (Edmonds et al., 2013; "Newspaper: Daily Readership," 2014; "Watching, Reading, and Listening to the News," 2012); in contrast, 34% of young people (ages 18–29) turned to late-night television and comedy shows for news (Pew Research Center, 2004). More recent surveys of audience habits have also found little indication that Gen Xers (33–47 years old) and Millennials (18–31 years old) will become heavier news consumers in the future (Kohut, 2013). By 2010, most young people in the United States (ages 18–24) looked more to *The Colbert Report* (80%) and *The Daily Show With Jon Stewart* (74%) for news than to traditional journalism outlets ("Americans Spending More Time Following the News," 2010). As a result, both shows have attracted significant academic attention. While some scholars considered them a new type of journalism, others argued that they promote cynicism rather than civic engagement.

3. Baym and Jones (2013) edited a collection on news parody across the globe, in which diverse authors analyze the impact of *TDS* and other different adaptations of news satire in countries such as Australia, France, India, Hungary, and Denmark, among others.

This chapter analyzes *Last Week Tonight With John Oliver* in relation to the academic debates and scholarly work generated by its successful predecessors. First, after offering an overview of U.S. TV satire's history, I review and organize some of the most relevant research on the "journalistic" and sociopolitical role of *TDS* and *TCR* in order to contextualize *LWT* in relation to the evolution of political infotainment in the United States. Second, I analyze how *LWT* not only fills gaps left by mainstream media but also seeks to complement *TDS* and *TCR*, taking satire to a more international, investigative, and activist level. This chapter shows the increasing intention of these shows to take a more active role in impacting the sociopolitical reality that they criticize. Because American political infotainment (and especially, the shows analyzed in this chapter) has been internationally influential, this chapter also serves to illuminate the debates about the genre for use in the analysis of the Latin American cases, which have remained academically unexplored. It finally offers conclusions in relation to the state of U.S. satiric infotainment in the post-network, Trump era.

SATIRE'S SELF-REFERENTIAL TRADITION IN U.S. TELEVISION

Created by comedians Lizz Winstead and Madeleine Smithberg, *TDS* premiered on cable's Comedy Central on July 22, 1996. It continued an important tradition of Anglophone satire (Swift and Twain being two of the most famous and foundational literary figures), which did not make an easy entrance into television.

> [Satire] is not a genre or format that has shifted and adapted to the modes of production or industrial imperatives the way in which soap operas, quiz shows, and sitcoms have from network radio to early TV to the network era and beyond. Instead, it represents a convergence of audience tastes, shifting programming strategies, and the gradual evolution of satiric and parodic television in other formats that has led to the current state of satire TV. (Gray, Jones, & Thompson, 2009, p. 19)

While the late 1950s and early 1960s were vibrant decades for social criticism and satire, very little of that agitation found its way into television. Network executives were intending to appeal to as many people—and to alienate as few advertisers—as possible. While comedians such as Lenny Bruce and Mort Sahl reached popular audiences with LP records, satire was mainly developed in print media. It first cultivated a countercultural, underground scene during the 50s, but it grew in the following decade: "With the young, witty, urbane John Kennedy in the White House, satiric expression, long a resource for cultural dissent, became for many American liberals a source of affirmation and a sign of better days to come" (Kercher, 2006, p. 194). In this context, two TV shows managed to incorporate satire into their formats: *The Smothers Brothers Comedy Hour*, which launched the faux presidential run of Pat Paulsen in 1968, and Rowan and Martin's *Laugh-In*. Since then, however, as noted by David Marc, "American television has always been better at satirizing itself than politics" (Gray et al., 2009, p. xvi). As part of TV's self-referential tradition, a rare and pioneer example of press satire was David Frost's *That Was the Week That Was* (1962–1963 in England, 1964–1965 in the United States). During the 1970s, TV began its attempts to reach smaller educated, urban young audiences through cutting-edge humor. News parody was repopularized with *Saturday Night Live*'s "Weekend Update" segment (1975–present) and, later, HBO's *Not Necessarily the News* (1982–1990), which was modeled after BBC's *Not the Nine O'Clock News*. The conservative period of George H. W. Bush was the political context for a breakthrough of self-referential TV satire: The late 1980s saw the birth of *The Simpsons*, the longest running sitcom ever, which exemplified the potential of parody as a media literacy educator about the techniques and rhetoric of televisual texts and genres (Gray, 2005). "Almost every television genre has been parodied in one episode or another. The show toys with American social vices by playing with American television, realizing that in a televised nation, social satire must often be both on and about television" (Gray et al., 2009, p. 24). In many ways, *The Simpsons* created the televisual space for the current satiric boom, establishing self-referential TV satire as the norm. Becoming an iconic example of a cable show finding its way into the American network lineup, the show also marked the milestone for post-network television and TV comedy. *The Simpsons'* influence can be observed, for example, in the launch of the cable channel Comedy Central in 1991 and its strategy of using political humor and satire as a means of branding itself (Jones, 2010). Since then, American TV network late-night shows and cable TV have included higher doses of irreverent political humor, self-referential parody, and biting social satire. Examples include *Politically Incorrect* and *Real Time With Bill Maher, Dennis Miller Live, The Chris Rock Show, The View, The Late Show With David Letterman, South Park,* Michael Moore's *TV Nation* and *The Awful Truth, Chapelle's Show,* and *Da Ali G Show,* among others. Within this group, as recalled by Winstead, *TDS* added new components to TV satire and to its subgenre of "press satire" or "fake news":

We were not just going to make fun of the news and the talking heads that were everywhere. We were going to make fun of them by becoming them. We would operate as a news organization while acting like a comedy show. It simply had never been done before. We were sure we would have a hit if we used all the news conventions—the set, the graphics, the music, the format—all to expose the ways our media had elevated celebrity and scandal to an importance that used to be reserved for war and politics and corporate malfeasance. We would have correspondents and send them to all the newsworthy events, blending in with the rest of the press corps, highlighting how ridiculous they had become. (Winstead, 2012, pp. 219–220)

THE DAILY SHOW WITH JON STEWART: SATIRE CHALLENGES JOURNALISM

On October 15, 2004, comedian Jon Stewart, the host of the "fake news" program *The Daily Show*, appeared on *Crossfire*, a debate show broadcast on the news channel CNN. *Crossfire* was hosted by two pundits, one of whom was presented as being "from the right" (Tucker Carlson) and one "from the left" (Paul Begala). During the interview, Stewart criticized the talk show hosts for debasing journalism in the name of political debate and made an appeal for "civilized discourse," a "responsibility to public discourse," and "to stop hurting America" with partisan hackery and theater that masquerades as news on CNN. Stewart's appearance on *Crossfire* was widely watched on TV and online.[4] A few months after Stewart's criticisms of the show, *Crossfire* was canceled, and Tucker Carlson was fired from CNN. Stewart's critiques resonated with millions, and voiced the audience's frustration with the news media. For Boler and Turpin (2008), it was a liminal moment of contemporary news media history, similar to Colbert's performance at the 2006 White House Correspondents' Dinner, in which the comedian delivered a harsh critique of the media and George W. Bush's administration—with Bush himself sitting close to Colbert—in front of hundreds of political and media figures.[5]

While Stewart has appeared in other "real" news shows and confronted other pundits for not doing responsible journalism, the *Crossfire* episode remains an iconic moment in which one of the most

4. The *Crossfire* episode, with more than 10 million views, is available in YouTube: https://www.youtube.com/watch?v=aFQFB5YpDZE
5. Stephen Colbert at the 2006 White House Correspondents' Dinner: https://www.youtube.com/watch?v=2X93u3anTco

influential infotainers of the country articulated his ideas on the role of journalism in democracy, positioned his own role as a comedian in an ambiguous and powerful discursive place, voiced the concerns that promoted a debate on the damaging potential of contemporary media, and concretely intervened in the mediascape by playing a part in the cancellation of a television news show. While Stewart's performance on *Crossfire* happened outside the codes of his comedy show, it was in many ways a crystallization of what *TDS* had been targeting intensely after the 9/11 attacks and during the Bush administration: the role that mainstream news media has in framing the sociopolitical reality. This focus had begun earlier, though. When Jon Stewart replaced Craig Kilborn as host of *TDS* in January 1999 (in the waning years of the Clinton administration and the Monica Lewinsky scandal), a significant change happened. The show became more strongly focused on politics and how it was framed in the national media, in contrast to the pop culture focus during Kilborn's era. According to Junod (2011), Stewart wanted the show to be more competitive, almost in a newsgathering sense, and he wanted it to have a stronger point of view. Operating under a production routine similar to that of newsrooms (Kakutani, 2008), the writers (such as Ben Karlin, former editor of the satirical newspaper *The Onion*) were essential in shaping the voice of the show,[6] which for many observers became clear with "Indecision 2000," the show's parody of that year's presidential campaign in which George W. Bush was elected president of the United States. During this campaign, the correspondents went on the road, mixing with real journalists. According to Stephen Colbert, then a correspondent for *TDS*,

> The more we got to meet people in the media, it was—Oh! You're fucking retarded! You don't care! The pettiness of it, the strange lack of passion for any kind of moral or editorial authority, always struck me as weird. We felt like, we're serious people doing an unserious thing, and they're unserious people doing a very serious thing. (Smith, 2010, p. 4)

Since then, *TDS*'s correspondents have gone on the road to record specials from cities hosting the Democratic and Republican National Conventions, and all the electoral coverage has culminated in live election night specials.

6. Winstead (2012) describes the *TDS* writers as "guys who looked beyond the headlines and dug deeper. Guys who barely had two nickels to rub together, and when they did they would take one of them and buy a copy of *Harper's* with it. The news was in their blood, not just a writing submission tailored for the job" (p. 223–224).

Following the 9/11 attacks and the invasion of Iraq, the Bush administration and the polarized mainstream media offered the political satirists some of the best material they could hope for. The show focused more closely not just on politics but also on the apparatus of policymaking and the White House's efforts to manage the news media. At the same time, it targeted conservative media outlets—like Fox News—which were (and continue to be) significantly challenging to the dominant journalistic norms of modern news media and the role that they play in the construction of political reality. As Jones and Baym (2010) noted, these challenges extend beyond the (re)introduction of partisanship into news coverage and include how we know and distinguish truth from falsehood. Grondin (2012) described the confrontation between *TDS* and the conservative media as a mediated reenactment of the U.S. culture war, specifically a continuation of the clash between conservative and liberal views of morality at the end of the Cold War, which cut across racial, gender, religious, ethnic, and class lines in American society. Grondin posed that today's culture war takes shape in infotainment TV, in which Stewart was a key culture warrior. In this context, as a reaction to the right-wing, conservative movement led by Fox News, *TDS*'s main strategy has been to interrogate the representations of the day's events that mainstream media seek to establish as truth, unveiling the artifice in contemporary news practices. The label of "fake news" allows the show to say what traditional journalism cannot. This is probably why Stewart has so insistently rejected the label of "journalist": "Never claiming to be news, [the show] can hardly be charged with being illegitimate journalism; either by the political structure it interrogates or the news media it threatens" (Baym, 2005, p. 273). A pertinent example of this is when Bernard Goldberg, political commentator for Fox News, demanded Stewart be as tough toward his liberal guests as with Fox and conservatives. In response, Stewart argued:

> You can't criticize me for not being fair and balanced. That's your slogan, which by the way, you never follow . . . To say that comedians have to decide whether they are comedians or social commentators—comedians do social commentary through comedy. That's how it's worked for a thousand years. I have not moved out of the comedian's box toward the news box. The news box is moving towards me. (*The Daily Show*, April 20, 2010)[7]

7. The video is available online: http://thedailyshow.cc.com/videos/v8fs1v/bernie-goldberg-fires-back

Similarly, *TDS*'s role was summarized in a dialogue between Stewart and Bill Moyers in 2003. Moyers said, "I do not know whether you are practicing an old form of parody and satire . . . or a new form of journalism." Stewart replied, "Well then that either speaks to the sad state of comedy or the sad state of news. I can't figure out which one. I think, honestly, we're practicing a new form of desperation" ("Bill Moyers talks with Jon Stewart on *NOW with Bill Moyers*, July 11, 2003"). These statements evidence Stewart's ambivalence about acknowledging a journalistic role in his comedy. Nevertheless, in the context of a decline in democratically useful news and public affairs programming, many scholars have shown how *TDS* has offered, in several cases, a much better informative job than mainstream media (Borden & Tew, 2007; Faina, 2012; Smolkin & Groves, 2007) and created a greater impact on serious political debate than most of its predecessors (Day, 2011). For example, after comparing news items "reported" by *TDS* with the same stories covered by CNN that focused on news reports of the 2004 presidential campaign, Jones (2007) showed how *TDS*'s faux journalistic style allowed the show to question and dispel the manipulative language coming from the presidential campaign and the media's coverage, while also reframing the important issues at stake.

TDS's deconstruction of news and political rhetoric is developed through the practice of "political culture-jamming," which adds a subversive interpretation of the dominant political brands to the public sphere. It jams the continuous stream of political images through the proliferation of humorous, dissident images that exploit leverage points—factual errors, logical contradictions, and incongruities—in both the dominant political discourse and the media that disseminate it (Warner, 2007). In a country with no national press council and where the government cannot enforce accountability of the media due to privileges the First Amendment affords the press, this becomes a tool to enforce accountability. Painter and Hodges (2010) found that *TDS* holds traditional broadcast media accountable in four distinct ways: by pointing out falsehoods, by pointing out inconsistencies, by pointing out when inconsequential news is blown out of proportion, and by critiquing the very nature of broadcast news. Likewise, Feldman (2007) maintained that professional journalists understand the program not as challenging the legitimacy of serious news but as challenging the news media to think more responsibly about what journalism should look like today. Feldman observed that some have begun to reevaluate the consensual notions of professional practice, like the news/entertainment and objectivity/subjectivity distinctions. In a media environment in which an increasingly savvy public realizes that mainstream news are no more "real" than *TDS* is "fake" (Jones, 2007), news becomes defined by a set of arbitrary cultural practices open for reconsideration. In this sense, Baym (2005) posited that *TDS* can be better understood not as "fake news" but as an experiment in journalism, an "alternative journalism" that questions conventions of public speech and how we make sense of the political world. Like most relevant satire, *TDS* is ultimately a struggle about meaning.

While there is debate on *TDS*'s real effects on audiences (Amarasingam, 2011; Baumgartner & Morris, 2006; Feldman, 2013; Feldman & Young, 2008; Hmielowski, Holbert, & Lee, 2011; Hoffman & Thomson, 2009; Holbert, Hmielowski, Jain, Lather, & Morey, 2011; Holbert, Lambe, Dudo, & Carlton, 2007; Holbert, Tchernev, Walther, Esralew, & Benski, 2013; Morris, 2009; Polk, Young, & Holbert, 2009; Xiaoxia, 2008, 2010; Young, 2013; Young Mie & Vishak, 2008), Feldman (2007) noted that the show's effective application of irony and satire implies a shared understanding between communicator and receiver. In this sense, the show might encourage young viewers to tune into traditional forms of news so that they have the context necessary to appreciate the program's humor. In fact, the National Annenberg Election Survey found that young people who watch *TDS* are more knowledgeable about politics than nonviewers ("'Daily Show' Viewers Knowledgeable About Presidential Campaign," 2004). According to the survey, followers of *TDS* had a more accurate idea of the facts behind a presidential election than most others, including those who primarily got their news through viewing the national network evening newscasts and reading newspapers. A subsequent survey by the Pew Research Center (2007) also supported the contention that regular viewers of *TDS* tend to be more knowledgeable about news than audiences of other news sources. From another perspective, Kowalewski (2013) found that entertainment news programs like *TDS* influence the transfer of the media's agenda to the public's agenda similarly to traditional hard news. In other words, individuals react similarly to entertainment news and traditional hard news, and entertainment programs have the ability to set the public's agenda. Nevertheless, Baumgartner and Morris (2006) found that viewers of *TDS* also think more negatively about television news and politicians and exhibit more cynicism toward the electoral system and the news media at large. In this vein, some critics suggest that *TDS*'s irony damages the democratic process, as deconstruction through ridicule and laughter leads to cynical nihilism. Hart and Hartelius (2007) accused Stewart of making cynicism attractive and profitable, while Colleta (2009) suggested that *TDS* doesn't have any efficacy beyond mere entertainment and that its self-referential irony undermines social and political engagement, creating disengaged viewers who prefer outside irreverence to discerning, engaged politics. Nevertheless, others have pointed out that Stewart has gone beyond humor and also adopted a sincere tone to voice his and society's concerns about the news media's role in democracy, as he did in the *Crossfire* episode. In this line, he (and Colbert) also organized in 2010 a "Rally To Restore Sanity," a spoof of the conservative Glenn Beck's "Restoring Honor" rally and Al Sharpton's "Reclaim the Dream" rally. Stewart's gathering took place at the National Mall in Washington, DC; about 215,000 people attended. The rally's purpose was to provide a venue for attendees to be heard above what Stewart described as the extreme portion of Americans who "control the conversation" of American politics. His argument was that the political extremes demonize each other and engage in counterproductive actions and that his rally was promoting reasoned discussion. While Stewart's rally was criticized as innocuous, a few years later Stephen Colbert took satiric activism to a new dimension.

THE COLBERT REPORT: SATIRIC ACTIVISM AS A REACTION TO SPECTACLE'S TRUTHINESS

On March 10, 2011, Stephen Colbert announced on his show the creation of his own political action committee (or super PAC), named "Americans for a Better Tomorrow, Tomorrow." It was a reaction to the Supreme Court's 2010 *Citizens United v. Federal Election Commission* (FEC) ruling, which lifted restrictions on the amount of money that corporations could spend to influence political elections based on their free speech rights. Colbert's super PAC, which reported raising more than $1 million in its January 2012 filing with the FEC, showed how several political players were using the system and demonstrated the blurred distinctions between the process and "money laundering." As part of the more-than-a-year-long skit, Colbert announced in 2012 his intention to run for "President of the United States of South Carolina" and signed provisionally the control of his super PAC to Jon Stewart, pointing to the evident connections between super PACs and political candidates and parties. David Carr of *The New York Times* wrote about Colbert's political intervention: "Maybe the whole system has become such a joke that only jokes will serve as corrective" (Carr, 2011). Before dissolving the super PAC at the end of 2012, Colbert received a Peabody Award for offering "innovative means of teaching American viewers about the landmark court decision." In 2014, the Annenberg Public Policy Center reported that the Colbert super PAC segments increased viewers' knowledge of PACs and campaign finance regulation more successfully than other types of news media ("Stephen

Colbert's Civics Lesson: Or, How a TV Humorist Taught America About Campaign Finance," 2014).

Colbert's super PAC, however, was not his first incursion into the serious realms of politics outside the comedy's box. On September 24, 2010, the comedian testified in character before a House subcommittee regarding legislation intended to facilitate legal protections for migrant farm workers. Invited by Committee Chair Zoe Lofgreen, Colbert humorously described his experience participating in the United Farm Workers' "Take Our Jobs" program, where he spent a day working alongside migrants in the fields. At the end of his presentation, he broke character, and explained his position:

> I like talking about people who don't have any power, and this seems like one of the least powerful people in the United States are migrant workers who come and do our work, but don't have any rights as a result . . . And, you know, "Whatsoever you do for the least of my brothers," and these seem like the least of our brothers right now . . . Migrant workers suffer and have no rights.[8]

While some of these incursions into the "real" world were widely criticized by the media as ineffective or unserious, other observers noted the way this sort of satiric activism was reinforcing the role of *TDS* and *TCR* as tools for educating the audiences on sociopolitical issues and as instruments to teach media literacy:

> Through the on-program and off-program performances, then, Stewart and Colbert are able to say things the news media either can't or won't say. In the process, they offer extended civic lessons—on media literacy, on worker's rights and conditions, on campaign financing, on the failures of worker's compensation programs—in ways that, again, news media typically fail to do, or do so poorly. And significantly so, they offer newer frames of interpretation or terms of debate than those already present in the political and journalistic establishment. (Jones, Baym, & Day, 2012, p. 56)

Colbert's interventions on reality became the most controversial aspect of a complex fictional character, whose overall satiric goal has been described as "to lay bare the mendacities of the neoconservative social and neoliberal economic hegemony in the United States" (Combe, 2015, p. 301). While the show has also been perceived as useful "to

---

8. Colbert's testimony in Congress on September 24, 2010, can be accessed at https://www.youtube.com/watch?v=nxeIO4pW05s

affirm progressive race-consciousness, reflect on the influence of racial constructions throughout history, expose White privilege, and refute reactionary White victim narratives" (Rossing, 2012, p. 44), its carnivalesque humor continued the main role established by *TDS*: to challenge the authority of traditional news operating as a critic of the press (Meddaugh, 2010). With his show's debut in October 2005, Colbert promised to "tear the news a new one," "feel the news for you," and concluded that, "right or wrong, I'm right, and you are wrong." As part of his project to "give people the truth, unfiltered by rational argument," he also introduced his concept of "truthiness," Merriam-Webster's 2006 Word of the Year, which *New York* magazine called "the summarizing concept of our age" (Sternbergh, 2006). The term refers to the substitution of emotion for rational thinking and to the valuation and celebration of perception, certainty, and feeling, irrespective of the facts (Jones & Baym, 2010). After explaining that the country is divided, not between "red and blue" but between "those who think with their heads, and those who know with their heart," Colbert said:

> Anybody who knows me knows I'm no fan of dictionaries or reference books. They are elitist. Constantly telling us what is or isn't true or what did or didn't happen. Who's Britannica to tell me the Panama Canal was finished in 1914? If I want to say it happened in 1941, that's my right. I don't trust books. They're all fact and no heart. (*The Colbert Report*, October 17, 2005)[9]

Presenting a dichotomy between head and heart, Colbert's concept of truthiness functions as a challenge to those who would disregard fact to preserve belief (Baym, 2009), which clearly relates to his main object of criticism: American right-wing media and its distortion of reality. Playing a parody of a right-wing pundit with a deep disregard both for accuracy and political correctness, Colbert cannot be understood apart from Bill O'Reilly, Fox's self-proclaimed "culture warrior" in the fight against liberalism. As noted by Conway, Grabe, and Grieves (2007), O'Reilly constructs a fearful and simplistic world of heroes and villains fighting over some imagined American way of life. His most recurrent villains are terrorists and illegal immigrants, but he also includes academics, non-Christians, and both left-leaning and politically neutral media. On the other hand, he claims the virtuous are the right-leaning media, Republicans, Christians, and a vague idea of the American people. Colbert mimicked O'Reilly's megalomaniacal and xenophobic rhetoric. Performing his notion of truthiness,

9. http://www.zippcast.com/video/5d6929198e462e39f38

Colbert satirically demonstrated how the media and its authoritative voice spread lies: "A majority of Americans thought Hitler was a great guy. That's a fact. I just made up that fact, but that doesn't keep it from being a fact" (*The Colbert Report*, August 10, 2006).

As can be noted, Colbert's notion of truthiness announced the unfortunate rise of Oxford Dictionary's 2016 International Word of the Year: "post-truth," an adjective that denotes a circumstance "in which objective facts are less influential in shaping public opinion than appeals to emotion and personal belief." Recent elaborations on today's post-truth era are deeply connected with the election of Donald Trump as the president of the United States, an era in which the president's counselor coined the term "alternative facts" to rebrand abject lies, Trump himself disseminates falsehoods on Twitter, and the administration dismisses as "fake news" the criticisms and accusations of the media.

Exposing how truthiness and sensationalism dominate public discourse, Colbert's goal was to dismantle what philosopher Harry Frankfurt called "bullshit," statements that "avoid, elude, dissuade questions of accurate representation" (Frankfurt, 2005, p. 33). Colbert's satiric tactic, then, was to bullshit in order to expose bullshit. These sorts of techniques are similar to what Geoffrey Baym (2010) called "neo-modern" journalism: the embracement of postmodern styles in order to reject "the postmodern logic of spectacle and simulacrum and the now-commonplace assumption that truth is relative and fact a product of power" (p. 126). In this sense, for Baym, Stewart and Colbert are really modernists at heart: "I argue that underlying the postmodern form, there is a quite modernist agenda, a critique of news and an interrogation of political power that rests on a firm belief in fact, accountability, and reason in public discourse (Jones & Baym, 2010, p. 281). On the other hand, Combe (2015) defends the inherent postmodern condition of these satiric shows and especially of *TCR*. For Combe, Colbert's concept of truthiness goes way beyond lampooning those who think with their guts or those who use bullshit for their personal gain. The real significance behind Colbert's truthiness is the more complex and disturbing idea that all truth is truthy: "No statement achieves (or deserves) the status of Ultimate Being. No matter how Universal-seeming, any verity is a contrivance and a construction fashioned from a particular set of circumstances" (Combe, 2015, p. 306). Thus, Colbert did not engage in Truth Wars with Bill O'Reilly or any other Fox News pundit; he and Stewart engaged instead in Epistemology Wars with his opponents: "His purpose is not to replace a false Truth with a true Truth. Through the exercise of situationally accurate circumstances, Colbert aims to identify, dismantle and replace a worse (meaning ill-constructed) point of view with a better (meaning well-constructed) point of view" (Combe, 2015, p. 306).

To the critique that *TCR* and *TDS* trivialize "the seriousness of both the politicians and the satire, turning everything into one big meta-joke" (Colleta, 2009, p. 866), Combe (2015) has also reaffirmed his post-modernist defense of the satiric shows, criticizing the attempts to either expect "a Transcendental Signified" in satire or equating postmodern satire with nihilism. "Far from advocating No Meaning, postmodernism proposes many meanings—an infinite amount based in contextuality, not perpetuity" (Combe, 2015, pp. 299–300). Some research on audience effects might actually support this postmodern condition of satire. In the case of *TCR* in particular, the political ideology of the viewer becomes a crucial factor—many conservative viewers actually thought that Colbert only pretended to be joking and he genuinely meant what he said (LaMarre, Landreville, & Beam, 2009). Similarly, Baumgartner and Morris (2008) found that viewers in general had a more positive perception of Republicans after watching the show. In this sense, *TCR*, similar to Sacha Baron Cohen's work, illustrated the ambivalent nature of multi-layered and elaborate satire: The satiric intentions do not necessarily align with the audience's interpretations and, in many cases, contradict them. In other words, Colbert, as a parody of conservatives, was mainly clever and fun for educated liberals in the same way that Borat was clever and fun for cosmopolitans. Like Baron Cohen's exaggerated characters, Colbert's fictional character reached an end. In September 2015, a few months after the end of *TCR* in December 2014, Colbert replaced David Letterman as the host of CBS's *The Late Show*. Befitting the difference between a niche cable half-hour and a network variety hour, the comedian reinvented himself with "a Wes Andersonian spirit of meticulously curated, experimental-yet-preservationist play" (Poniewozik, 2015). In contrast to Colbert's ambiguous satire, and at a time when Stewart had also retired from *TDS*, John Oliver, a former *TDS* correspondent and the natural heir to the tradition, filled the satiric infotainment gap with direct, nonambiguous, confrontational, and in-depth pieces.

LAST WEEK TONIGHT WITH JOHN OLIVER: SATIRE AS INVESTIGATIVE REPORTING AND SOCIAL AGITATION

In June 2014, prior to the opening of the soccer World Cup in Brazil, John Oliver exposed the corrupt, manipulative, and immoral practices of FIFA, the Fédération Internationale de Football Association, and its president, Sepp Blatter, in a 13-minute segment. Putting aside FIFA's recurrent bribery scandals, Oliver explained the federation's "comically grotesque" operating principles in the questionable organizing of the World Cup, such as reaping the profits of the event while leaving the host country with the costs, forcing Brazil to repeal a public-safety law that banned the sale of alcohol in stadiums in order to allow Budweiser's advertising, the construction of a $270 million stadium in a Brazilian city without a professional soccer team, and FIFA's ludicrous tax-exempt status as a nonprofit, among others. He also derided Sepp Blatter's sexist comment suggesting that the way to boost interest in women's soccer is by having the players wear tighter shorts and highlighted the irregularities of positioning the 2022 World Cup in Qatar, a country where 120-degree summer temperatures will not only result in the deaths of the construction project workers but will also make the world's largest sporting event uncomfortable and dangerous for viewers and players alike. The online video of the show, which has more than 11 million views on YouTube,[10] became viral and was part of a series of accusations and rants that Oliver, a soccer fan and former aspiring player himself, elaborated against FIFA. Less than a year after the airing of *LWT*'s first segment, FIFA top officials were arrested on corruption charges in June 2015, and Oliver revisited the topic with updates on the current state of the institution. "I don't know what I'm more surprised by," Oliver said about the investigation that led to the arrests, "that FIFA officials were actually arrested or that America was behind it. It took the country who cares the least about football to bring down the people who have been ruining it." In spite of the arrests, Blatter was still reelected to a fifth term as FIFA president. "The problem is that all the arrests in the world are gonna change nothing as long as Blatter is still there, because to truly kill a snake, you must cut off its head, or in this case, its asshole," Oliver added before making a plea to the World Cup's sponsors, like Adidas, Budweiser, and McDonald's, to withdraw their support from Blatter's mafia. "Budweiser, if you pull your support and help get rid of Blatter, I will put my mouth where my mouth is, and I will personally drink one of your disgusting items," the host said, while adding that he would wear one of Adidas's "ugly shoes" and take a bite out of every item on the dollar menu at McDonald's. A few days later, Blatter resigned amid reports he was under investigation. Although it wasn't confirmed that the sponsors really had anything to do with Blatter stepping down, Oliver fulfilled his promises in the next show, which ended

10. https://www.youtube.com/watch?v=DlJEt2KU33I

with him drinking a bottle of beer. "Bud Light Lime may taste like your tongue is angry with you," Oliver said, "but, after Sepp Blatter leaving, to me it tastes delicious." *Adweek* reported that Budweiser's twitter mentions jumped 525% after Blatter quit and called it "the John Oliver effect." *CBS Sports* suggested that the host was "the hero behind Sepp Blatter's FIFA resignation," after *The Washington Post* had already headlined: "FIFA head Sepp Blatter crushed by John Oliver."

Oliver's tenacity against the corruption of the FIFA did not stop with Blatter's resignation. When former FIFA VP Jack Warner, indicted on corruption and bribery charges, went on Trinidad and Tobago's TV to share his own claims against FIFA, *LWT* bought their own airtime on Trinidadian TV. Oliver called on Warner to release as much incriminating evidence against FIFA as possible. Warner hit back with a 3-minute video set to overly dramatic music in which he called the British Oliver an "American foreigner" and a "comedian fool." Oliver responded on his show by exposing Warner's sloppy video editing skills that used the top Google result for "epic and dramatic music" to exaggerate his argument. "We both have our flaws. People say I'm not a good listener, for example. Just as I've said that you diverted $750,000 in Haiti Relief Funds into a bank account you controlled. And sure, we may both dispute those charges, but my point is neither of us is perfect. So to you I say this Jack, if you really want to continue trading shit-talking videos with increasingly high production elements, then consider your challenge accepted, my friend," Oliver said before fire rained down on his set. While there was no answer from Warner this time, Oliver kept the FIFA scandal in the public eye by criticizing Blatter's attempt to "clean his image" by appearing side by side with Russian President Vladimir Putin and paying bail with a combination of Rolex watches and a Ferrari. Oliver also reveled in the flight of FIFA's sponsors, such as Visa, InBev, and McDonald's. "You know your organization is in trouble when McDonald's says it is 'not satisfied,'" said Oliver. "This is coming from the maker of grayish brown meat circles, tiny condensed chicken mistakes and, once a year, shamrock shakes, AKA a leprechaun's diarrhea."

The FIFA case exemplifies how *LWT* has participated in public debate: first, by covering thoroughly a topic and keeping it on the news agenda; second, by pleading for real actions (or sanctions), intervening directly on the issue, and engaging in debates with the protagonists; and third, by following the case and not letting it get buried in the news cycle. In other words, the show's strategy was to report, denounce, call for action, and remain a watchdog on the evolution of the case. With a similar approach to the controversial, "boring," and complex issue of "net neutrality" described at the beginning of this chapter, *LWT* generated a real impact on the way the FIFA scandal was framed and discussed in the transnational media. While it would be difficult to measure the specifics of the impact, Oliver's online viral videos were cited and linked in the most prominent international publications that covered the FIFA scandal, and Oliver's sustained satiric accusations on the corrupt practices of the institution became news themselves, expanding the Oliver effect in setting the public and international agenda that led to Blatter's resignation.

Called by *The Guardian* (2014) "the star of TV counter-culture," Oliver has repeatedly attacked corporate America and has covered other intricate topics, such as climate change, the death penalty, the wealth gap, paid family leave, the amount of hidden sugar in food, civil forfeiture, the false hopes of lotteries, and government surveillance, among other issues that could barely be considered "entertaining" rather than "audience kryptonite" (Carr, 2014). Nevertheless, during its first year, *LWT* had an average audience of four million viewers who tuned in every week, and two million more watched online the next day. Then, many of those online videos became viral, reaching up to 12 million views and counting. According to *The Washington Post*, Oliver has found a particular niche online by perfecting the art of the viral rant (Yahr, 2014). Diverse news and entertainment media (such as *Time, The Huffington Post,* and *Slate*) have also taken advantage of the "Oliver effect" by participating in the ritual of quickly embedding his videos and hoping to get more traffic and interactions in social media.

Broadcast on Sunday nights at 11 p.m., right after HBO's blockbuster hit "Game of Thrones," each half-hour episode (with no commercials) contains an explanation of a complicated topic from the weekly news agenda, which is frequently turned into agitprop comedy. *Rolling Stone* magazine has described Oliver's pieces as "virtuosic long-form segments, which can stretch to 15 minutes or more, gliding along a Phillipe Petit–worthy line between wonky didacticism and absurdist jokes," adding that they are "like nothing else on television" (Hiatt, 2014, p. 41). As can be noted from the examples described, a main difference between *LWT* and *TDS/TCR* is the in-depth and lengthy treatment of stories, which not only seeks to inform the audience but also, in many cases, to encourage them to take action. While Stewart and Colbert had significant interventions in the real world, Oliver is, according to scholar Dannagal Young, "offering an explicit call to action that's unique. He's interacting with a topic, not just commenting or issuing a broad judgment" (Helmore, 2014). For Young, "contemporary satirists have been reluctant to compromise their status as outsiders, but people on the Left have grown frustrated with satirists who are adept at identifying problems but rarely cross over into agitation" (Helmore, 2014).

In contrast to *TDS* and *TCR*, *LWT* is not a faux newscast or a parody of TV pundits. It has not spent much time mocking the absurdity of cable news or even using its footage. *LWT*'s sources respond to its particular investigative nature. "It's impossible to avoid some stuff about cable news, when it's just so bad," Oliver said. "But generally, we've been forced to look to other sources, because some of the stories we were looking at weren't really covered on cable news. So, the stuff that we've been using for stories has been more from Bloomberg, Al-Jazeera, BBC International or foreign news agencies like India Today. That's where we've been finding the stuff that we need to tell the story," said Oliver to *Rolling Stone* (Hiatt, 2014). *LWT* has assumed this investigative role in times when investigative journalism has declined in the United States. Due to the economic crisis and shrinking audiences, traditional journalism outlets have drastically reduced or gotten rid of their investigative teams (Frank, 2009), distancing themselves from their watchdog role that had its peak during the Watergate era. Investigative reporting has been the first target for news organizations looking to make cuts because it's usually expensive work (it takes more time and more experienced journalists to produce, and it often involves legal battles): "Assigned to cover multiple beats, multitasking backpacking reporters no longer have time to sniff out hidden stories, much less write them. In Washington, bureaus that once did probes have shrunk, closed and consolidated" (Walton, 2010). As noted by Houston (2015), surveys by the American Society of News Editors and the Pew Research Center estimated that about 20,000 daily newspaper editorial jobs have been lost—a 36% decline since the peak of 56,900 newsroom jobs in 1989. The membership of Investigative Reporters and Editors, a professional association, fell more than 30% from 2003 to 2009. Applications for Pulitzers are down more than 40% in some investigative categories, a fall reflected in other competitions. While nonprofit muckraking organizations have mushroomed in the last decade (there are 106 of them in 47 countries), most of these have budgets less than $50,000 and five or fewer people on staff (Coronel, 2013). In this context, a popular satiric infotainment show such as *LWT* offers a prominent place for investigations, infusing the muckraking tradition with humor and punch lines as narrative storytelling techniques at the service of a deeper public interest story.

Stewart's influence on Oliver's new take on satiric infotainment is evident. Oliver, who spent seven years as the "Senior British Correspondent" at *TDS* and even guest-hosted it during eight weeks in the summer of 2013 while Stewart was on leave, has clearly stated his mentor's influence in his career and comedic approach. Nevertheless, there are important differences between them. The main one is, of course, that Oliver is a foreigner. Born in Birmingham, brought up in Bedford, and educated at Cambridge, the comedian has described himself as a child of the Thatcher era, a period marked by the consolidation of economic liberalism and social conservatism, accompanied by the promotion of "traditional moral values" (Ball, 2013). The British experience has been difficult to translate to the American mediascape. After former tabloid editor Piers Morgan, the British figure that replaced Larry King, was fired from CNN, many critics pointed out the difficulties of British media personalities to assimilate and connect with American audiences (Carr, 2014). This disconnection is more profound than just a difference in accent. For the particular case of satire, Orr (2015) analyzed the differences between contemporary British and American TV political satires, suggesting that the latter is infused with a U.S. "national fable of undaunted naiveté" (p. 8). English comedian Ricky Gervais, cocreator of the original British version of *The Office* and the person who recommended that Stewart hire Oliver at *TDS*, described this difference in an interview with *Time* magazine:

> Americans are more "down the line." They don't hide their hopes and fears. They applaud ambition and openly reward success. Brits are more comfortable with life's losers. We embrace the underdog until it's no longer the underdog. We like to bring authority down a peg or two. Just for the hell of it. Americans say, "have a nice day" whether they mean it or not. Brits are terrified to say this. We tell ourselves it's because we don't want to sound insincere but I think it might be for the opposite reason. We don't want to celebrate anything too soon. Failure and disappointment lurk around every corner. This is due to our upbringing. Americans are brought up to believe they can be the next president of the United States. Brits are told, "It won't happen for you." (Gervais, 2011)

Oliver, whose rather working-class accent "seems impressively posh to most Americans" (Hiatt, 2014, p. 39), illustrates these distinct approaches. An example of Oliver's British take on satire can be traced back to January 2009, when he covered Barack Obama taking the oath of office in Washington, DC, in front of hundreds of thousands of euphoric people cheering for the first Black president and the end of the Bush era. In the midst of a climate of hope and change, Oliver offered an alternative interpretation of the historic event: "Is it exciting? Yes! Are people setting themselves up for inevitable disappointment? Of course they are! Do they realize that yet? Absolutely not!"[11] Obama had, at that moment, been

11. http://thedailyshow.cc.com/videos/65oswg/inauguration-day-unity

president for less than a minute. In an interview with *Rolling Stone*, Oliver explained that he had "a similar kind of euphoric feeling in 1997 when Tony Blair was elected" (Hiatt, p. 41). This mix of fatalism and skepticism that distinguishes British from American humor is also part of the essential distinction between Stewart and Oliver:

> Stewart is, at his core, filled with hope. He seems pretty sure that if both political parties could embrace civility, if Fox News turned less nutty, if the media as a whole got more serious, America and the wider world could move forward. To Oliver, though, our global predicaments are all-but-immutable black comedy, which feels about right for an age of ISIS, Ebola, extreme climate change, and Vladimir Putin. (Hiatt, p. 40–41)

The distinct ideological premises of British and American humor, in fact, reflect different sociocultural realities and people's perception of the elites: "American politicians still enjoy a degree of deference from their colleagues, the press, and (occasionally) the public that their counterparts across the pond couldn't dream of" (Orr, 2015, p. 8). In spite of this, U.S. satire has increasingly connected with the British sensibility in the last years, or in the words of the veteran English broadcaster Jeremy Paxman: "British political satire is arguably enjoying a golden age—but in America" (Sherwin, 2014).

Oliver's foreignness also seems to have influenced his agenda of international topics: *LWT* has devoted more attention than his predecessors to foreign stories (not explicitly connected with the United States) and included more foreign associations in his jokes. *LWT*'s segments explaining the Brazilian government corruption scandal and its ridiculous political candidates, Ecuador's President Correa's despotism against social media criticism (Correa even replied to Oliver on Twitter), Maduro's desperate populism in Venezuela, the Armenian genocide, Yemen diplomacy, the Hungarian internet tax, the European Far Right, the anniversary of the Tiananmen Square massacre in China, and Hong Kong protests over its electoral system, among others, have been examples of the show's broad international scope explained for a U.S. audience, a considerably ethnocentric society that has experienced an increasing decline in foreign news coverage during the past decades. Similar to what has happened to investigative reporting, many news organizations have shrunk their budgets and closed their offices abroad or drastically reduced the number of full-time foreign correspondents. Between 1988 and 2010, international news coverage declined 56% on TV networks such as NBC, ABC, and CBS. The front page newshole for foreign affairs stories decreased from 27% in 1987 to

11% in 2010 (Willnat & Martin, 2012). In this sense, *LWT* has also added a cosmopolitan value to U.S. satiric infotainment.

U.S. NEWS SATIRE IN THE POST-NETWORK ERA

LWT complements what I call a "satiric triumvirate" that has established a critical dialog with three of the main functions and practices of journalism in the United States: information, opinion/analysis, and investigation. While Stewart focused on deconstructing the daily news agenda (the informative function of daily journalism) and Colbert tackled the inconsistencies and absurdities of pundits (opinion/analysis), Oliver focuses on investigative journalism with thorough reporting and longer in-depth pieces. Of course, all these areas are interconnected and overlap one another, and all the shows have critically tackled the various journalistic aspects at some point, but their focus defined their different intentions (and possible effects).

The evolution of this "satiric triumvirate" also shows how these infotainment shows have increasingly attempted to intervene in the real world of politics—from Stewart's Rally To Restore Sanity and Colbert's super PAC to Oliver's agitprop pieces encouraging his viewers to take action and his confrontations with public figures. Rejecting any type of journalistic role and accountability, these contemporary court jesters have progressively moved from infotainment to activism outside of the comedy box. This attitude can also be seen as a response to the criticisms related to the innocuous and cynic role of satire and its potential alienation of audiences.

During the past decades, the context for satiric infotainment has also changed in the United States. While *TDS* gained influence as an oppositional voice to the Bush administration and Colbert exhibited the ideological tensions during Obama's government, Oliver works with the political scenario of President Donald Trump, an entertainer himself. Soon before Trump was elected, Oliver delivered a national apology, taking blame for the rise of the Republican presidential nominee. "It is frankly hard to believe that there was a time when people thought a Trump candidacy would be funny," he said in *LWT* before showing a clip from 2013 when he joked about the possibility. It was a moment in which the political reality challenged the absurdist logic of satire, opening the door for "alternative facts" and "fake news" becoming key expressions to understand the tense relation between the U.S. government and the media. Nevertheless, in the Trump era, satire has remained relevant and combative, evidencing the thin-skinned nature of the president who embarked on Twitter wars with several comedians who parodied him and his collaborators. Documentary filmmaker Michael Moore has actually called to "fight Trump with an army of comedy" in order to expose his falsehoods and "nakedness," a confrontation between institutional cynicism and absurdist disbelief. Or as noted by Hennefeld (2017): "It will be a war of consensus between the propaganda of fake-fake news (as disinformation) and the critical apparatus of real-fake news (as comedic truth-telling)."

On the other hand, the rise of Trump and his misogynistic campaign matched a rebirth of racial tensions and xenophobic discourse. In this scenario, the U.S. satiric shows have also adapted to these circumstances. The fact, for example, that Oliver is a foreigner does not seem gratuitous nor does the selection of South African Trevor Noah as Stewart's replacement at *TDS*. In times when American ethnocentrism and its negative impact on the rest of the world have become evident, it seems necessary to include new voices and points of view and more diversity in the satiric resistance. Other programs like *The Nightly Show With Larry Wilmore* and *Full Frontal With Samantha Bee*—both comedians were former contributors to *TDS*—are also examples of this effort toward more diversity in terms of race and gender in U.S. satiric infotainment. More recently, Nussbaum (2017) associated the misogynistic Trump's campaign with an "explosion of female comedy." For example, comedian Melissa McCarthy's hilarious *SNL* parody of Sean Spicer, the White House press secretary, has already promoted a tendency of women willing to play and ridicule members of Trump's administration.

From another perspective, the TV business and viewing trends have also irrevocably changed since Stewart began hosting *TDS* in 1999. In the post-network era, social media and multiplatform communication have altered news cycles. As noted by Weiner (2015), viewers—especially the ones who have been satiric TV's core demographic (ages 18–34)—expect to have content available in a variety of platforms (smartphone applications, Xbox consoles, YouTube, Roku, Hulu, Netflix, Amazon, among others). While any traditional media outlet faces a similar challenge, networks such as Comedy Central, owned by the media conglomerate Viacom, deal with a particular paradox: What to do when your main demographic stops watching television? After Stewart announced his retirement in 2015, Viacom's stock dipped 1.5% because of the perception that ratings, as well as advertising income, would continue to decline (Comedy Central's ratings were down 30% among its target audience, year over year, in the first quarter of 2015). It does not mean, however, that people are not watching their content, but, as network executives argue, they are doing it in ways that traditional "linear" ratings don't capture nor do they reflect multiplatform viewing habits (Weiner, 2015). In other words, in terms of advertising, the money is still in the linear world and satire's young audience is multilinear. While networks like Comedy Central still make most of their money from affiliate fees, advertising, and licensing fees, executives are addressing new modes of viewing: by betting on Web-born talent, devising shows with digital platforms in mind, and bringing greater diversity to the network's programming (Weiner, 2015). CC Studios, a Comedy Central division charged with developing digital-only series, has already produced successful shows that stemmed from independent Web projects, which are considerably cheaper to produce. Similarly, Funny or Die, the Emmy-winning comedy video-hosting website launched in 2007, is already a prevalent example of the production of new risqué satiric projects. In 2014, for example, comedian Zach Galifianakis interviewed President Barack Obama on his online show "Between Two Ferns," hosted by Funny or Die. The video, in which they talked about the Affordable Care Act in the midst of absurdist jokes, already has more than 30 million views. In September 2016, in the midst of the controversial campaign against Donald Trump, presidential candidate Hillary Clinton also appeared on the online show. It is not difficult to imagine, then, that the next influential satiric voices will probably come from digital development.

REFERENCES

Amarasingam, A. (Ed.). (2011). *The Stewart/Colbert effect: Essays on the real impacts of fake news*. Jefferson, NC: McFarland.

Americans spending more time following the news. (2010). *Pew Research Center*. Retrieved from http://www.people-press.org/2010/09/12/americans-spending-more-time-following-the-news/

Ball, J. (2013). The Thatcher effect: What changed and what stayed the same. *The Guardian*. Retrieved from http://www.theguardian.com/politics/2013/apr/12/thatcher-britain

Baumgartner, J., & Morris, J. (2006). The Daily Show effect. *American Politics Research*, 34(3), 341–367.

Baumgartner, J., & Morris, J. (2008). One "nation," under Stephen? The effects of *The Colbert Report* on American youth. *Journal of Broadcasting & Electronic Media*, 52(4), 622–643. http://dx.doi.org/10.1080/08838150802437487

Baym, G. (2005). *The Daily Show*: Discursive integration and the reinvention of political journalism. *Political Communication*, 22(3), 259–276.

Baym, G. (2009). Stephen Colbert's parody of the postmodern. In J. Gray, J. Jones, & E. Thompson (Eds.), *Satire TV: Politics and comedy in the post-network era* (pp. 124–146). New York, NY: NYU Press.

Baym, G. (2010). *From Cronkite to Colbert: The evolution of broadcast news*. Boulder, CO: Paradigm.

Baym, G., & Jones, J. (Eds.). (2013). *News parody and political satire across the globe*. New York, NY: Routledge.

Bill Moyers talks with Jon Stewart on *NOW With Bill Moyers*, July 11, 2003. *PBS*. Retrieved from http://www.pbs.org/moyers/journal/archives/stewart_ts.html

Boler, M., & Turpin, S. (2008). *The Daily Show* and *Crossfire*: Satire and sincerity as truth to power. In M. Boler (Ed.), *Digital media and democracy: Tactics in hard times*. Cambridge, MA: MIT Press.

Borden, S. L., & Tew, C. (2007). The role of journalist and the performance of journalism: Ethical lessons from "fake" news (seriously). *Journal of Mass Media Ethics*, 22(4), 300–314.

Cable and internet loom large in fragmented political news universe. (2004). *Pew Research Center*. Retrieved from http://www.pewinternet.org/2004/01/11/cable-and-internet-loom-large-in-fragmented-political-news-universe/

Carr, D. (2011, August 21). Comic's PAC is more than a gag. *The New York Times*. Retrieved from http://www.nytimes.com/2011/08/22/business/media/stephen-colberts-pac-is-more-than-a-gag.html?_r=0

Carr, D. (2014, November 16). John Oliver's complicated fun connects for HBO. *The New York Times*. Retrieved from http://www.nytimes.com/2014/11/17/business/media/john-olivers-complicated-fun-connects-for-hbo.html?_r=1

Colleta, L. (2009). Political satire and postmodern irony in the age of Stephen Colbert and Jon Stewart. *Journal of Popular Culture*, 42(5), 856–874.

Combe, K. (2015). Stephen Colbert: Great satirist, or greatest satirist ever? *The International Communication Gazette*, 77(3), 297–311.

Conway, M., Grabe, M. E., & Grieves, K. (2007). Villains, victims, and the virtuous in Bill O'Reilly's "No-Spin Zone": Revisiting world war propaganda techniques. *Journalism Studies*, 8(2), 197–223.

Coronel, S. (2013). Why investigative reporting is on life support. *The International Consortium of Investigative Journalism (ICIJ)*. Retrieved from http://www.icij.org/blog/2013/01/why-investigative-reporting-life-support

"Daily Show" viewers knowledgeable about presidential campaign. (2004). *Annenberg Public Policy Center*. Retrieved from http://www.annenbergpublicpolicycenter.org/daily-show-viewers-knowledgeable-about-presidential-campaign/

Day, A. (2011). *Satire and dissent*. Bloomington, IN: Indiana University Press.

Dowd, M. (2006). America's anchors. *Rolling Stone*. Retrieved from http://web.archive.org/web/20070818095819/http://www.rollingstone.com/news/coverstory/jon_stewart_stephen_colbert_americas_anchors

Edmonds, R., Guskin, E., Mitchell, A., & Jurkowitz, M. (2013). Newspapers: By the numbers. *The State of the News Media 2013*. Retrieved from http://www.stateofthemedia.org/2013/newspapers-stabilizing-but-still-threatened/newspapers-by-the-numbers/

Edmonds, R., Guskin, E., Rosenstiel, T., & Mitchell, A. (2012). Newspapers: Building digital revenues proves painfully slow. *The State of the News Media 2012*. Retrieved from http://www.stateofthemedia.org/2012/newspapers-building-digital-revenues-proves-painfully-slow/

Faina, J. (2012). Public journalism is a joke: The case of Jon Stewart and Stephen Colbert. *Journalism*, 14(4), 541–555.

Feldman, L. (2007). The news about comedy. *Journalism*, 8(4), 406–427.

Feldman, L. (2013). Learning about politics from *The Daily Show*: The role of viewer orientation and processing motivations. *Mass Communication & Society*, 16(4), 586–607. http://dx.doi.org/10.1080/15205436.2012.735742

Feldman, L., & Young, D. G. (2008). Late-night comedy as a gateway to traditional news: An analysis of time trends in news attention among late-night comedy viewers during the 2004 presidential primaries. *Political Communication, 25*(4), 401–422. http://dx.doi.org/10.1080/10584600802427013

Frank, L. (2009). The withering watchdog. *PBS*. Retrieved from http://www.pbs.org/wnet/expose/2009/06/the-withering-watchdog.html

Frankfurt, H. (2005). *On bullshit*. Princeton, NJ: Princeton University Press.

Fuller, J. (2012). *What is happening to news? The information explosion and the crisis of journalism*. Chicago, IL: University of Chicago Press.

Gervais, R. (2011). The difference between American and British humour. *Time*. Retrieved from http://time.com/3720218/difference-between-american-british-humour/

Gray, J. (2005). Television teaching: Parody, *The Simpsons*, and media literacy. *Critical Studies in Media Communication, 22*(3), 223–238.

Gray, J., Jones, J., & Thompson, E. (Eds.). (2009). *Satire TV: Politics and comedy in the post-network era*. New York, NY: NYU Press.

Grondin, D. (2012). Understanding culture wars through satirical/political infotainment TV: Jon Stewart and *The Daily Show*'s critique as mediated re-enactment of the culture war. *Canadian Review of American Studies, 42*(3), 347–370.

Hachten, W. (2005). *The troubles of journalism* (3d ed.). Mahwah, NJ: Lawrence Erlbaum.

Hart, R. P., & Hartelius, E. J. (2007). The political sins of Jon Stewart. *Critical Studies in Media Communication, 24*(3), 263–272. http://dx.doi.org/10.1080/07393180701520991

Helmore, E. (2014, June 14). How John Oliver started a revolution in US TV's political satire. *The Guardian*. Retrieved from http://www.theguardian.com/tv-and-radio/2014/jun/15/john-oliver-started-a-revolution-in-us-tv-political-satire

Hennefeld, M. (2017). Fake news: From satirical truthiness to alternative facts. *New Politics*. Retrieved from http://newpol.org/content/fake-news-satirical-truthiness-alternative-facts

Hiatt, B. (2014, October 9). John Oliver is mad as hell. *Rolling Stone*, pp. 38–43.

Hmielowski, J. D., Holbert, R. L., & Lee, J. (2011). Predicting the consumption of political TV satire: Affinity for political humor, *The Daily Show*, and *The Colbert Report*. *Communication Monographs, 78*(1), 96–114. http://dx.doi.org/10.1080/03637751.2010.542579

Hoffman, L. H., & Thomson, T. L. (2009). The effect of television viewing on adolescents' civic participation: Political efficacy as a mediating mechanism. *Journal of Broadcasting & Electronic Media, 53*(1), 3–21. http://dx.doi.org/10.1080/08838150802643415

Holbert, R. L., Hmielowski, J., Jain, P., Lather, J., & Morey, A. (2011). Adding nuance to the study of political humor effects: Experimental research on Juvenalian satire versus Horatian satire. *American Behavioral Scientist, 55*(3), 187–211. http://dx.doi.org/10.1177/0002764210392156

Holbert, R. L., Lambe, J. L., Dudo, A. D., & Carlton, K. A. (2007). Primacy effects of *The Daily Show* and national TV news viewing: Young viewers, political gratifications, and internal political self-efficacy. *Journal of Broadcasting & Electronic Media, 51*(1), 20–38. http://dx.doi.org/10.1080/08838150701308002

Holbert, R. L., Tchernev, J. M., Walther, W. O., Esralew, S. E., & Benski, K. (2013). Young voter perceptions of political satire as persuasion: A focus on perceived influence, persuasive intent, and message strength. *Journal of Broadcasting & Electronic Media, 57*(2), 170–186. http://dx.doi.org/10.1080/08838151.2013.787075

Holcomb, J. (2014). News revenue declines despite growth from new sources. *Pew Research Center*. Retrieved from http://www.pewresearch.org/fact-tank/2014/04/03/news-revenue-declines-despite-growth-from-new-sources/

Houston, B. (2015). 21st century muckraking: Investigative reporting unleashed. *Global Investigative Journalism Network*. Retrieved from http://gijn.org/2015/02/20/investigative-reporting-unleashed-from-withering-watchdogs-to-global-muckrakers/

Jones, J. (2007). Fake news versus real news as sources of political information: *The Daily Show* and postmodern political reality. In K. Rieget (Ed.), *Politicotainment*. New York, NY: Peter Lang.

Jones, J. (2010). *Entertaining politics: Satiric television and political engagement*. Lanham, MD: Rowman & Littlefield.

Jones, J., & Baym, G. (2010). A dialogue on satire news and the crisis of truth in postmodern political television. *Journal of Communication Inquiry*, *34*(3), 278–294.

Jones, J., Baym, G., & Day, A. (2012). Mr. Stewart and Mr. Colbert go to Washington: Television satirists outside the box. *Social Research*, *79*(1), 33–60.

Junod, T. (2011, October). Jon Stewart and the burden of history. *Esquire*. Retrieved from http://www.esquire.com/features/jon-stewart-profile-1011

Kakutani, M. (2008, August 17). Is Jon Stewart the most trusted man in America? *The New York Times*. Retrieved from http://www.nytimes.com/2008/08/17/arts/television/17kaku.html?pagewanted=all

Kercher, S. (2006). *Revel with a cause: Liberal satire in postwar America*. Chicago, IL: University of Chicago Press.

Kohut, A. (2013). Pew Research surveys of audience habits suggest perilous future for news. *Pew Research Center*. Retrieved from http://www.pewresearch.org/fact-tank/2013/10/04/pew-surveys-of-audience-habits-suggest-perilous-future-for-news/

Kovach, B., & Rosenstiel, T. (2001). *The elements of journalism: What newspeople should know and the public should expect*. New York, NY: Crown.

Kowalewski, J. (2013). Does humor matter? An analysis of how hard news versus comedy news impact the agenda-setting effects. *Southwestern Mass Communication Journal*, *28*(1), 1–29.

LaMarre, H. L., Landreville, K. D., & Beam, M. A. (2009). The irony of satire. *International Journal of Press/Politics*, *14*(2), 212–231.

Meddaugh, P. M. (2010). Bakhtin, Colbert, and the center of discourse: Is there no "truthiness" in humor? *Critical Studies in Media Communication*, *27*(4), 376–390. http://dx.doi.org/10.1080/15295030903583606

Mitchell, A., & Matsa, K. E. (2015). The declining value of U.S. newspapers. *Pew Research Center*. Retrieved from http://www.pewresearch.org/fact-tank/2015/05/22/the-declining-value-of-u-s-newspapers/

Mitchell, A., & Rosenstiel, T. (2012). *The state of the news media 2012: An annual report on American journalism*. Washington, DC: Pew Research Center's Project for Excellence in Journalism.

Morris, J. (2009). *The Daily Show with Jon Stewart* and audience attitude change during the 2004 party conventions. *Political Behavior*, *31*(1), 79–102. http://dx.doi.org/10.1007/s11109-008-9064-y

Newspaper: Daily readership. (2014). *Pew Research Center*. Retrieved from http://www.journalism.org/media-indicators/newspaper-readership-by-age/

Nussbaum, E. (2017). How jokes won the election. *The New Yorker*. Retrieved from http://www.newyorker.com/magazine/2017/01/23/how-jokes-won-the-election

Orr, C. (2015, March). Why the British are better at satire. *The Atlantic*. Retrieved from http://www.theatlantic.com/magazine/archive/2015/03/why-the-british-are-better-at-satire/384964/

Painter, C., & Hodges, L. (2010). Mocking the news: How *The Daily Show with Jon Stewart* holds traditional broadcast news accountable. *Journal of Mass Media Ethics*, 25(4), 257–274. http://dx.doi.org/10.1080/08900523.2010.512824

Polk, J., Young, D. G., & Holbert, R. L. (2009). Humor complexity and political influence: An elaboration likelihood approach to the effects of humor type in *The Daily Show with Jon Stewart*. *Atlantic Journal of Communication*, 17(4), 202–219. http://dx.doi.org/10.1080/15456870903210055

Poniewozik, J. (2015). Review: On "Late Show" premiere, Stephen Colbert tries to bring big back to late night. *The New York Times*. Retrieved from http://www.nytimes.com/2015/09/10/arts/television/late-show-with-stephen-colbert-review.html?_r=0

Press widely criticized, but trusted more than other information sources. (2011). *Pew Research Center*. Retrieved from http://www.people-press.org/2011/09/22/press-widely-criticized-but-trusted-more-than-other-institutions/

Rossing, J. P. (2012). Deconstructing postracialism: Humor as a critical, cultural project. *Journal of Communication Inquiry*, 36, 44–61.

Sherwin, A. (2014, September 1). Jeremy Paxman: Britain needs a new "Spitting Image" to restore faith in politics. *Independent*. Retrieved from http://www.independent.co.uk/news/media/tv-radio/jeremy-paxman-britain-needs-a-new-spitting-image-to-restore-faith-in-politics-9704394.html

Smith, C. (2010). America is a joke. *New York Magazine*. Retrieved from http://nymag.com/arts/tv/profiles/68086/

Smolkin, R., & Groves, E. (2007). What the mainstream media can learn from Jon Stewart. *American Journalism Review*, 29(3), 18–25.

Stephen Colbert's civics lesson: Or, how a TV humorist taught America about campaign finance. (2014). *Annenberg Public Policy Center*. Retrieved from http://www.annenbergpublicpolicycenter.org/stephen-colberts-civics-lesson-or-how-a-tv-humorist-taught-america-about-campaign-finance/

Sternbergh, A. (2006). Stephen Colbert has America by the ballots. *New York Magazine*. Retrieved from http://nymag.com/news/politics/22322/

Today's journalists less prominent. (2007). [Press release]. *Pew Research Center*. Retrieved from http://www.people-press.org/files/legacy-pdf/309.pdf

Walton, M. (2010). Investigative shortfall. *American Journalism Review*. Retrieved from http://ajrarchive.org/article.asp?id=4904

Warner, J. (2007). Political culture jamming: The dissident humor of "The Daily Show With Jon Stewart." *Popular Communication*, 5(1), 17–36.

Watching, reading, and listening to the news. (2012). *Pew Research Center*. Retrieved from http://www.people-press.org/2012/09/27/section-1-watching-reading-and-listening-to-the-news-3/

Weiner, J. (2015, June 18). Comedy Central in the post-TV era. *The New York Times*. Retrieved from http://www.nytimes.com/2015/06/21/magazine/comedy-central-in-the-post-tv-era.html?_r=0

Willnat, L., & Martin, J. (2012). Foreign correspondents: An endangered species? In D. H. Weaver & L. Willnat (Eds.), *The Global Journalist in the 21st Century* (pp. 495–509). New York, NY: Routledge.

Winstead, L. (2012). *Lizz Free or Die*. New York, NY: Penguin Group.

Xiaoxia, C. (2008). Political comedy shows and knowledge about primary campaigns: The moderating effects of age and education. *Mass Communication & Society*, *11*(1), 43–61. http://dx.doi.org/10.1080/15205430701585028

Xiaoxia, C. (2010). Hearing it from Jon Stewart: The impact of *The Daily Show* on public attentiveness to politics. *International Journal of Public Opinion Research*, *22*(1), 26–46. http://dx.doi.org/10.1093/ijpor/edp043

Yahr, E. (2014, June 10). HBO's John Oliver has found his late-night niche—viral rants. *The Washington Post*. Retrieved from https://http://www.washingtonpost.com/news/style-blog/wp/2014/06/10/hbos-john-oliver-has-found-his-niche-viral-rants/

Young, D. G. (2013). Laughter, learning, or enlightenment? Viewing and avoidance motivations behind *The Daily Show* and *The Colbert Report*. *Journal of Broadcasting & Electronic Media*, *57*(2), 153–169. http://dx.doi.org/10.1080/08838151.2013.787080

Young Mie, K., & Vishak, J. (2008). Just laugh! You don't need to remember: The effects of entertainment media on political information acquisition and information processing in political judgment. *Journal of Communication*, *58*(2), 338–360. http://dx.doi.org/10.1111/j.1460-2466.2008.00388.x

CHAPTER 3

Jaime Bayly's *El Francotirador*

*Peruvian Satiric Infotainment After Fujimori's
Media Dictatorship*

In 2009, Jaime Bayly, one of Peru's most influential TV journalists and celebrities, announced that he wanted to be the first bisexual, impotent, and agnostic president of Peru. He added that he also wanted to be the first lady. He launched an atypical electoral campaign, fueled by his irreverent TV show *El Francotirador (The Sniper)*, which combined political interviews, celebrity culture, and social and political satire. Bayly's yearlong virtual campaign increasingly gained attention and local and international media coverage. He even polled at 10% in Lima, the capital city, but ultimately dropped out of the race a few months before the election.[1]

Born in Lima in 1965, Bayly started as a newspaper reporter at the age of 15. He began interviewing politicians and celebrities on TV when he was 18 years old. He was quickly transformed into a national celebrity, as Lima's *enfant terrible*, and his life and career proceeded to be linked to scandals. He made recurrent media spectacles of his bisexuality, former drug addiction, suicidal intents, love affairs, political opinions, sexual impotence, literary works, and family life. He has participated in Peruvian and international show business and literary circles. While he exposed local politicians' and celebrities' secrets with a tabloid approach, he also criticized authoritarian

---

1. A previous version of this chapter was published as an article in the *Journal of Iberian and Latin American Studies* in 2015.

attitudes, conducted decisive interviews with opinion leaders, and acquired an influential and critical attitude toward recent governments in Peru. At the same time, he has been accused of being a delusional egomaniac, a postmodern buffoon, and a representative of Lima's right-wing and elite social class (*El País*, January 7, 2012).

This chapter analyzes how Bayly constructed his ambiguous and contradictory media persona during his 30-year career and how he capitalized on its political appeal during his electoral run while revealing social tensions in contemporary Peru, mainly based on inequality, exclusion, and ethnic and social discrimination (CVR, 2004; De la Cadena, 2011; Flores Galindo, 1994; Matos Mar, 1987; Nugent, 1992; Portocarrero, 1993; Thorp, Caumartin, & Gray-Molina, 2006; Thorp & Paredes, 2010; Vargas Llosa, 1996). Based on the analysis of his TV show *El Francotirador*, his newspaper columns, and the press coverage about him, Bayly's intense, controversial, and sometimes transgressive life in the media is read as an example of how entertainment replaces other argumentative and informative forms of political communication in Peru, a deeply divided society with fragile social institutions, precarious democracy, and a discredited political class that exist within a crisis of representation (Barrenechea & Sosa, 2014; Cotler, 2013; Crabtree, 2010; Dargent, 2009; Levitsky & Cameron, 2003; Tanaka & Vera, 2007; Vergara, 2013). Bayly's life in the media also illuminates how mass media spectacle became a contested arena to negotiate political power both during and since President Alberto Fujimori's authoritarian regime (1990–2000).

THE FUJIMORIZATION OF POLITICS AND MEDIA IN PERU

Spectacle and infotainment became key components of the authoritarian government of President Fujimori, which maintained tremendous control of the media. This control led to both flagrant cases of corruption and also a disproportionate growth of sensationalist media and the trivialization of national TV content. Fujimori used the media as a mouthpiece for the authoritarian regime to disqualify any oppositional figures through defamation and sexist, racist, and homophobic insults. The tabloid media became extremely popular, garnered high ratings and circulation, and mainly (but not exclusively) targeted the Peruvian lower classes. Evidence indicates that the government, through the National Intelligence Service, paid in cash for the biased coverage (Conaghan, 2002, 2005; Degregori, 2000; Fowks, 2000; Macassi, 2001; Wood, 2000). This strategy also shifted attention away from relevant social issues and developed a society with an appetite for spectacle and infotainment, to the detriment of freedom of expression. This period of Peruvian history has been called "Latin America's First Media Dictatorship,"[2] and Fujimori's presidency has been described as one of the best examples of the relations among neopopulism, neoliberalism, and mass media (especially television) in Latin America (Boas, 2005; Roberts, 1995; Weyland, 2001, 2003).

During Fujimori's administration, the media in general became frivolous and timid. Media spectacles grew, distracting public attention from national politics and violations of human rights. *Chicha*,[3] or sensationalist publications, became the most outrageous and "trashy" products. Designed to appeal to the less educated segment of the Peruvian population, these tabloids, displayed in all *kioskos* (street newsstands), used slang in headlines and news articles, portrayed partially nude females on the front page, and focused coverage on murders, rapes, and local celebrities (Gargurevich, 1991, 2000). At the same time, the government and the undermined media encouraged the success and popularity of new entertainment TV programs and infotainment formats, such as the talk show *Laura en América* and the paparazzi show *Magaly Teve*. Fully embracing sensationalism, a conservative rhetoric, and a paternalistic attitude toward the low-income classes, these were two of the most popular shows in Peru during the 1990s. Like most of the media, they served the government's authoritarian discourse in direct ways (as propaganda) and indirect ways (shifting attention away from relevant social issues).

While *Monos y Monadas*—an emblematic political satire magazine that is part of a rooted tradition of satirical writings in Peru—ceased publication after,[4] TV political humor was also co-opted by the regime. For

2. The Skylight Pictures online video "Latin America's First Media Dictatorship" shows how media were co-opted through the top-level corruption in Peru: https://www.youtube.com/watch?v=X0y5uXV11Os

3. The term *chicha*, a traditional Peruvian beverage, is also used to refer to the popular culture of Lima, a mix that reflects the intrinsic *mestizaje* of Peruvian contemporary society. In music and other cultural manifestations, it has developed an original aesthetic and narrative of popular life. But the media world appropriated the term for vulgar sensationalism.

4. Founded in 1905 by Leonidas Yerovi, the satiric magazine *Monos y Monadas* congregated some of the most important Peruvian writers of the time, such as Ricardo Palma, Abraham Valdelomar, and Manuel González Prada. Its first period only lasted 2 years. Seven decades later, the writer and humorist Nicolas Yerovi, Leonida's grandson, relaunched the magazine in 1978 during the military dictatorship. It congregated again a talented generation of writers, humorists, and cartoonists, such as Antonio Cisneros, Carlos Tovar "Carlín," Rafo León, and Juan Acevedo, who targeted the political elites and Peru's social contradictions. The second period of the magazine ended in 1984. A year later the magazine resumed publication, lasting until 1992, when it closed with Fujimori's self-coup on April 5. A new period started after the fall of Fujimori's regime in 2000, and lasted 3 years (Mendoza, 2005; Planas, 2000).

example, Carlos Alvarez, one of the most famous comedians of the last decades in Peru, was hired on the state TV channel to satirize opposition leaders and took part in Fujimori's electoral campaigns (Alonso, 2012; Hildebrandt, 2008; "Popular cómico peruano afirma que fue chantajeado por Montesinos," 2002; Vivas Sabroso, 1999). It is also important to note the existence of *Los Chistosos*, a satiric infotainment radio show hosted by veteran comedian Guillermo Rossini and other talented impersonators. Broadcast on *Radio Programas del Peru (RPP)*, a radio station also co-opted by the regime, the show, now more than 23 years on the air, tried to be neutral within a censored environment and mildly satirized diverse political tents ("'Los chistosos', 22 años de pasión por el humor," 2015; Pajares, 2012).[5] During the last year of the Fujimori regime, one of the few spaces critical of the government on national TV was the satiric infotainment show *Beto a Saber*, which demonstrated the power of the combination of political satire and journalism to critique the authoritarian regime (Alonso, 2010).

Fujimori understood the importance of media spectacle to obtain the best political use of the military's victories. For example, in 1992 the police captured terrorist leader Abimael Guzmán of the Shining Path, who was exhibited publicly in a cage with a black-and-white-striped uniform, pacing back and forth like an animal. The shocking images appeared worldwide. Fujimori used this event and its spectacular media framing as one of the main accomplishments of his government. The colonization of reality by saturating the media with startling images and floods of misinformation led to what Degregori (2000) called "the decade of the anti-politics." For Degregori, an emptiness of critical discourse in the political spheres and in the media marked the 1990s, where images and sensationalism ruled over debate, analysis, and argumentation, and consolidated a society of spectacle. Fujimori's government promoted staged, spectacular news and political infotainment combinations as part of the regime's media control mechanisms. Executed through the National Intelligence Service, these mechanisms were part of a wide network of corruption and mafia operations: Media owners and journalists were bribed to express a pro-government editorial stance and to unscrupulously attack members of the opposition through libel and defamation. The corruption during the Fujimori-Montesinos regime expanded to many other institutions and social sectors. Its exposure through videos, broadcast by an alliance of oppositional groups, led to Fujimori's resignation via fax in November 2000

---

5. After the fall of the Fujimori regime, the news parody show also made its way onto television as *24 minutos* and *24 minutazos*. According to Rossini, the show was canceled in democracy because President Toledo took offense to their parodies (Pajares, 2012).

while he was in Japan. Upon his extradition to Peru, he was subjected to a sensationalized trial and was sentenced in 2009 to 25 years in prison for violating human rights.

The precarious post-Fujimori democratic government inaugurated in 2001 faced a strong oppositional mainstream press. This press sought to recover its watchdog role, frequently using sensationalism to deliver accusations, a possible legacy of spectacle, but renamed "freedom of expression" in democracy. This was the case of *La Ventana Indiscreta*, an innovative show within the investigative journalism genre often criticized for sensationalism. In 2004, President Toledo accused the press of a "plot" to remove him from power through a series of corruption allegations involving his closest collaborators (Felch, 2004; Mahshie, 2005). During Alan Garcia's government (2006–2011), the media exposed high-profile corruption in the government until several of those critical journalists were fired from the main media outlets. In this context, Jaime Bayly, the nation's most controversial journalist and celebrity, launched an atypical presidential campaign in 2010 via his popular infotainment TV show *El Francotirador (The Sniper)*, which evidenced the power of satire and celebrity culture in Peru's fragmented society.

DISCRIMINATION, IDENTITY, AND HUMOR IN PERU

Discrimination and inequality in Peru reflect a historical process rooted in the Spanish conquest and colonial times. Spanish rule focused on a strong hierarchy, consisting of a privileged urban Spanish-descent population (White or "criollos") and a marginalized rural indigenous population ("indios"), with overlapping racial and class boundaries (Flores Galindo, 1994; Moreno & Oropesa, 2012; Portocarrero, 1993). "Mestizos," the offspring of Spanish and indigenous populations, added a layer of complexity to Peruvian social organization, accompanied by a preoccupation with ancestry to establish descent. Within these categories, fluidity has prevailed due to the imperfect demarcation of racial boundaries by social characteristics (De la Cadena, 2011; García, 2005; Thorp & Paredes, 2010). "Criollos" refers to "White" Peruvians as well as those of European descent and is usually associated with individuals from the coast, frequently considered members of the upper classes (García, 2005). In this sense, ethnic categories reflect social, geographic, and genealogical distinctions (Moreno & Oropesa, 2012). Similarly, the indigenous population is considered primarily rural and is comprised of segmented populations of Andeans and Amazonians. Smaller percentages of Blacks and Asians also became part of the ethnic mixture of the nation. In such a diverse country, lack of cohesive identities has been a constant debate. Nugent (1992) explained the Peruvian dynamics between social and ethnic groups as one based on contempt ("desprecio"). In practice, however, these dynamics are more complex: Boundary permeability is apparent among upwardly mobile individuals with indigenous backgrounds, who characterize themselves as "mestizo" to maintain consistency with their accomplishments (De la Cadena, 2011). This might explain partially why Peru is a country where concepts of ethnicity and race have been very much suppressed. In contrast to other Latin American countries with significant indigenous populations (such as Guatemala, Bolivia, and Ecuador), Peru lacks an indigenous identity (Thorp et al., 2006).[6] Nevertheless, the massive immigration from the Andes to Lima that began during the 1940s drastically changed the social organization of the country. Matos Mar (1987, 2004, 2012) called this process "desborde popular" (popular overflow), in which millions of people migrated from the poor, marginalized rural areas (the "Other Peru") to the cities, especially Lima (the "Official Peru"), constituting a huge cultural revolution. Those migrants from the provinces settled in territories in the peripheries of the city ("barriadas"), generating a struggling process of urbanization and new, unexpected social dynamics.

In time, the migrants from the provinces (the so-called urban-indians) were labeled with the polysemic identity term "cholo" (Quijano, 1980), which has been used in a pejorative sense but more recently also as an empowering identity term to proudly reflect the hybrid nature of the "New Peru." Initially discriminated against and marginalized, those millions of migrants from the Andes brought their culture but also adapted to the urban lifestyle, transforming Lima into the megacity of 9 million people that it is today. TV humor has tended to portray these social dynamics in a discriminatory manner, reproducing prejudiced stereotypes of marginalized ethnic groups (Sue & Golash-Boza, 2013). Two of the most controversial cases have been the characters La Paisana Jacinta and El Negro Mama. Created by comedian Jorge Benavides, these characters offensively parodied indigenous and Black Peruvians, respectively. Peruvian media humor has also developed a similar framing with other marginalized groups, such as LGBT

6. Key historical events—such as the Rebellion of Tupac Amaru in 1780, the war with Chile (1879–1883), the leftist military dictatorship of General Velasco (1968–1975), and the recent period of political violence between the state and the Shining Path (1980–2000)—led to the relative failure of an indigenous movement to emerge in the 20th century.

people. Homophobic, sexist, and racist jokes have always been part of most popular entertainment shows on national TV.

While discrimination, resentment, and inequality prevail, third and fourth generations of migrants from the rural areas to the city have prospered. Many of them are now successful entrepreneurs and have emerged as an expanding middle class. In the current context of the country's macroeconomic growth and the celebration of "progress" in Lima, the "cholification" of the city is perceived as a cultural fusion among the urban, the Andean, and the global (Ypeij, 2013). A "criollo" aristocrat himself, Bayly's various and contrasting identities then can also be interpreted as a result of this process of "cholification" in Peruvian society.

EL FRANCOTIRADOR AND THE PRESIDENTIAL ELECTIONS

On October 13, 2008, the news portal *Terra* published the following story in its entertainment section: "Jaime Bayly announces his presidential candidacy." "I am going to be the first homosexual and impotent Peruvian president," Bayly said on his show *El Francotirador*. The *Terra* story had these quotes:

> Some people think I am joking, but I will be a presidential candidate in 2011. I will gather 150,000 citizens' signatures, and I will propose some innovative ideas. I don't aspire to win, but I will be a candidate. Why? To fuck with the system! I don't want to change the country, just fuck with the system. Laugh, but I am going to be a candidate, you'll see . . . I would make a fantastic president. I'd start working every day at 1 p.m. from my house. I won't ever go to the Government Palace, nor will I travel to the provinces. (*Terra*, October 13, 2008)

On April 24, 2009, the international Spanish news agency EFE reported: "Jaime Bayly wants to be President and First Lady of Peru." The story quoted Bayly as saying, "I am bisexual, impotent, and agnostic. I am American, because I have an American passport, and I am not crazy enough to give it away. But I am also Peruvian, and I dream that the poor children of my country will be able to have the same education as my daughters" (*El Nuevo Herald*, April 24, 2009). In January 2010, his potential presidential candidacy got extensive national and international attention. He began to appear in two national polls, receiving 2%–3% of public support after the announcement of a political agreement between Bayly and veteran politician José Barba Caballero, who stated that Bayly would run as a candidate for Barba's political party *Cambio Radical* (Radical Change). The AFP news agency of France reported: "Popular TV host and writer Jaime Bayly said that he would run for President in the 2011 Peruvian elections as a provocation, but his idea was taken seriously by polls and politicians. And now it is difficult to determine if it is for real or part of his jokes" (*El Nuevo Herald*, January 21, 2010). At the same time, *El Comercio*, the country's largest-circulated newspaper, created a special section in its online edition named "Candidate Bayly." Bayly devoted a significant portion of his weekly show *El Francotirador* and his weekly column in the newspaper *Peru 21* to discussing his presidential candidacy and his platform. At this point, Bayly repeatedly mentioned his motivations for seeking office: 1) to make his mother happy; 2) to realize a goal for which he had prepared since childhood; 3) to use his experience and capabilities, which surpassed those of most politicians in power; and 4) to make use of his liberal ideas, held by no other candidate.

In February 2010, the prestigious English magazine *The Economist* described Bayly and his presidential ambitions in a news story:

Jaime Bayly, a writer of humorous novels of rather lesser stature, who is also a television talk-show host, has launched his candidacy for a presidential election due in April 2011. Like Mr. Vargas Llosa, Mr. Bayly is a liberal. But he is a highly irreverent one. Mop-haired and rumpled, he talks freely about his bisexuality (he says that at the moment he prefers women but that this might once again change); his taste for mood-altering pills that are apparently damaging his liver; his past cocaine habit and his continuing fondness for an occasional joint. His television programs, broadcast in Colombia and Peru (he previously worked in Miami), mercilessly mock Venezuela's leftist president, Hugo Chávez.

His policies are just as politically incorrect. He favors legalizing abortion and same-sex marriages. He would eliminate centuries-old privileges enjoyed by the Catholic Church. He wants to abolish the armed forces and spend their budget on improving state schools. In another constitutional proposal—this one smacks of populism—he would cut the number of lawmakers in Peru's single-chamber Congress from 120 to just 25. He defies Peruvian nationalism by saying that the government should not have filed a claim against neighboring Chile over their maritime-border dispute, because it will not win.

A survey this month by Ipsos-APOYO, a polling firm, shows there is no clear favorite in a crowded field of presidential wanabees. Only 22% backed the leading candidate, Luis Castañeda, the mayor of Lima. Mr. Bayly has the support of 5%. He appeals to young voters, and could tap into the national frustration with traditional politicians. But he is from the Lima upper class. It remains to be seen whether he can appeal to poorer Peruvians. Or indeed whether he will run. Humor, seriousness and narcissism fight for supremacy within Mr. Bayly's ego. He may have some fun keeping Peru guessing. In a recent weekly column he mused about turning 50 in 2015, and said that by then he plans to write, travel, have sex and smoke pot—not be "president of Peru or any other tribe." (*The Economist*, February 25, 2010)

Numerous local journalists, intellectuals, social scientists, opinion leaders, politicians, celebrities, and even the president of the country discussed, interpreted, and analyzed Bayly's presidential campaign. His appealing media character, which is composed of a variety of attributes that often seem contradictory, helped draw attention to his political intentions. The presidential campaign was not his first incursion into politics. In 1990, Bayly actively supported the presidential candidacy of writer and 2010 Nobel Prize winner Mario Vargas Llosa, who lost to political outsider Alberto Fujimori. In 2001, he developed a political campaign for the "blank vote," urging citizens to manifest their nonacceptance of the electoral process. At the same time, his show played a major role in the 2001 and 2006 presidential elections and became a decisive factor in Lima's 2010 municipal elections.

During his 30-year media career, Bayly established ambiguity as a central feature of his character. He built an iconic personality whose identity allowed him to walk the line between media circus and influential journalism, and between cosmopolitan, commercial literature and the folkloric spectacle of the local jet set. He crossed social barriers by means of the television screen. He flirted with collective homophobia. He stung both the right and the left, simplifying all types of discourse. He knew the political power of laughter and that being educated was not a priority for opinion leaders in a society of spectacle—it was more important to be fun. Bayly's chameleonic discourse made him influential in diverse spheres that were not easily reconciled. His ambiguous character combined contrasting discourses, appealing to different audiences (and potential voters). Even if some people condemned some aspects of his character, they could feel positively about other aspects. Based on his TV show *El Francotirador*, his newspaper columns, and press coverage about him, some of Bayly's ambiguous configurations, highlighted and interpreted below, contribute to understanding how he combined apparently contradictory discourses to validate his strategies, exert influence, and gain media attention and popular support (in electoral or ratings terms), especially during his presidential campaign, while revealing, framing, and dissimulating contradictions and tensions within Peruvian society.

BAYLY IS A JOURNALIST—BUT ALSO A COMMERCIAL ENTERTAINER

Bayly began reporting at age 15 for the newspaper *La Prensa*, working with other right-wing, young journalists of his generation—the so-called "Young Turks" who became some of the most influential journalists in Peru. Bayly also wrote a novel—*The Last Days of the Press* (1996)—in which he portrayed the newspaper environment during the early 1980s, the democratic period that followed Velasco's military dictatorship. In his youth, he was talented and precocious, writing about politics, culture, and sports. He transitioned to television as a serious political commentator for the program *Pulso* (1984). After appearing on various news programs, Bayly got his own show in 1991, *Qué hay de nuevo? (What's new?)*, which became the "official talk show" that established "who's who" in Peru's cultural, celebrity, and cosmopolitan circles (Vivas, 2001). Bayly adapted American television genres and took inspiration from the stand-up comedy tradition, talk shows, and late-night shows—particularly *The David Letterman Show* and *Larry King Live*. He then invented his own style of doing local television, combining stand-up comedy, local popular culture, gossip and scandals, edgy political interviews, and entertainment reporting. During Fujimori's authoritarian regime, Bayly spent several years living abroad, publishing fiction books, and working on international TV. In 2001, he returned to Peru and inaugurated *El Francotirador*, in which he incisively interviewed political candidates in the restored democracy. He asked a candidate if she was a virgin, revealed the ignorance of other candidates on political issues, and asked ex-president Alan Garcia if he was crazy. He then called media attention to the case of an unacknowledged daughter of presidential candidate Alejandro Toledo, who was later forced to admit his parental ties.

At the same time, the show's formula evolved into a more affected style in which Bayly, with a dark suit and a funny haircut, sat in the middle of the stage. He pontificated and delivered monologues in between interviews, in front of the camera but also in front of a live audience that interacted with him. He became a transgressive mediator between the political elite and the masses, who were represented by some dozens of attendees in the studio. He frequently referred to the audience during the interviews or monologues, promoting applause and cheers from them, creating complicity with his viewers, and framing his interactions with powerful people as "us" against "them." Bayly asked the questions that nobody else was asking in the media, voiced popular concerns, and tapped into sensational curiosity, thus bringing the powerful and famous down to earth.

When talking about political and social national issues, he portrayed himself and his team as professional journalists.[7] He was included in an anthology of the most accomplished journalists of the country and was considered one of the best interviewers in Peru (Salinas, 2008). Bayly's columns appear in several international newspapers and other media outlets. He played the role of someone informed, with an insider's perspective of the power structure and an accumulated knowledge of the country's news cycle. He used this configuration to consolidate his political image. During his "presidential campaign," he repeated several times that because of his journalistic experience he knew how the system worked and had met and confronted the most influential people in the country. At the same time, his recurrent adversarial and satirical attitudes about powerful people also configured him as someone whom the powerful feared. He remained the sassy and risqué journalist who conducted the important interviews that garnered headlines nationwide.

However, when facing a critical press, Bayly often mocked the seriousness and alleged respectability of journalists, creating the impression that he was above them. When accused of developing the "media circus" and promoting general vulgarity, he responded that his role was to entertain the people and give "humor and laughter" to the audience (*El Comercio*, February 8, 2010). He argued that TV is the most democratic medium because every citizen can change the channel. So, if he wanted to talk about banalities, exhibit his sexual life, or kiss an interviewee on the lips, he could do it. People decide if they want to watch those shows, and, according to him, weekly ratings (to which he frequently referred) best reflected this. With postmodern self-referentiality, he created complicity with the audience when his show won (and even when it lost) the ratings war against other TV programs. Ratings, like surveys, measured his influence, validated his strategies, and set his agenda. His discourse, then, inevitably linked to commercial terms.

Bayly remained very conscious of his commercial value and cited it several times on his show. When he had a problem with the TV station, he threatened to resign, implying that the owners and directors of the TV station would lose advertising money if he left. Usually, these problems with the owners and board of directors—problems that Bayly strategically aired on the show—came from discordance with the political stance of the show. For example, he dedicated an entire show to attacking Baruch Ivcher,

7. In a personal interview I conducted with Sonia Suyon, an investigative journalist for Bayly's show, she told me about the journalistic routines that the production team developed to make the show and prepare the material for the interviews.

the owner of the station, Frecuencia Latina, accusing Ivcher of censorship. Bayly criticized Ivcher's efforts to limit his freedom of expression and for being against his presidential candidacy. "I don't need Baruch or this TV station. Modestly, I think that the TV station loses more than me with my resignation," Bayly said on his show (*El Comercio*, February 22, 2010). In this sense, he relied on his commercial value as an entertainer to support his journalistic independence.

Bayly's journalist/entertainer configuration connected with recent Peruvian political infotainment history. It reflected the use of tabloid papers and entertainment media by Fujimori for political purposes and the trend toward tabloidization in journalism during the restored democracy. The fact that Bayly's virtual presidential candidacy was covered both in political and entertainment sections also reflected the tension between news and entertainment in Peruvian media, where even *El Comercio*, the right-wing family-owned paper of record, has embraced sensationalism and partisanship. Commercial pressures and concentration of the media have worsened this situation. The Grupo El Comercio, the biggest media conglomerate of Peru, owns almost 80% of the newspaper market in addition to TV, cable, radio, and internet media outlets. In fact, as we will note later, Bayly was later hired by *El Comercio* during the presidential election runoff to support the right-wing candidate and attack the left-wing one. *El Comercio* has also been accused of representing conservative elite viewpoints and firing critical journalists from its staff (Knight Center for Journalism in the Americas, May 30, 2011). In this sense, the tensions between news and entertainment, partisanship and independence, and sensationalism and critical/watchdog reporting in Peru are also linked to concentration of the media, another symptom of the country's inequalities. Depending on the context, Bayly evidenced and dissimulated these tensions by combining journalistic transgression and commercial success.

BAYLY IS A CELEBRITY—BUT ALSO A WRITER

A personality of Peruvian television for almost 30 years, Bayly had enormous success, which led to programs in several other Spanish-speaking countries and in the United States. As a protagonist in the evolution of mass media over recent decades, he managed to avoid going out of style. He understood the need to be flexible and to know how to reinvent himself, and the power of scandals to maintain his relevance. He managed to stay in Latin America's news agenda. This made him become one of the most famous Peruvian celebrities in the region, a transnational commodity in a globalized world. He bragged about his close friendships with other Latin pop icons like Shakira, Enrique Iglesias, and Joaquin Sabina. He also dined with the president (and wrote about it). He frequently met with intellectuals and writers such as Mario Vargas Llosa, whom he considered a mentor. At the same time, many Peruvian celebrities said they consider Bayly a sort of "intellectual."

In spite of his celebrity lifestyle, Bayly describes himself primarily as a writer, one who works on TV to maintain his comfortable standard of living. Since his 1994 novel *Don't Tell Anyone*, he has published more than a dozen books. He won the prestigious Herralde Prize and emerged as a finalist for a Planeta Award. At first dismissed as a "light" writer by the Peruvian literary establishment, in recent years critics have acknowledged both his literary and commercial merits. Bayly's first homoerotic novels, written in the first person in simple and explicit language, portrayed Lima's upper-class environment, youth entitled by their privileged status, gay love, homophobia, and the self-destructive compulsion toward drug use. In these stories, Bayly mercilessly depicted Peru's celebrities, politicians, and people from his social circle. With an intentionally autobiographical tone, his books always danced around the line between reality and fiction. While in Peru writers tended to polarize into irreconcilable regional groups (Andeans versus Criollos, for example), Bayly tried to be global, with con-siderable success. During his presidential campaign, while he was also promoting his latest novel, he said in an interview with Argentinean news-paper *Clarin*: "I don't think that one can be a presidential candidate and a writer at the same time. I think those are incompatible vocations, and if I ever have to choose one, I will stick with my vocation as a writer" (April 6, 2010).

However, while Bayly used his show to promote his books, he rarely covered literary issues or interviewed other creative writers. He preferred to interview pop celebrities and to cover sensational news and frivolous topics. He reproduced the disconnection between cultural worlds in Peru and the tension between the so-called "high culture" and the popular/mass culture in a country where only the literate elite enjoy access to quality higher education. For the masses, there is TV and celebrity culture. While there is a TV in 99% of urban Peruvian households, studies show that ine-quality in access to education prevails in the country (Salazar, 2011). Bayly became an exceptional bridge that connected social classes through sen-sationalism; his popular autobiographical books (focused on local gossip, celebrities, and Lima's upper-class secrets) were written in an accessible language for the urban masses and became best sellers, and his irreverent TV programs obtained high ratings in the upper classes, because they were a space for the social and political elite to connect with the less privileged groups. For the popular classes, he became an indiscrete window, allowing a peek into a privileged world from which they were excluded. However, Bayly rarely incorporated his popular audience into an intellectual debate or the discussion of critical cultural topics.

BAYLY IS BISEXUAL—BUT ALSO A FAMILY MAN

Beginning with his first novel, Bayly described himself as bisexual—a person who "sometimes likes a man and sometimes a woman." As such, he presented himself as someone who belongs to an oppressed minority, someone who knows what it is like to fight against prejudice, particularly Peruvian society's brutal homophobia. This sexual configuration, however, also helps maintain the media's eye on his sexual scandals. He exhibits his sexual life and relationships on his show and in writings, even naming and introducing several of his lovers. For example, he said that he was the lover of famous local actor Diego Bertie. The actor rejected this claim and said that they were only friends. Then, Bayly began a media campaign satirizing Bertie's attitude, trying to force him out of the closet. The Bayly-Bertie affair dominated headlines for several weeks. In this way, Bayly portrayed himself as someone not afraid to declare who he is and with whom he sleeps. He did not respect the privacy of others. He fosters the idea of honesty beyond limits, positioning himself in a discursive place above social prejudices. He disregards the local gossip he generates and wants the public to follow him into this bubble. During the campaign, he also frequently talked about his affairs with men and about his last Argentinean male lover.

At the same time, Bayly was also a respected family man. Bayly always referred to his daughters as the main loves of his life and to his ex-wife, Sandra Masías, as the woman with whom he would always be in love. He devoted entire shows to declaring his love for his family and always stressed that he would give them anything. In fact, he wrote several columns stating how much money he paid to keep them happy (including the most expensive education, luxuries, trips, and apartments). He also referred frequently to his mother, whom he called a "saint." He acknowledged that she, a wealthy, conservative, and generous member of a religious congregation, has "suffered enough for having a son like him." In a gesture of familial commitment, he interviewed her for Mother's Day. He consistently portrayed her as an understanding, stoic woman who always fought to keep the family together and at peace. His relationship with these women was totally in line with the social values and Lima's upper-class sensibilities.

According to such norms, the man should be a successful provider of his women's material and emotional needs.

Despite this professed familiar commitment, during his virtual presidential campaign, Bayly introduced the Peruvian audience to his 21-year-old lover, Silvia Núñez del Arco, a beautiful upper-middle-class woman. Presented also as a writer, she said Bayly impressed her when they first met at a broadcast of one of his shows. While publicly apologizing to his wife and his male Argentinean lover, Bayly portrayed her as the woman who saved him from sexual impotence and declared that he wanted her to be the mother of his next child. With Núñez del Arco, Bayly's intimate panorama became complete: an aristocratic mother, a classy wife, educated daughters, and a gorgeous young mistress. Thus, he projected the archetype of the successful White male in a sexist, classist, and patriarchal society. Fitting this archetype allowed Bayly's bisexuality to be tolerated in a society with fixed gender roles, a society that has been considered the most homophobic in Latin America (*Publimetro*, May 27, 2013).

BAYLY IS A WHITE ELITE—BUT ALSO A POPULAR CULTURE ICON

Bayly, the black sheep of an aristocratic family, went to one of the most exclusive schools in the country. Then he studied a few semesters of law in the most prestigious local private university, dropping out to develop his media career. Members of his family held important private-sector and public positions—bank directors, powerful businessmen, and influential politicians. For example, his uncle Roberto Letts, a millionaire, owned one of the most important mines in Peru, especially significant because the country's main economic activity is mining. During Bayly's virtual presidential campaign, he wrote a column criticizing the mining industry and he called his uncle a "cabrón de mala entraña" (a bad-hearted bastard). After his uncle's death, Bayly used several shows to speculate on the size of his inheritance, declaring that if he received the money, it would help support his presidential campaign. He interviewed members of his family, talked with a clairvoyant about the issue, and even delivered monologues speaking to the spirit of his uncle. The local media covered the reading of the will, and to his surprise, Bayly was excluded. On the next show, Bayly interviewed a different uncle, Ricardo Letts (brother of Roberto), one of the country's most prominent leftists and another black sheep of the family, who was also excluded. Bayly's mother, however, received a good portion of the fortune. Bayly said his mother told him not to worry about his presidential campaign's expenses.

The economic aspect of his character drew interest. Bayly maintained an image of living well but also of saving money. He said he was no millionaire but kept "some savings" in the bank. He proposed funding his presidential campaign through an atypical economic organization. He did not fundraise or ask for money from any powerful economic group—as most candidates do—in order to not owe any favors in case he became president. He said this would avoid corruption in his possible future government. He would instead use his TV show as his primary means of publicity and would use his family's money or, in the worst-case scenario, some of his savings for the campaign. This appealing discourse about the campaign's economic underpinning reinforced the idea that money and social capital are necessary to participate actively—and avoid corruption—in a Peruvian democracy.

During his presidential campaign, Bayly tried to portray himself as someone doing a public service for the country by running for president. But pointing to his commercial celebrity, some critics said that he was just using his presidential campaign to drive up TV ratings. He responded in an interview: "They don't know me well. There are times to joke and other times to take things seriously. Being a candidate is a serious issue. If I were as frivolous as they say, I would not be a candidate. I would stay on TV making money and publishing my books and columns . . . Now I have another dream: to work five years for the poor children of my country" (*El Comercio*, January 17, 2010). A few months later, he aborted his campaign, stating that the president's salary would not maintain his family's lifestyle.

Bayly always acknowledged being raised as part of the elite but presented himself as an enlightened, rebellious upper-class individual—sometimes even as a class traitor. He revealed the intimacies of the upper class, criticized their values, and publicly aired their gossip. This appealed to popular audiences because it seemed to level people. Though Bayly shared and reproduced many of Lima's upper-class prejudices, his on-air charisma crossed race, educational, and class lines using the universal language of lowbrow humor. At the same time, his media career forced him to be in touch with popular tastes. He frequently interviewed local pop culture icons. Several of them from the middle or lower classes have made their way into show business. They were always grateful for these interviews because it gave them greater public exposure and an opportunity to promote their shows and performances on one of the most-watched national TV shows. Several of them also acknowledged their class differences with Bayly and, in a subtle way, thanked him for the attention. Bayly mocked them and sometimes ridiculed them. He assumed a patriarchal attitude toward these subaltern subjects. One of the most visible popular icons on Bayly's show was an obese, provincial folkloric singer named Tongo. For Ubilluz (2010), the relationship between Tongo and Bayly was a tutelary bond: A man from informal capitalism asked a man of elite circles for access to formal capitalism. The power distance between the two characters related to what Ubilluz called "the "postmodern creole subject," an apolitical individual exclusively concerned with his social mobility in the framework of late capitalism whose social goal is linked to the will of the boss.

Bayly's promotion of Tongo made the singer wealthy and famous in Peru. Tongo not only made Bayly godfather of his child, but he also composed and sang the musical hit that launched Bayly's campaign, "Jaime for President."[8] The lyrics of this song reveal how the popular classes might have perceived Bayly: "He was a very different kid from the rest/ In spite of having everything, he liked equality/ This kid became a man in the middle of injustice and evil/ Intelligent and very bright, he will give us the solution/ Jaime, Jaime, Jaime Bayly/ Jaime for president." That same night on the show, Bayly told Tongo, "I won't be able to win the election without your help. I need your popular appeal and your song to connect with the masses." His relationship with Tongo exemplified Bayly's utilitarian and condescending attitude toward Peru's popular classes and culture, a similar attitude to the one that the conservative political elite maintains in the country.

BAYLY IS A PROGRESSIVE—BUT ALSO CONSERVATIVE

In a widely discussed column, Bayly described his main political ideas and positions toward the presidency—what he called his "government plan" (*Peru 21*, June 6, 2010). Most of these ideas were highly controversial and innovative in the electoral agenda, and some could be considered very progressive in Peruvian society. For example, Bayly's political platform supported gay marriage, abortion, and the legalization of drugs. According to some polls, most Peruvians did not agree with these ideas (*El Comercio*, February 13, 2010).

Bayly also called for a more secular Peruvian state, one without privileges for the Catholic Church. Some of his other political ideas—decreasing the military budget, significantly increasing funding for education and the police, and reducing the number of representatives in Peru's unicameral Congress—were popularly supported. His main populist appeal was,

8. The video can be accessed at: http://www.youtube.com/watch?v=eLNMySR_RhU

however, to make education for poor children a priority in his potential government.

Even though Bayly has always been linked to the Peruvian right wing, during his campaign he described his political stance as "liberal or libertarian left," comparable to José Luis Rodríguez Zapatero in Spain (*La República*, February 18, 2010). However, in another column, Bayly analyzed the other presidential candidates and concluded:

> The difference between the six candidates that defend the current economic system and my possible presidential candidacy is the following: I also support the basic lines of the current economic model, but the other candidates are, in essence, conservatives, anti-liberals, clerics, pro-military, mercantilists, the old Peruvian right wing supported by cassocks and bayonets . . . I want Peruvians not only to stop being poor but to also become freer to decide on our personal lives . . . My possible candidacy has a modern, liberal and anti-establishment sense. It condenses a protest message against the insertion of the state into issues of personal freedom. It is not enough to support political and economic freedom; we have to defend freedom mainly in the sphere of moral individuality. (*Peru 21*, February 3, 2010)

Bayly's defense of the neoliberal economic system was not the only conservative element in his political discourse. He also offered to pardon Fujimori, who was incarcerated for human rights violations. Bayly argued that Fujimori had already paid for his sins and that the "good things" Fujimori did in his government (such as the stabilization of the economy through neoliberal policies and privatizations and the defeat of terrorist left-wing groups) were more important than the "bad things"—namely repression, corruption, human rights violations, censorship, and limits on freedom of expression. Bayly's conservative interpretation of recent Peruvian social conflicts remained obvious, for example, in his show criticizing the "Museo de la Memoria" ("Memory Museum"), a project seeking to present an exhibition explaining the causes of the 23-year violent conflict between the state and armed terrorist groups, which caused roughly 70,000 deaths. The project, directed by Mario Vargas Llosa and promoted by Alan García's government, was funded by international donations. Bayly criticized Vargas Llosa, President García, and the museum idea.[9] After humorously simplifying the bloody period of violence in Peru, he said that he was "not sure if Peruvians need a museum to remember how the terrorists brutally

---

9. The video can be accessed at: http://www.youtube.com/watch?v=N7yJEcAu9Rc

hurt the country." He added that if he were the director, he would simplify the issue: "I would put Abimael Guzmán [the leader of the Shining Path] naked in a room. And that would be the entire museum. If one wants to know more, we can say, 'This crazy, disturbed man wanted to capture power with a terrorist ideology.' If you want to touch him, you have to pay more. He can even yell, spit, or say a Maoist thing." This oversimplification of recent Peruvian history not only revealed Bayly's acceptance of right-wing violence but also shadowed one of the main reasons for political turmoil in the country: inequality and discrimination against indigenous and rural people (CVR, 2004). In fact, a few years before his campaign, Bayly said on his show that people from the Andes were less intelligent than people from the cities because of the lack of oxygen in those areas. He used this idea to explain why they voted for a left-wing candidate, manifesting their inconformity with the current system.

Bayly's ideological position, however, became more ambiguous when dealing with his own political interests. Consider his coverage of the 2010 municipal elections during his presidential campaign. Lourdes Flores, the leader of the traditional right-wing party Partido Popular Cristiano (PPC), was favored to become mayor of Lima. After Bayly said he would not run as a candidate for the political party Cambio Radical, he publicized his interest in running as presidential candidate for the PPC. However, Lourdes Flores did not support his candidacy. After initially being sympathetic to her candidacy, Bayly began to attack her systematically on his show, accusing her of having connections with drug trafficking. He even aired recordings of Flores's private phone conversations. Bayly instead supported the leftist candidate, Susana Villaran, who later won the election as the first female mayor of Lima. Bayly's biased coverage, highly discussed by the Peruvian media, was considered a decisive factor in the final results. His municipal electoral coverage contributed, according to Bayly, to termination of his contract with Frecuencia Latina TV. The severance coincided with his announcement to drop his presidential campaign.

The next example of intersection between Bayly's political ambivalence, professional ethics, and his own interests came during the last two months of the Peruvian presidential elections, in which he did not participate. By then, Bayly lived in Miami with a new show, a new wife, and a new baby. The two candidates in the presidential runoff were on both sides of the political extremes: right-wing Keiko Fujimori, daughter of Alberto Fujimori, and leftist Ollanta Humala. Most conservative and mainstream media conducted an overwhelming campaign against Humala, favoring Fujimori (Knight Center for Journalism in the Americas, May 30, 2011). During this campaign, Bayly was hired by America Television for $800,000 to attack

Humala for 12 programs on a show hosted from Miami and broadcast nationally in Peru. Despite Bayly's efforts, Peruvians elected Humala president on June 6, 2011.

The 2011 presidential election in Peru exemplified a pivotal moment of political polarization in a fragmented society that is trying to construct a new national identity based on the celebration of "progress." Paradoxically, Peruvian progress (mainly identified as sustained macroeconomic growth based on the mining industry during the past decade) has generated violent social protests in rural areas of the country affected by the expansion of powerful industries and unjust policies about their territories and natural resources. In this tense social scenario—also apparent in new dynamics of social mobility in Lima, increasing consumption by the population, radicalization of the left wing, and right-wing partisan media—Bayly's character channeled all these tensions toward his own political and commercial ambitions. His ideological ambivalence allowed him to appeal to different social sectors until he exposed his vacuity, disguised as idealism. Then he wrote in the third person: "The loser has lost again. But he is not willing to surrender. The loser knows that if someone calls him in five years [for the next election], he will wear the boxing gloves again to fight clean and passionately for his ideals" (*Peru 21*, June 6, 2011).

THE BAYLY EFFECT AND THE NEW PATHS OF PERUVIAN SATIRE

Bayly constructed his media character through ambiguity and contradiction—he is openly bisexual, but a family man; he is a respected writer, but also an outrageous showman; he is an experienced journalist, but a celebrity; he is high class, but with popular sensitivity; he is progressive on some issues (legalization of drugs and abortion, anticlerical, antimilitary), but is conservative in others (economic policies, interpretation of the period of political violence in the country, supporter of authoritarian right-wing governments); and he is cultivated and informed, but his interpretations on national issues are banal simplifications. He developed all these ambiguities and apparent contradictions through humor and satire, exploiting postmodern cynicism through a discursive integration of news, politics, entertainment, and celebrity culture. Crossing and connecting diverse spheres, this appealing ambiguity manifested itself as political power, as exemplified in Bayly's presidential campaign and his influential role in several Peruvian elections.

Jaime Bayly's *El Francotirador* was also a democratic consequence of the Fujimorization of media and politics during the 1990s, a symbol of spectacle's influence on the national agenda. This program showed that mass media, especially television, provide a privileged site on which to perform neopopulism. After the decadent role played by shameful re-ality/talk shows and the paparazzi on national TV during Fujimori's media dictatorship, the popularity of *El Francotirador* confirmed that politics could never go back to serious and stilted formats. Moreover, Bayly's role in the 2001, 2006, 2010, and 2011 elections in Peru showed that entertainment had become a preeminent arena for politics in a so-ciety with no solid political parties or institutions. His performance as a potential presidential candidate also demonstrated that the scope of media goes beyond influencing political trends; they can also create their own candidate, portrayed as an outsider of traditional politics through telepopulism.

Fujimori's media heritage was reflected in Bayly's use of sensationalism and his evident preference for tabloid content and treatment of news, as well as through his overt manipulation of information according to per-sonal and political interests. While Bayly was the result of a process of tabloidization in Peruvian media, his discourse (even in its most lowbrow version) was different from that of the "chicha" press, other sensational media, and popular entertainment. In a country where the newspaper *El Trome*, a sensationalist tabloid owned by the conservative media conglom-erate Grupo El Comercio, is the most read newspaper in the country, the producers of popular tabloid media use local popular language in order to connect with the masses. Tabloid newspapers use slang, the people's street language. Bayly did not. He imposed his verbose speeches (with abundant metaphors, repetitive synonyms, and "difficult" words) in order to consolidate his intellectual authority over the popular classes and other celebrities. And yet he included elements and popular figures of the "chicha" culture to create a hybrid world that "criollos," "mestizos," and "cholos" could admire without being compromised, a space where they could learn (and laugh) about the "others" without suspending their own identities. At the same time, Bayly used tabloid journalism to nor-malize a hegemonic voice of class contempt and conservative politics, but also amplified his dissenting voice on sexuality and some progressive approaches. In this scenario, celebrity proved an essential component of Bayly's discourse. Not only known for his "well known-ness" and irrever-ence, he was also featured as a powerful personality of the country—in contrast to the powerless elitism of ordinary celebrities. While today's politicians want to be portrayed as celebrities, Bayly has been a celebrity with political ambitions. He used oversimplification, distraction, and dis-tortion as rhetorical instruments to develop what DeMott (2003) called "junk politics"—politics that personalizes and moralizes issues instead of clarifying them. Narcissistic and entitled, Bayly also dissolved the boundaries between the public and the private in media discourse through an exhibitionism disguised as freedom. He performed an idealized version of freedom by creating an appealing image of honesty without limits.

In this process, Bayly has been the partial author and the text of his media persona. Through his novels, columns, and TV shows, he produced various faces and discourses to diverse and overlapping audiences. However, he has been an open text that offered the possibility of multiple readings—readers could hold on to whichever of his configurations suited their ideological and moral beliefs better. While there is no available audience research on Bayly's reception, his popularity in Lima and many other Peruvian and Latin American cities is evident. It is not clear, however, how the people of the Andean and rural areas might have perceived him. He appealed to mainly urban citizens. This is why since the beginning of his virtual campaign, political scientists and commentators manifested their skepticism about Bayly's real possibilities to be a strong presidential candidate beyond Lima. Bayly's character seemed to effectively navigate diverse segments of urban population, but he did not seem to be able to reach the poor rural Peruvians. His racist, conservative, and classist remarks highlighted his inability to comprehend those realities. However, he did appeal to diverse citizens of Lima, including the emerging middle class produced by decades of migration to the capital city. As shown in this chapter, Bayly's character offered the emerging middle class the possibility to peek into a privileged world from which they were traditionally excluded; his TV audience and readers were allowed into the intimate spaces of the social aristocracy, political elites, and celebrity circles through the "democratizing" medium of television and mass media. In times when there is a perceptible anxiety about "progress" and social mobility in Lima, Bayly was also appealing to diverse segments because he was successful, transgressive, deviant, and powerful—a rare combination in Peruvian society. At the same time, Bayly's multilayered persona offered guidance into how to capitalize commercially and politically on a society's lack of cohesive identities. His ambiguous and contradictory attributes offered several of those identities a space within his persona.

Bayly's diverse and contrasting identities also connected with the idea of the New Peru based on "fusion." In a country where the idea of "mestizaje" has been used to support national discourses, Bayly's hybrid character also reflected the hybrid nature of contemporary Peruvian culture (the so-called "chicha" or "cholo" culture) as well as the hybrid nature of contemporary media ("political infotainment" being itself a hybrid product of today's discursive integration). Recent Peruvian satire in other platforms has targeted Peru's sociopolitical contradictions from new angles. From a hybrid journalistic point of view, the magazine *Dedomedio* and the news portal *Utero.pe* have used an irreverent and satiric style to frame politics for young urban audiences. *El Diario de Curwen*, a popular satiric infotainment YouTube channel, has developed viral videos on sociopolitical issues such as labor laws that affect young people or sexist ideas about feminist protests. The online satiric TV show *GCU (Gente Como Uno)* parodies the conservative and ignorant perspectives of mainstream TV journalism, exposing Peruvian prejudices in public discourse. *El Panfleto*, an online satiric newspaper in the spirit of *The Onion*, has also aggressively criticized issues of race, identity, and sociocultural privilege in the country. These satiric manifestations suggest that many of the tensions that Bayly's character reflected are still predominant issues for critical humor in Peru.

The fact that Bayly has become a famous regional figure in Latin(o) American show business through his TV show in Miami also evidences the dialogue between local and regional celebrity culture in today's global media. In Miami, his style is toned down and his discourse adapted for an international audience: He aggressively attacks Latin American leftist regimes (especially Castro's dictatorship in Cuba and the Chavez/Maduro autocracy in Venezuela) while also cohosting many of his shows with his young wife. His cosmopolitan style—impregnated with his sociopolitical contradictions—seems to resonate with Latin American audiences (he has actually hosted successful TV shows in other Latin American countries, where he is also known for his literary work). Nevertheless, he remains a Peruvian phenomenon: an aristocrat court jester who was able to negotiate his limits for transgression due to his chameleonic identity that appealed to diverse social sectors. In this sense, the next chapter offers an interesting contrast: A role similar to the one that Bayly played in Peru was fulfilled in Mexico by a deeply marginal character, revealing sociocultural differences between the two countries.

REFERENCES

Alonso, P. (2010). Entrevista a Beto Ortiz. *Dedo Medio*, 32–36.

Alonso, P. (2012). Carlos Álvarez: "Se les ha hecho difícil imitarme." *Terra*.

Barrenechea, R., & Sosa, P. (2014). Peru 2013: La paradoja de la estabilidad. *Revista de Ciencia Política*, 34(1), 267–292.

Boas, T. C. (2005). Television and neopopulism in Latin America: Media effects in Brazil and Peru. *Latin American Research Review*, 40(2), 27–49.

Conaghan, C. M. (2002). Cashing in on authoritarianism: Media collusion in Fujimori's Peru. *Harvard International Journal of Press/Politics*, 7(1), 115–125.

Conaghan, C. M. (2005). *Fujimori's Peru: Deception in the public sphere*. Pittsburgh, PA: University of Pittsburgh Press.

Cotler, J. (2013). Las paradojas de la democracia peruana. In B. Revesz (Ed.), *Miradas cruzadas: política públicas y desarrollo regional en Perú* (pp. 55–88). Lima, Peru: Instituto de Estudios Peruanos.

Crabtree, J. (2010). Democracy without parties? Some lessons from Peru. *Journal of Latin American Studies, 42*(2), 357–382.

CVR. (2004). Hatun Willakuy. Versión abreviada del Informe Final de la Comisión de la Verdad y Reconciliación. Lima, Peru.

Dargent, E. (2009). *Demócratas precarios: élites y debilidad democrática en el Perú y América Latina*. Lima, Peru: Instituto de Estudios Peruanos.

De la Cadena, M. (2011). Reconstructing race: Racism, culture and mestizaje in Latin America. *NACLA Report on the Americas, XXXIV*(6), 16–23.

Degregori, C. I. (2000). *La década de la antipolítica: auge y huida de Alberto Fujimori y Vladimiro Montesinos*. Lima, Peru: Instituto de Estudios Peruanos.

DeMott, B. (2003). *Junk politics*. New York, NY: Nation.

Felch, J. (2004). Have Peru's press heroes gone too far? *Columbia Journalism Review, 43*(2), 43–47.

Flores Galindo, A. (1994). *Buscando un inca: identidad y utopía en los Andes*. Lima, Peru: Horizonte.

Fowks, J. (2000). *Suma y resta de la realidad: medios de comunicación y elecciones generales 2000 en el Perú*. Lima, Peru: Friedrich Ebert Stiftung.

García, M. E. (2005). *Making indigenous citizens: Identities, education, and multicultural development in Peru*. Stanford, CA: Stanford University Press.

Gargurevich, J. (1991). *Historia de la prensa peruana, 1594–1990*. Lima, Peru: La Voz Ediciones.

Gargurevich, J. (2000). *La prensa sensacionalista en el Perú*. Lima, Peru: Fondo Editorial PUCP.

Hildebrandt, C. (2008, November 19). La "rata" y el ratón. *Diario La Primera*. Retrieved from http://www.diariolaprimeraperu.com/online/columnistas-y-colaboradores/la-rata-y-el-raton_27603.html

Levitsky, S., & Cameron, M. (2003). Democracy without parties? Political parties and regime change in Fujimori's Peru. *Latin American Politics and Society, 45*(3), 1–33.

"Los chistosos", 22 años de pasión por el humor. (2015, May 24). *La República*. Retrieved from http://larepublica.pe/impresa/ocio-y-cultura/2379-los-chistosos-22-anos-de-pasion-por-el-humor

Macassi, S. (2001). *Prensa amarilla y cultura política en el proceso electoral*. Lima, Peru: Asociación de Comunicadores Sociales Calandria.

Mahshie, A. (2005). A media plot against the president or a case of incompetence? *IPI Global Journalist, 11*(2), 18–19.

Matos Mar, J. (1987). *Desborde popular y crisis del Estado*. Lima, Peru: Instituto de Estudios Peruanos.

Matos Mar, J. (2004). *Desborde popular y crisis del Estado: veinte años después*. Lima, Peru: Fondo Editorial del Congreso del Perú.

Matos Mar, J. (2012). *Perú: estado desbordado y sociedad nacional emergente*. Lima, Peru: Universidad Ricardo Palma.

Mendoza, R. (2005, June 20). "Monos y monadas": La risa inteligente. *La República*. Retrieved from http://larepublica.pe/20-06-2005/monos-y-monadas-la-risa-inteligente

Moreno, M., & Oropesa, R. S. (2012). Ethno-racial identification in urban Peru. *Ethnic & Racial Studies, 35*(7), 1220–1247.

Nugent, J. G. (1992). *El laberinto de la choledad*. Lima, Peru: Fundación Friedrich Ebert.

Pajares, G. (2012, September 14). "En corrupción, los presidentes han sido parejos." Entrevista a Guillermo Rossini. *Peru 21.*

Planas, E. (2000). Monos se quedan. *Caretas, 1648.*

Popular cómico peruano afirma que fue chantajeado por Montesinos. (2002). *EFE.* Retrieved from http://www.eluniverso.com/2002/08/21/0001/14/81FAA97C8 D87402DAC1C8877D3085BEA.html

Portocarrero, G. (1993). *Racismo y mestizaje*. Lima, Peru: Sur.

Quijano, A. (1980). *Dominación y cultura: Lo cholo y el conflicto cultural en el Perú*. Lima, Peru: Mosca Azul Editores.

Roberts, K. M. (1995). Neoliberalism and the transformation of populism in Latin America: The Peruvian case. *World Politics, 48*(1), 82–116.

Salazar, M. (2011, January 31). Peru: Rural education reflects ethnic, socioeconomic inequalities. *IPS—Inter Press Service.* Retrieved from http://www.ipsnews. net/2011/01/peru-rural-education-reflects-ethnic-socioeconomic-inequalities/

Salinas, P. (2008). *Rajes del Oficio (2)*. Lima, Peru: Planeta.

Sue, C. A., & Golash-Boza, T. (2013). "It was only a joke": How racial humour fuels colour-blind ideologies in Mexico and Peru. *Ethnic & Racial Studies, 36*(10), 1582–1598.

Tanaka, M., & Vera, S. (2007). Perú: entre los sobresaltos electorales y la agenda pendiente de la exclusión. *Revista de Ciencia Política, volumen especial*, 235–247.

Thorp, R., Caumartin, C., & Gray-Molina, G. (2006). Inequality, ethnicity, political mobilisation and political violence in Latin America: The cases of Bolivia, Guatemala and Peru. *Bulletin of Latin American Research, 25*(4), 453–480.

Thorp, R., & Paredes, M. (2010). *Ethnicity and the persistence of inequality: The case of Peru*. New York, NY: Palgrave Macmillan.

Ubilluz, J. C. (2010). *El francotirador*: el programa (de clase) de Jaime Bayly. *El Grito.* Retrieved from http://www.elgritoperu.org/files/2010/Marzo/10/664563_ Ubilluz.pdf

Vargas Llosa, M. (1996). *La Utopía Arcaica: José María Arguedas y las ficciones del indigenismo*. Mexico City, Mexico: Fondo de Cultura Económica.

Vergara, A. (2013). *Ciudadanos sin república: cómo sobrevivir en la jungla política peruana?* Lima, Peru: Planeta.

Vivas, F. (2001). *En vivo y en directo: una historia de la televisión peruana*. Lima, Peru: Universidad de Lima.

Vivas Sabroso, F. (1999). No es broma. *Caretas, 1581.*

Weyland, K. (2001). Clarifying a contested concept: Populism in the study of Latin American politics. *Comparative Politics*(1), 1–22.

Weyland, K. (2003). Neopopulism and neoliberalism in Latin America: Unexpected affinities. *Studies in Comparative International Development, 31*(3), 3–31.

Wood, D. (2000). The Peruvian press under recent authoritarian regimes, with special reference to the autogolpe of President Fujimori. *Bulletin of Latin American Research, 19*(1), 17–32.

Ypeij, A. (2013). Cholos, incas y fusionistas: el Nuevo Perú y la globalización de lo andino. *European Review of Latin American and Caribbean Studies, 94*, 67–82.

CHAPTER 4

Brozo's *El Mañanero*

Televisa's Grotesque Clown as Transgressive
Journalism in Mexico

In November 2014, a wax sculpture of Brozo, *el payaso tenebroso* ("the creepy clown"), joined the look-alikes of 230 of Mexico's most prominent historical figures in politics, sports, and the arts that reside in Mexico City's Wax Museum. The tribute came 14 years after Brozo's news show, *El Mañanero*, first aired on TV and broke into the world of political communications in Mexico. The brainchild of comedian Victor Trujillo, Brozo has been considered one of the most identifiable "journalists" in the country ("Micha, Alatorre, Dóriga, Aristegui y Rocha, los comunicadores con mejor imagen en México: Parametría," 2015). According to *Forbes* (2015), Brozo was at one point the most influential Mexican journalist on Twitter.

This chapter analyzes the character of Brozo in the context of Mexico's carnivalesque tradition and based on the satirical impunity of a fictional and marginal character that has come to embody the voice of the country's working class. Brozo is the buffoon that, through critical and vulgar humor, can speak truths without fear of repercussions in a country infamous for its high levels of corruption and violence against journalists. It also examines Brozo as a political communicator who reached the pinnacle of his influence within the Mexican media landscape from his rostrum at Televisa, one of the most powerful media conglomerates in the world, with a questionable tradition of fealty to the politically powerful. In this way, this chapter looks at Brozo's transgressive role since the end of Mexico's one-party rule in 2000 and, in particular, the PRI's return to power in 2012.

CORRUPTION, MEDIA CONCENTRATION, AND VIOLENCE AGAINST JOURNALISTS IN MEXICO

For more than seven decades (1929–2000), the Revolutionary Institutional Party (PRI) held an authoritarian regime in Mexico disguised as a democracy. The writer Mario Vargas Llosa called this single-party system "a perfect dictatorship," which was sustained with the help of political repression, institutionalized corruption, electoral fraud, control of the workers' unions, and a corrupt press. During the PRI's regime, it was common for reporters to receive payola (known as "embutes," "chayos," or "chayotes) from officials or politicians to cover their versions of the news, while media owners received payments disguised as political ads, subsidies, and other fiscal benefits (Alves, 2005).

During this period, media concentration in Mexico was also incentivized through a tacit alliance between the PRI and Televisa, the largest media conglomerate in the country and one of the chief participants in the entertainment industry worldwide (Calleja, 2012; Fernández, 1982; Mancinas, 2007; Mejía, 1998; Sosa & Gómez, 2013; Trejo, 1985; Villamil, 2010). Thanks to this relationship, Televisa operated as a de facto monopoly for decades. Its owner and founder, Emilio "The Tiger" Azcárraga Milmo, considered himself "a soldier of the PRI." After the end of the Cold War, the implementation of neoliberal economic policies, and the wave of democratization in Latin America during the 1990s, the PRI's regime began to crumble under the weight of corruption, a result of the political system's decay. The constant pressure from other political parties—like the National Action Party (PAN) from the right side of the political spectrum and the Democratic Revolution Party (PRD) from the left—and civil society added to the tensions between reformers and hardliners within the PRI. In addition, an independent press had slowly begun to emerge (Alves, 2005; Hughes, 2008), which played an important neutral role in the 1997 federal elections, when for the first time the PRI lost its majority of seats at Mexico's Chamber of Representatives. By then, and after the 1997 electoral reform allowed political parties to purchase airtime from media groups for their electoral campaigns, Emilio Azcárraga Jean, Azcárraga Milmo's son, was already saying that democracy was "good business."

The political opposition's momentum consolidated with the PAN's victory in the presidential election of 2000, which brought Vicente Fox to power and put an end to the PRI's 71 years of political dominance. During Fox's administration, discussions started to draft a law to put media at the service of the democratic efforts; however, they resulted in the scandalous "Televisa Law" of 2006 (crafted in marathon daylong sessions and approved in fewer than 2 weeks), which favored the media giant (Esteinou Madrid & Alva de la Selva, 2009; Gaytán & Fregoso, 2006). The "Televisa Law," or Federal Law of Radio and Television, deregulated the digital frequency spectrum, a public good of the country, conceding it to Televisa (and TV Azteca) free of monetary costs.

After the polarizing presidential election of 2006, which concluded in a virtual tie, Felipe Calderón (the PAN's candidate) ascended to power facing protests from thousands of followers of Andrés Manuel López Obrador (the PRD's candidate), who questioned the results of the election. In the midst of this political crisis, Calderón's administration launched an unprecedented war against drug trafficking. The initiative led to a countrywide bloodbath—more than 121,000 people were killed during Calderón's 6 years in power ("Más de 121 mil muertos, el saldo de la narcoguerra de Calderón: Inegi," 2013)—without any practical results. In this violent scenario, journalism became one more victim of the war against drugs. According to the *Committee to Protect Journalists* (2014), Mexico has become one of the most dangerous countries for journalists. From 2000 to 2014, Mexico's National Commission for Human Rights (CNDH) documented the deaths of 88 journalists or media workers who were allegedly killed for reasons related to their work. Eighty-nine percent of the attacks against journalists in Mexico remain unpunished, according to the Knight Center for Journalism in the Americas (2014).

During Calderón's administration, the electoral reform of 2007 sought to limit the amount of airtime available for the purchase of political ads, which would have meant a reduction in TV networks' profits. Media companies were furious and characterized the reform as an attack on freedom of expression. Even though Televisa still received plenty of privileges from the state, many of the network's journalists attacked the measure. In the midst of a crisis of legitimacy and the much criticized and inefficient war against drug trafficking, Calderón had to relent; he still needed the support of the large media companies:

> [Calderón's administration] supported hundreds of concessions that violated the Court's criteria, lobbied for the television networks before Congress so they would be exempted from taxation, failed to keep its promise with the PRI and PRD to help push for a new media law, delayed as long as possible its order calling for a third television network, and wrongfully intervened with regulatory agencies so that their actions would be favorable to the television networks'

interests. The cherry on top was the approval of the merger between Iusacell and Televisa, which became the largest concentration of communication assets in the country's history.[1] (Calleja, 2012)

Calderón's submission to private media networks was a contrast to the support Televisa gave the PRI during the presidential election of 2012. A "factic (or de facto) power" (Lay, 2013) because of its influence on the public agenda and political decisions, Televisa's partisan coverage was for many a decisive factor in the electoral success of the PRI's candidate Enrique Peña Nieto, the former governor of the State of Mexico. The electoral results sparked a wave of criticisms and protests against the media, specifically Televisa, for misinforming its audience and not playing its democratic role in the elections (Parish, 2012). One of the consequences was the creation of the citizens' movement YoSoy132, initially integrated by Mexican students, which called for the democratization of the mass media and the repudiation of the media conglomerates' imposition of Peña Nieto as the president of Mexico. After his inauguration, however, Peña Nieto approved a controversial reform to the country's telecommunications law, which was supposed to break the media duopoly of Televisa and TV Azteca, according to *El País* (2013, 2015). However, some critics have described it as a political instrument that ultimately benefited Televisa and harmed América Móvil, property of the multimillionaire business magnate Carlos Slim, according to the Knight Center for Journalism in the Americas (2013).

In this political and media context, Brozo became one of Mexico's most influential "journalists," first from his launch pad at an independent channel and, starting in 2002, from Televisa, the heart of the country's media and de facto power.

BROZO, THE DECADENT CLOWN, AS A JOURNALIST

The character of *Brozo, the creepy clown*, began as the antithesis of the stereotypical and fondly remembered *Bozo, the friendly clown*, who entertained

1. "[El gobierno de Calderón] refrendó cientos de concesiones violando el criterio de la Corte, se convirtió en el cabildero de las televisoras ante el Congreso para que les excentaran impuestos, incumplió su palabra ante el PRI y el PRD para impulsar una nueva ley de medios, aplazó hasta lo último de su mandato la tercera cadena nacional de televisión y de manera indebida injirió en los órganos reguladores para que sus actos fueran en beneficio de los intereses de las televisoras. La cereza en el pastel fue la aprobación de la concentración Iusacell-Televisa que significa la mayor concentración de recursos comunicacionales como nunca en la historia de este país."

children on TV during the 1970s. While Bozo recited innocent stories to children and used clean humor, Brozo is a bawdy, misogynistic, politically incorrect clown with a raspy voice. With his green hair and decadent aspect, Brozo is a bitter and incensed character who speaks with resentment and cynicism. He uses sour humor and vulgar expressions to criticize the social and political realities of the country, with a special focus on Mexico's elites. In contrast to Brozo, Victor Trujillo, the character's creator and alter ego, is a comedian and an educated political commentator who has worked as a radio and television host as well as a voiceover actor.

In addition to the intentional contrast with Bozo's name, "Brozo" is also a derivative of the word "broza," a Mexican colloquialism that refers to "vulgar people" and that, according to the Royal Spanish Academy, alludes to waste or garbage. These two meanings reinforce his links to the country's working and marginalized classes. At the same time, the fictional origin of the character also alludes to his marginal configuration: Brozo was born in the Santa Martha Acatitla prison, where his mother (Brozamaría) was serving time for attempted murder. When she was released, she abandoned him in her cell. Brozo left prison when he reached puberty and traveled to Tijuana, where he learned drug traffickers had killed his mother. He experienced the hardships of living in the streets and earned a living telling stories. That's how he made his public debut in 1988 at a Mexico City bar. He spoke to the patrons with a husky voice and proclaimed: "Things are fucked up and they're going to get worse."[2] He insulted the audience, made fun of the president, and joked about the claims of electoral fraud during the 1988 presidential election. That same year, the character of Brozo made his first televised appearance on the state TV channel Imevisión (which was privatized in 1993 and became TV Azteca) on the TV show *La Caravana* ("The Caravan"), in which he restyled classic tales—like "The Steadfast Tin Soldier," "Peter Pan," "Don Quixote," and "The Little Prince"—into vulgar and lewd versions. Many of these stories were later compiled in the book *Cuentos Tenebrosos* ("Creepy Tales"). The preamble to all his stories was: "Kids, do you want me to tell you a story? No? Well, too bad, because I'm going to tell it to you anyway." In this way, perhaps, he also announced his future as a news commentator.

Nowadays Brozo's most recognizable and influential role is as the host of the popular newscast *El Mañanero* ("The Early Riser"), which has taken many forms over the years, from its radio broadcast starting in 1994 to

2. "La cosa está de la chingada y se va a poner peor."

its debut on Mexican television in 2000.[3] The name of the show alludes, jokingly, to a brief sexual encounter in the morning. Under this premise, Brozo has commented on the news, interviewed members of the political, social, and cultural elites, and, in many instances, determined the national agenda. In a *New York Times* article on Brozo (2002), Trujillo explains his approach to journalism using comedy as the parting point:

> Comedy has always seemed the best way to deliver hard news. And within the realm of comedy, the best personality is one who is not vulnerable to attack. Brozo is misogynous. He is an alcoholic, a drug addict, irresponsible and dirty. There's nothing anyone can call him that he has not called himself. (Thompson, 2002)

By 2001, Brozo's influence as a TV commentator was already evident: He was the first to cover the 9/11 terrorist attacks, and his broadcast was one of the most widely seen in local programming (Gaytán & Fregoso, 2002).[4] After hosting shows in Imevisión and CNI Canal 40, Brozo went to Televisa in 2002. Though Trujillo had been a constant critic of the media giant and had suggested he would never work for it, a new chapter for *El Mañanero* began at Televisa. For many critics, Brozo had sold out. However, Trujillo made sure that his program maintained its critical stance against those in power and has rejected numerous times claims of possible censorship at Televisa.

One of the most controversial stories that Brozo broke was his March 2004 exclusive on the acts of corruption of René Bejarano, a federal representative and the PRD's coordinator at the Legislative Assembly in Mexico City. After receiving a video from a PAN congressperson that showed Bejarano accepting bribe money from a businessman, Brozo broadcast it on his program. Coincidentally, Bejarano was giving an interview in another Televisa studio nearby. Unaware of the video's existence, Bejarano agreed to appear on *El Mañanero*, where he was confronted by the clown

3. His most remembered infotainment programs are the different versions of *El Mañanero, El Circo de Brozo,* and *El NotiFiero. El Mañanero* was first broadcast on radio in Grupo ACIR in 1994. It was a successful show and, in 2000, it made its television debut on CNI Canal 40. In January 2002, the show migrated from TV Azteca to Televisa. After his wife's death, Víctor Trujillo decided to end the show on June 2, 2004. The show returned to the radio waves through W Radio from 2012 to 2014. In its latest incarnation, *El Mañanero* was broadcast on Televisa's Foro TV channel at 6:30 a.m. from Monday to Friday until June 2016.

4. Part of the program aired on September 11, 2001, can be seen here: https://www.youtube.com/watch?v=qGk2TIJvOp0

and was exposed. With that, Brozo's reputation as one of the most incisive journalists in Mexican television was consolidated. Thinking back on
those first years with Televisa, Trujillo told the magazine *Chilango* (2009,
p. 2): "Brozo was at the top. We wanted to go into the news but we didn't
plan to be covered by the media, to be interviewed, to be talked about in
newspapers in Germany [*Spiegel*], France [*Le Monde Diplomatique*], the
gringo newspapers [*Seattle Times*], in Spain [*La Voz de Galicia*]." After the
Bejarano case, Trujillo received death threats and, according to his closest
collaborators, there were attempts to link him to drug trafficking to dis-
credit him. By then, Brozo had already become an influential voice in the
public debate who regularly interviewed the most prominent political
leaders. "If Superman can bend beams by looking at them, then Brozo can
devour any politician that you put in front of him,"[5] Trujillo told the newspaper *El Universal* (2005).

In its last incarnation, *El Mañanero* was broadcast from 2010 to June
2016—a 2-hour show that aired at 6:30 a.m. Monday to Friday on Televisa's
Foro TV channel. The backstage was made up of a solemn structure with
classical columns, as if it were a temple or institutional building, with several images of Brozo (illustrations, paintings, caricatures) as a pop culture
icon. A trumpet blared and an off-camera voice announced the start of
the show: "And we're off!" Brozo introduced the program with that day's
date and would add: "Scoundrels, we are alive, only for today."[6] That's how
the first segment of the show started, in which Brozo commented on the
most important topics on the political agenda and shared the top headlines
of the day. For example, a few days after the forced disappearance of 43
students from Ayotzinapa, in Iguala, Guerrero, on September 26, 2014,
Brozo editorialized on the national tragedy: He denounced the degree to
which the government and organized crime have fused, before satirically
criticizing the prosecutor in charge of the case.[7]

The next important segment of the show was called "Debatitlán, the
knights of the political table."[8] This segment used to start with images
of a woman in a thong and a mask dancing to a bolero or another bar
music song. After this carnivalesque wink, the tone would turn serious. In
Debatitlán, Brozo was accompanied by four other traditional commentators

5. "Si Superman dobla varillas con la mirada, pues Brozo puede comerse al político
que le pongas."
6. "Chamacos, estamos vivos, sólo por hoy."
7. Brozo's monologue on the topic can be seen here: https://www.youtube.com/
watch?v=EXl9cDibbtg
8. "Debatitlán, los caballeros de la mesa polaca."

and analysts who were dressed formally, like in any other political analysis show on TV. The commentators, mediated by Brozo, would discuss the news of the day. For example, on January 23, 2015,[9] one of the commentators explained how that day's discussion was going to break down: First, he proposed to talk about the political and administrative problems of the country (starting with the "shipwreck of a commissioner in Michoacán"); then, to talk about topics related to political violence in Mexico; and finally, to review the internal movements of the main political parties. On the table sat a sign that read "119 days"—a reminder of the time that had passed since the tragedy of Ayotzinapa in Iguala, a topic that *El Mañanero* covered extensively for 2 years, until the show ended in June 2016.

Finally, "The Informative Fence" ("La Vaya Informativa") was the show's international segment, in which several fictional correspondents would report real news from sets simulating different parts of the world. For example, John Lemon reported about the dramatic drop in fines issued and people arrested by the New York City Police Department,[10] Juan Naranjo reported from Spain on an art exhibit in Madrid about corruption,[11] or Jean Piña reported from South Carolina about the United States' immigration laws.[12]

One of the controversial aspects of the show was the character of Brozo's secretary, the woman wearing a bikini and a mask who he would call his "Reata" ("leash").[13] The way Brozo treated this character led to criticisms, including a complaint that was filed before the Chamber of Representatives' Commission on Gender Equality for possible violations of women's human rights and dignity ("Comisión del Senado verificará "El Mañanero" de Brozo, por considerarlo 'sexista y discriminatorio,'" 2012). Similarly, the renowned writer Carlos Monsiváis criticized Brozo's humor as "inconsistent and shamefully homophobic" (Thompson, 2002). His critics, however, also understand the transgressive scope of the clown who mocks the powerful: His vulgarity connects with a popular audience who feels represented (and avenged) by the clown's criticisms of the ruling class. Or in the words of journalist Álvaro Cueva: "Brozo represents the dreams and vices of Mexican society" (Thompson, 2002).

9. This episode can be watched here: https://www.youtube.com/watch?v=Jv8N_-xeDi8 Other segments of Debatitlán can be seen here: https://www.youtube.com/watch?v=P56oSyoST-M; https://www.youtube.com/watch?v=puhUfbLvhiA

10. https://www.youtube.com/watch?v=Y89Af5VzcRY

11. https://www.youtube.com/watch?v=ki59Yuab-ro

12. https://www.youtube.com/watch?v=n09DuXTqYx8

13. One of the Reata's appearances can be seen here: https://www.youtube.com/watch?v=tLGygyl27ZY

Following the tradition of the buffoon, Brozo uses vulgar humor to voice the average citizen's dissatisfaction. He also criticizes, parodies, and mocks the country's leaders, authorities, and powerful figures without suffering major consequences. Ruggiero (2007) analyzed Brozo's character as a buffoon with subversive humor who mocks the Mexican elite as stupid, immoral, and illegal. For example, Brozo attacked and mocked Enrique Peña Nieto, before he became the PRI's presidential candidate, for his lack of book smarts and his political opportunism.[14] Peña Nieto had appeared at a book presentation at the International Book Fair and was ridiculed after a journalist asked him which books had influenced him the most. Peña Nieto confused the names of the titles and authors. Brozo used the event to deconstruct satirically the politician's improvised and superficial speech. Not only did Brozo expose Peña Nieto's inconsistencies in literary topics, but he also unveiled how these public demonstrations of cultural and learned authority are propagandistic farces. Finally, after mocking Peña Nieto's public appearance, Brozo incorporated the audience into his criticism of the powerful: He began to read the hilarious and irreverent messages his followers had posted on Twitter. In this way, he directed a collective, carnivalesque space from which to cast stones to the powerful.

Brozo's function, however, was not limited to offering commentary and analysis; he also resorted to direct confrontation. In an interview with Peña Nieto in 2012,[15] shortly before his presidential election, Brozo went over some of the most critical issues in the national agenda, channeling at several times the voice of thousands of Mexican citizens outraged with institutional corruption and the widespread violence across the country. With similar authority and in the midst of a humoristic, circus-like environment, Brozo had an extensive interview with Andrés Manuel López Obrador, the PRD's presidential candidate in 2006.[16] The conversation was humorous and filled with over-the-top comments, but Brozo also asked (and asked again) deep and incisive questions (for example, Brozo asked about Subcommander Marcos' support of López Obrador's presidential run, the candidate's ties to the corporate class, taxes, etc.). Similarly, in 2006 he also interviewed the PAN's candidate, Felipe Calderón,[17] who was

14. The video can be watched online here: https://www.youtube.com/watch?v=xAafGUVDyvk
15. https://www.youtube.com/watch?v=TSGh28BdxeA
16. https://www.youtube.com/watch?v=vZm2UEcFPlY; https://www.youtube.com/watch?v=jA1ZaDnyQq4
17. https://www.youtube.com/watch?v=SaM3l91Wigo

leading in the polls at that time and was eventually elected as the country's president. During that interview, besides discussing the most prominent political issues, Brozo even managed to get the candidate to share details from his private life. Three years later, Brozo used his show to confront Calderón's government about his campaign promises (or lies).[18] These interviews with the most prominent members of the Mexican political elite are good examples of how Brozo positioned himself as the influential buffoon who confronts the powerful. The interviews would even often begin with an acknowledgement of any history or relationship between the interviewer and interviewee, which cemented the clown himself as a member of the political elite. Through his grotesque outfit and marginal configuration, this foul and vulgar character positioned himself in a critical, immune, and privileged place within Televisa, the real court where the structure of Mexican power was judged during the country's democratic transition after 71 years of authoritarian regime:

> Whatever Brozo says is news in this country. Because he is not a man, because he is a character, he can have total and absolute freedom of expression without suffering any consequences. He represents the opening of Mexico, the opening of the government of Fox and the opening of Televisa. He is a symbol of the new era we are living in this country. (Cited in Ruggiero, 2007, p. 9)

Subversive and transgressive humor has a long tradition in Mexico. Since colonial times, literature—like the poetry of Sor Juana Inés de la Cruz (Jhonson, 2000) or the prose of Fernández de Lizardi (Ozuna, 2004)— already showed a critical streak toward social and political elites. This is a tradition that grew richer with authors like Jorge Ibargüengoitia, Augusto Monterroso, and Carlos Monsiváis. In the press, *El Hijo del Ahuizote* was a satirical cartoon magazine founded in 1885 that held a solitary critical stance against the repressive dictatorship of Porfirio Díaz (Díaz-Duhalde, 2010; Escamilla Gil, 1982).[19] In the 20th century, critical humor also found spaces in theater and the modern audiovisual mass media. Starting in 1911, a type of traveling theater known as a *carpa* ("tent") became very popular

18. https://www.youtube.com/watch?v=kYYru_cM8YM
19. There is an ample tradition of satirical magazines and political cartoons in Mexico. Two current examples are the magazine *El Chamuco y los Hijos del Averno* and the animated online cartoon "Mario Netas," published on the newspaper *Reforma*'s website, and later co-opted by Televisa under the name "Terapia Intensiva." The column "Politica Cero" by Jairo Calixto Albarrán is another example of satire in traditional media, while the radio program El Weso (broadcast by Televisa's W Radio) also uses sociopolitical humor.

and remained so until the end of the 1960s (Granados, 1984; Merlín, 1995). Unlike traditional circuses, the theatrical presentations at the carpas were simple and without elaborate sets. They mixed satire, musical acts, and other genres closely related to popular entertainment. Combining the medieval Spanish and Aztec traditions of the public theater, the carpas first developed in Mexico City and then spread throughout the country, and their performances were accessible to the budgets of the lower classes. With an air of anarchist comedy, the carpas also offered a space for social criticism and dissident humor (Alzate, 2010; Pilcher, 2001). Their characters included marginal stereotypes like the "pelado," a trope figure that was immortalized by Cantinflas, a character played by actor Mario Moreno (Esterrich & Santiago-Reyes, 1998). Raised in a poor neighborhood, mestizo and working class, Cantinflas had the appearance of a vagabond, used popular slang, made fun of the middle class and elites, and questioned social differences (Pilcher, 2000, 2001; Stavans, 1995). Cantinflas became a symbol of Mexican national identity; his creator was called Mexico's Charles Chaplin and gained great political influence.[20] One of Cantinflas' most memorable aspects was the way in which he talked, which incorporated slang, wordplay, and double entendres.

Like Cantinflas, Brozo also incorporates popular oral tradition and has his own particular vocabulary. For example, one his most famous phrases was "Prau, Prau," which he used to refer, among other things, to sex. Trujillo coined the phrase at a time when it wasn't possible to talk about sex or refer to it directly on Mexican television during prime time; he used verbal experimentation, along with his audience's complicity, to avoid censorship.

Though Brozo shares important characteristics with carnivalesque characters of Mexico's audiovisual culture (like Cantinflas and Roberto Gómez Bolaños' El Chavo del Ocho), it is essential to go back to his most distinctive characteristic: Brozo is a journalist, comments on the news, interviews and criticizes real members of the political elite, and influences the media's public agenda. Brozo's programs are broadcast from news studios that acquire a carnivalesque touch by combining serious or traditional elements with extravagant or absurd ones. His shows have included traditional news commentators and parodic characters who play the roles of correspondents, traffic reporters, or other journalists. In this way, Brozo reaffirms the global tendency toward satirical infotainment at a time when

20. Cantinflas' success in the 20th century is perhaps only comparable to the celebrity of El Chavo del Ocho, a marginal character created by comedian Roberto Gómez Bolaños (or "Chespirito") who also questioned injustices and social differences.

traditional journalism, to a large degree still financed in Mexico by the state ("El gobierno: Gran financiador de la prensa en México," 2015), continues to face a great economic and legitimacy crisis.

BROZO AND THE POLITICAL AGENDA

El Mañanero's last show was broadcast on June 24, 2016. In this farewell episode, Brozo presented the results of a survey conducted by his show through social media (Twitter and Facebook), which posed the following question: "Taking in mind your expectations and disenchantments, who would you have voted for in 2012?" More than 31,000 people voted on Twitter, producing the following results: First place was a tie between the PAN candidate Josefina Vásquez Mota and the PRD candidate Andrés Manuel López Obrador, followed by Gabriel Quadri (of the relatively young New Alliance Party, or PANAL) with 10% of the vote and, in last place, the PRI's Enrique Peña Nieto, Mexico's current president, with 6% of respondents' votes. On Facebook, more than 50,000 people voted with similar results, though they placed López Obrador in first place, with 52% of the votes, and Peña Nieto in last with 4%. After presenting these negative results for the current administration, Brozo offered a summary of the most important national issues that he covered in the last 6 years, the period of *El Mañanero's* final phase on Foro TV. The clown gave particular emphasis to the violence, the human rights violations, and the symbiosis between organized crime and public entities:

> We reached this new chapter for *El Mañanero* with a country thrown into turmoil, kids, by organized crime. We saw how organized crime consolidated its strength in some states of the republic, and it became impossible to distinguish between those who were supposed to be the good guys and the bad ones. We learned that in Mexico, killings that somewhere else would have shook the earth, here they only made us feel outrage for a few months. We saw how little by little the country's most emblematic touristic spots were turned into criminal plazas: Acapulco, Ixtapa, Zihuatanejo, Cancún, Veracruz, they all live in fear and anxiety because of the symbiosis between criminals and the police . . . and the worst came in 2014: . . . [that year] showed us that those who should uphold the peace in the country can take down the enemy with no other judgment than that of the bullets. And then, hell. Not only for the parents, relatives and classmates of the 43 students who have been missing since September 26. Those in power wanted to tell us a [version of the] truth that, for them, was the one that had to go down in history, but no one believed them. . . . They went after

the international mission that came to remove the veil, to pull down the pants of the historic lie. They disparaged those who came with the international organizations and dared to show us our reality—how sensible—just because they declared that here, in our dear and beloved Mexico, torture is systematic and human rights are not respected . . .[21,22]

After reiterating the implications of the disappearance of the 43 students from Iguala, Brozo placed the blame on institutional corruption, the disconnect between political parties and the citizenry, and the opposing interests of the country's leaders and an unequal society with high levels of poverty:

> We witnessed the unthinkable signing of a Pact for Mexico, which was born from the PRD and PAN's weakness and led to the creation of a series of constitutional and structural reforms that sought to modernize a country that never existed outside the politicians' minds. Research revealed that more than 60 percent of all people in Mexico live in poverty and that more than 80 percent of this country's wealth is in the hands of a very small group. . . . Every morning we hear about the fights between the political parties, about the disagreements in Congress, about the corrupt actions of public servants, from those at the very top to the scapegoats.[23]

21. "Llegamos a esta nueva etapa de El Mañanero con un país convulsionado, niños, por el crimen organizado. Vimos cómo en algunos estados de la república la delincuencia organizada afianzaba su fuerza y ya no se podía distinguir entre los que se supone eran los buenos y quiénes eran los malos. Supimos que en México por las matanzas que en otro lado habrían causado un terremoto devastador, aquí sólo se sentía indignación por unos meses. Vimos cómo poco a poco los lugares más emblemáticos del turismo nacional se convertían en plazas de criminalidad: Acapulco, Ixtapa, Zihuatanejo, Cancún, Veracruz, viven en zozobra por la simbiosis entre criminales y policía . . . Y lo peor llegó en el 2014: . . . nos mostró que quienes deben velar por la paz de la nación pueden abatir al enemigo sin mediar juicio alguno más que el de las balas. Y luego, el infierno. No sólo para los padres, familiares y compañeros de 43 jóvenes estudiantes que desde el 26 de septiembre están desaparecidos. Y los del poder nos quisieron contar una verdad que para ellos tenía que pasar a la historia, pero nadie la creyó. . . . Se lanzaron en contra de la misión internacional que vino a desenmascarar, a bajarle los calzones a la mentira histórica. A quiénes se atrevieron desde los organismos internacionales a mostrarnos nuestra realidad, los descalificaron, qué sensibilidad, sólo porque declararon que aquí, en el México lindo y querido, la tortura es sistemática, que no se respetan los derechos humanos . . ."
22. The June 24, 2016, episode can be seen here: https://www.youtube.com/watch?v=uGSpu-gt-Nk
23. "Fuimos testigos de la firma impensable de un Pacto por México, nacido de la debilidad del PRD y del PAN, y a partir de ahí se fraguó la confección de unas reformas constitucionales, estructurales, que buscaban modernizar a un país que nunca existió más que en la mente de los políticos. Las mediciones nos revelaron que más del 60% de los mexicanos viven en la pobreza y que muy pocos acumulan más del 80% de la riqueza en este país. . . . Todas las mañanas nos enteramos de las pugnas de los partidos, de

And finally, Brozo reminded his audience about the constraints on freedom of expression and journalism in Mexico:

> We witnessed real estate scandals and we witnessed how the person who investigated and discovered those conflicts of interest was taken off the air. . . . There were two permanent elements on our screens. I'm not talking about this hair or this red nose, which are only a matter of aesthetics and eroticism. From the beginning of this new chapter on the screen you're watching, there's a black ribbon that reminds us of the everyday mourning for our fellow reporters and journalists who have died doing their job. . . . It reminds us that the collateral victims are in the thousands and that the lack of safety makes brothers and sisters of us all.[24]

After noting the violence against journalists, Brozo alluded to one of the most controversial attacks against freedom of expression in Mexico during the administration of Enrique Peña Nieto: the termination of Carmen Aristegui, one of the most recognizable and trusted journalists in the country, from the radio network MVS in March 2015. According to the firm, Aristegui was fired because of her program's support of Mexicoleaks, a digital platform for citizen reports. However, for many observers the real reason was the work by Aristegui and her investigative team in unveiling the First Lady's real estate scandal (Martinez Ahrens, 2015). The team of journalists revealed that the presidential couple's luxurious mansion, estimated to be worth about $7 million, was obtained from one of the Mexican government's main contractors. The scandal, which came to be known as "Peña's White House," affected the president's image in and outside the country (Nájar, 2015). On the episode of *El Mañanero* aired on March 16, 2015, Brozo gave a detailed summary of the case, defended Aristegui, and suggested that the government had interfered to have the journalist and her team fired. "It is very regrettable, very regrettable to lose journalistic spaces and even more so at times like these . . . the voices that

los desacuerdos en el Congreso, de los actos de corrupción de los servidores públicos, desde el más alto hasta el del chivo expiatorio."

24. "Fuimos testigos de los escándalos inmobiliarios y fuimos testigos de que quien investigó y descubrió esos conflictos de interés fue sacada del aire. . . . Dos elementos fueron permanentes en nuestra pantalla. No estos pelos ni esta nariz roja, que sólo son una cuestión de estética y eroticidad. Desde el inicio de esta nueva etapa en nuestra pantalla que están viendo, hay un crespón, hay un moño negro, que nos recuerda el luto cotidiano por nuestros compañeros reporteros y periodistas muertos en el ejercicio de su oficio. . . . Nos recuerda que las víctimas colaterales se cuentan por miles y que la orfandad de seguridad nos hermana a todos."

inform, the voices that are part of the profession that must say what no one wants to hear, should be abundant,"[25] Brozo said.[26] According to several local media, the online video in which Brozo criticized Aristegui's termination was blocked by Televisa in the United States ("Televisa bloquea video en el que "Brozo" censura despido de Carmen Aristegui," 2015). Months later, on August 24, 2015, after Peña Nieto's suspicious exoneration in the "White House" case, Brozo referred once again to Aristegui's unfair departure and to the loss of confidence in the government. He gave his verdict: "The president lost by winning."

That critical and confrontational attitude against the president and his administration was constant during El Mañanero's last incarnation.[27] Brozo not only made fun of Peña Nieto on a regular basis—he often mocked the president by calling him "Henry Monster Peña Nieto"—he also even called for his resignation. This happened after one of the biggest scandals of Peña Nieto's administration: the escape of Joaquín "El Chapo" Guzmán Loera, leader of the Sinaloa Cartel and the most powerful drug trafficker in Mexico, from a maximum security prison on July 11, 2015, using a clandestine tunnel that was almost a mile long. Guzmán had already escaped from prison once in 2001 and was recaptured in February 2014. Brozo began his coverage on July 13, 2015, highlighting Peña Nieto's previous vow that Guzmán would not escape again, something that the president said would be "unforgivable." After that, he mocked the current administration and its ineffectiveness, listed specific shortcomings in the maximum security prison that held Guzmán, and, after stating that such a jailbreak "can only be done with tons of money," he suggested that authorities must have been complicit in the escape. Finally, he posed a question: "What has to happen in this country for someone to resign?"[28] Guzmán's escape, of course, continued in the national and international news agenda, and El Mañanero covered it extensively. On July 20, 2015, after Peña Nieto returned from a trip abroad and issued a statement, Brozo once again emphasized the government's responsibility in Chapo's prison break:

25. "Es muy lamentable, muy lamentable que se pierdan espacios para el ejercicio del periodismo y más en estos momentos . . . Deben sobrar voces para la información, para el oficio que debe sustentarse en decir lo que nadie quiere escuchar."

26. Video of the March 16, 2015, episode can be seen here: https://www.youtube.com/watch?v=3V5xh4UfMtQ

27. Another example of Brozo's critical attitude toward the government was the show that aired on December 1, 2015, in which he listed the campaign promises Peña Nieto had not yet fulfilled after 3 years in office. It can be seen here: https://www.youtube.com/watch?v=nnwER-_EkTw

28. The episode that aired on July 13, 2015, on Chapo's prison escape can be seen here: https://www.youtube.com/watch?v=kiWT3pA_zgU

Look, Mr. President, the Mexican people are not angry. We aren't some mutts that just got attacked with stones; we aren't abandoned women either. Authorities' failures, unfortunately, happen every day. More than being angry or furious, we are fed up, because we are all very aware that impunity and corruption have gone too far, and they have already penetrated the country's institutions deeply. What good would pouting do when we know that the government, of any political party, fails to fulfill its first and foremost responsibility, which is to protect the integrity of its citizens?[29],[30]

And in another segment of that same episode, Brozo called the president and his interior minister "schmucks" ("peleles") and repeatedly asked for their resignations ("Brozo arremete contra Peña y su gobierno; El Chapo 'los trató como peleles', dice," 2015).[31] After El Chapo was recaptured months later, on his show that aired on January 12, 2016, Brozo criticized how the government celebrated it: "The way in which he escaped was as unforgivable as the way in which they celebrated. They wanted to make the affair so heroic that they even sang the national anthem; it seemed like capturing 'El Chapo' put an automatic end to the violence the country has been experiencing for the last 20 years,"[32] Brozo said ("Es imperdonable cómo celebraron, critica Brozo a EPN y su Gabinete tras recaptura de 'El Chapo'," 2016).

Brozo's critical and irreverent attitude toward the PRI's government contrasts with Televisa's habitual and historic stance. For some analysts, however, Brozo's criticisms helped further the media giant's interests: "On the one hand, Televisa seeks to convey to its audiences the idea that it also provides spaces for critical opinions, but, on the other one, and given its drop in earnings, there is a strong, veiled complaint against the federal government for the changes in the allocation of government advertising

29. "Mire, presidente, no es ira lo que tenemos los mexicanos. No somos unos perros que agarraron a pedradas; tampoco somos unas mujeres abandonadas. Las fallas de la autoridad, por desgracia, son el pan nuestro de cada día. Lo que sí hay, más que enojo e ira, es hartazgo, porque ya nos consta a todos que la impunidad y la corrupción han llegado muy lejos, y ya penetraron hondo en las instituciones del país. ¿De qué valdrían los pucheros cuando sabemos que el gobierno, del partido que sea, incumplen con la primera tarea que tiene, que es resguardar la integridad del ciudadano?"

30. The episode that aired on July 20, 2015, can be seen here: https://www.youtube.com/watch?v=wld9SLR1YO8

31. Brozo made this call during the round table discussion on July 20, 2015: https://www.youtube.com/watch?v=Q992vudNCL0

32. "Igual que fue de imperdonable cómo se les fugó, es imperdonable cómo lo celebraron. Tan heroico quisieron hacer el asunto que hasta cantaron el Himno Nacional, parecía que con la captura de 'El Chapo' Guzmán se acababa automáticamente la violencia que vive el país desde hace 20 años."

funds and in the electoral law that have forced media networks to cede free airtime to political parties" (Fregoso, 2015).[33] All of this occurred within the context of a 39.9% decline in Grupo Televisa's profits, according to the Mexican Stock Exchange (BMV), after a drop of 16.4% in Televisa's advertising sales, due to being forced to cede airtime to political parties and candidates during electoral periods (Barragán, 2015). Despite these skeptical interpretations and the show's prominence, *El Mañanero* was canceled in June 2016 as part of several changes to Televisa's programming. Trujillo was relocated to a new Televisa comedy show, *Peladito y en la Boca* ("Naked and in the Mouth"), which was promptly canceled for low ratings. In May 2017, after declaring that "We are living the last years of national TV" (Marín, 2016), Trujillo brought Brozo and *El Mañanero* back through digital platforms, inaugurating a new online era for his iconic and popular character.

CONCLUSIONS

Brozo's case finds its place inside the tension between the carnival as a liberating or subversive space and its current co-optation by a tabloid and corporate culture. On the one hand, he has been an influential agent of criticism against social and political elites during Mexico's democratic transition after 71 years of censorship and control by the PRI's monolithic and authoritarian system. In the midst of institutionalized corruption, Brozo has been part of the democratic urge to be able to criticize the powerful within the public discourse. Operating within the tradition of the carnival-esque buffoon, this clown has also obtained critical impunity in a medium where violence against journalists, whether it's from government officials or organized crime, is common. He also has built on the transgressive tradition of marginal characters (like Cantinflas) in Mexican culture and, in this way, echoes the outrage of a large percentage of the country's population that does not feel represented or defended by its institutions. In a country tired of political disappointments, Brozo turns the outrage, impunity, and anger into something a bit more digestible with his humor, cynicism, and

33. "Por una lado, Televisa busca dejar entre la audiencia la idea de que también da voz a opiniones críticas, pero, por otro, y ante la caída de sus ganancias, se esconde un fuerte reclamo al Gobierno Federal por los cambios en la asignación de publicidad oficial y en la Ley Electoral que obliga a los medios de comunicación a ceder tiempo gratis a los partidos políticos."

vulgarity. Similar to the way in which Mexican culture relates to death—instead of fearing it, it mocks and parodies it—Brozo applies this attitude to the current national tragedy. He does it in an intelligent way, but he's not elitist or condescending; he doesn't alienate his viewers with the habitual high-sounding intellectualism of most political commentators. Thus, Brozo's character allows a class marginalized by the political and intellectual elite to become participants in the public discussion. Brozo opens a door for Mexico's working class to have an opinion about politics.

On the other hand, Brozo's carnivalesque impunity exists within the confines of Televisa's media hegemony. Though it would be useful to have a detailed content analysis to evaluate whether there have been substantial changes in his coverage before and after joining Televisa, it is evident that his critical discourse operates within the commercial constraints of the media giant's capitalistic structure. How much this specifically affects his approach to the country's political power is also a pertinent question to shed light on aspects of media's freedom of expression and Mexico's democracy. Another important question is how much Televisa can use Brozo's satirical transgression as an element to negotiate or generate pressure when confronted with the government's legislative changes regarding the country's media networks, which undoubtedly affect their profits.

Brozo's influence and celebrity do not just evidence the erosion in authority of traditional journalism, but also the consolidation of a tabloid mentality with the transmutation of political communications into a circus-like spectacle. With the self-referential (and meta-referential) sense of humor associated with postmodern media, the tradition of satirical infotainment to which Brozo belongs continues to grow and evolve in Mexico. Another case is *El Pulso de la República* ("The Pulse of the Republic"), a satirical, independent program broadcast through YouTube since 2013 that has quickly turned into one of the most influential and popular spaces of the new medium. Like Jon Stewart and Stephen Colbert, Chumel Torres (the creator and host of *El Pulso de la República*) critically parodies the news agenda. After the show's YouTube success, Televisa tried to recruit Torres, just like it did with Trujillo. But unlike Brozo, Torres did not accept and told the media giant: "You are the enemy" (Breiner, 2014). The new digital media landscape will likely open paths for greater independence within the emerging phenomenon of satirical infotainment. However, in countries where TV and radio are still the main forms of mass communication, the government's pressures and big media conglomerates' co-optation attempts continue to be recurring strategies.

REFERENCES

Alessandrini, Y. (2005, September 4). Víctor Trujillo: "Metí a Brozo a la congeladora." *El Universal*. Retrieved from http://archivo.eluniversal.com.mx/nacion/129139. html

Alves, R. (2005). From laptog to watchdog: The role of the press in Latin America's democratization. In H. de Burgh (Ed.), *Making Journalists* (pp. 181–202). London, U.K.: Routledge.

Alzate, G. (2010). Dramaturgy, citizenship, and queerness: Contemporary Mexican political cabaret. *Latin American Perspectives*, 37(1), 62–76.

Badgen, S. (2014). 89% de ataques contra periodistas mexicanos siguen impunes, según comisión de derechos humanos. Retrieved from https://knightcenter. utexas.edu/es/blog/00-15504-89-de-ataques-contra-periodistas-mexicanos-siguen-impunes-segun-comision-de-derechos-h

Barragán, D. (2015). La TV abierta agoniza: Televisa y Azteca ya no venden como antes y sus deudas crecen. *Sin Embargo*. Retrieved from http://www. sinembargo.mx/08-07-2015/1406317

Breiner, J. (2014). Mexican blogger builds a business out of political satire. *News Entrepreneurs*. Retrieved from http://newsentrepreneurs.blogspot.mx/2014/ 03/mexican-blogger-builds-business-out-of.html

Brozo arremete contra Peña y su gobierno; El Chapo "los trató como peleles", dice. (2015, July 21). *Proceso*. Retrieved from http://www.proceso.com.mx/ 411217/brozo-arremete-contra-pena-y-su-gobierno-el-chapo-los-trato-como-peleles-dice

Calderon, V. (2013, June 10). Peña Nieto promulga la reforma de telecomunicaciones de México. *El País*. Retrieved from http://internacional.elpais.com/ internacional/2013/06/10/actualidad/1370885658_536894.html

Calleja, A. (2012). La concentración mediática en México. *Café Político*. Retrieved from http://mx.boell.org/sites/default/files/aleida2mediatica.pdf

Comisión del Senado verificará "El Mañanero" de Brozo, por considerarlo "sexista y discriminatorio". (2012). *Sin Embargo*. Retrieved from http://www.sinembargo. mx/24-04-2012/215403

Díaz-Duhalde, S. (2010). El Hijo del Ahuizote. *Revista de Critica Literaria Latinoamericana*, 36(72), 510–512.

El gobierno: Gran financiador de la prensa en México. (2015). *Arena Pública*. Retrieved from http://arenapublica.com/articulo/2015/08/17/4153

Es imperdonable cómo celebraron, critica Brozo a EPN y su Gabinete tras recaptura de "El Chapo". (2016, January 12). *Sin Embargo*. Retrieved from http://www. sinembargo.mx/12-01-2016/1596461

Escamilla Gil, G. (1982). *El Hijo del Ahuizote*: Semanario feroz, padre de más de cuatro. *Revista Mexicana de Ciencias Políticas y Sociales*, 28(109), 117–122.

Esteinou Madrid, J., & Alva de la Selva, A. (Eds.). (2009). *La Ley Televisa y la lucha por el poder en México*. Mexico City, Mexico: Fundación Friedrich Ebert.

Esterrich, C., & Santiago-Reyes, A. M. (1998). From the Carpa to the screen: The masks of Cantinflas. *Studies in Latin American Popular Culture*, 17, 33.

Fernández, F. (1982). *Los medios de comunicación masiva en México*. Mexico City, Mexico: Juan Pablos.

Fregoso, J. (2015, July 26). "Brozo" exige renuncia de EPN pero es Televisa, quiere más dinero y poder: Académicos. *Sin Embargo*. Retrieved from http://www. sinembargo.mx/26-07-2015/1425153

Gaytán, F., & Fregoso, J. (2002). Del pánico a la banalidad en la tragedia. Terrorismo y medios de comunicación en México. *Revista Chasqui, 77*. Retrieved from http://www.redalyc.org/pdf/160/16007707.pdf

Gaytán, F., & Fregoso, J. (2006). La ley Televisa de México. *Revista Chasqui, 94,* 40–45.

Granados, P. (1984). *Carpas de México: leyendas, anécdotas e historia del teatro popular.* Mexico City, Mexico: Editorial Universo.

Hughes, S. (2008). The media in Mexico: From authoritarian institution to hybrid system. In J. Lugo-Ocando (Ed.), *The media in Latin America* (pp. 131–149). Maidenhead, NY: Open University Press.

Jhonson, J. G. (2000). Humor in Spain's American colonies: The case of Sor Juana Inés de la Cruz. *Studies in American Humor, 3*(7), 35–47.

Lay, I. (2013). Medios electrónicos de comunicación, poderes fácticos y su impacto en la democracia de México. *Revista Mexicana de Ciencias Políticas y Sociales, 217,* 253–268.

Mancinas, R. (2007). El desarrollo de grupos de comunicación en México. *Razón y Palabra, 59*. Retrieved from http://www.razonypalabra.org.mx/anteriores/n59/varia/rmancinas.html - au

Marín, N. (2016, December 2). "Son los últimos años de la TV": Brozo. *El Universal.* Retrieved from http://www.eluniversal.com.mx/articulo/espectaculos/television/2016/12/2/son-los-ultimos-anos-de-la-tv-brozo

Martínez, A. (2013). Diputados en México aprueban reforma de telecomunicaciones: Un resumen. Knight Center for Journalism in the Americas. Retrieved from https://knightcenter.utexas.edu/es/blog/00-13262-diputados-en-mexico-aprueban-reforma-de-telecomunicaciones-un-resumen

Martinez Ahrens, J. (2015, March 16). La periodista Carmen Aristegui, despedida de la cadena MVS. *El País.* Retrieved from http://internacional.elpais.com/internacional/2015/03/16/actualidad/1426481984_041673.html

Martínez, J. (2015, March 12). México rompe el histórico duopolio de la televisión. *El País.* Retrieved from http://internacional.elpais.com/internacional/2015/03/12/actualidad/1426124159_306125.html

Más de 121 mil muertos, el saldo de la narcoguerra de Calderón: Inegi. (2013). *Proceso.* Retrieved from http://www.proceso.com.mx/348816/2013/07/30/mas-de-121-mil-muertos-el-saldo-de-la-narcoguerra-de-calderon-inegi

Mejía, F. (1998). Del canal 4 a Televisa. In Miguel Angel Sánchez de Armas (Ed.), *Apuntes para una historia de la televisión mexicana* (pp. 19–98). Mexico City, Mexico: Televisa/Revista Mexicana de Comunicación.

Merlín, S. (1995). *Vida y milagros de las carpas: la carpa en México 1930–1950.* Mexico City, Mexico: Instituto Nacional de Bellas Artes.

Micha, Alatorre, Dóriga, Aristegui y Rocha, los comunicadores con mejor imagen en México: Parametría. (2015). *Etcétera/Parametría.* Retrieved from http://www.etcetera.com.mx/articulo/micha,_alatorre,_doriga,_aristegui_y_rocha,_los_comunicadores_con_mejor_imagen_en_mexico_parametria/35182/

Nájar, A. (2015, March 16). El escándalo que condujo al despido de la destacada periodista mexicana Carmen Aristegui. *BBC Mundo.* Retrieved from http://www.bbc.com/mundo/ultimas_noticias/2015/03/150315_ultnot_mexico_mvs_radio_despide_aristegui_az

Ozuna, M. (2004). Don Catrín de la Fachenda de Fernández de Lizardi o el humor como purga social. In I. Lerner, R. Nival, & A. Alonso (Eds.), *Actas del XIV Congreso de la Asociación Internacional de Hispanistas, IV: Literatura hispanoamericana* (pp. 505–513). Newark, DE: Cuesta.

Parish, N. (2012). Mexico's media monopoly vs. the people. *Fortune*. Retrieved from
    http://fortune.com/2012/09/14/mexicos-media-monopoly-vs-the-people/
Pilcher, J. (2000). El signo de la mugre: Cantinflas, cross-dressing, and the creation of
    a Mexican mass audience. *Journal of Latin American Cultural Studies, 9*(3), 333–
    348. http://dx.doi.org/10.1080/13569320020010756
Pilcher, J. (2001). *Cantinflas and the chaos of Mexican modernity*. Wilmington,
    DE: Scholarly Resources.
Ruggiero, T. E. (2007). Televisa's Brozo: The jester as subversive humorist. *Journal of
    Latino-Latin American Studies (JOLLAS), 2*(3), 1–15.
Sosa, G., & Gómez, R. (2013). En el país Televisa. In O. Rincón (Ed.), *Zapping
    TV: el paisaje de la tele latina* (pp. 83–97). Bogota, Colombia: Fundación
    Friedrich Ebert.
Stavans, I. (1995). The riddle of Cantinflas. *Transition, 67*, 22–46.
Televisa bloquea video en el que "Brozo" censura despido de Carmen Aristegui.
    (2015). *Proceso*. Retrieved from http://www.proceso.com.mx/398827
Thompson, G. (2002, January 14). Now the morning news is earthy and unsparing.
    The New York Times. Retrieved from http://www.nytimes.com/2002/01/14/
    international/americas/14MEXI.html
Trejo, R. (Ed.). (1985). *Televisa, el quinto poder*. Mexico City, Mexico: Claves
    Latinoamericanas.
Vallejo, M. (2009). Brozo: el drama tras el payaso. *Chilango*, 1–5. Retrieved
    from http://www.chilango.com/general/nota/2009/04/22/
    brozo-el-drama-tras-el-payaso-parte-1
Villafranco, G. (2015). Los periodistas más influyentes en Twitter
    en 2015. *Forbes*. Retrieved from http://www.forbes.com.mx/
    los-periodistas-mas-influyentes-en-twitter-en-2015/
Villamil, J. (2010). *El sexenio de Televisa*. Mexico City, Mexico: Grijalbo.
Witchel, E. (2014). Getting away with murder: CPJ's 2014 Global Impunity Index
    spotlights countries where journalists are slain and the killers go free.
    Committee to Protect Journalists. Retrieved from https://cpj.org/x/5a16

CHAPTER 5

Peter Capusotto y sus videos

Satire, Identity, and Spectacle During Kirchner's Argentina

*P*eter *Capusotto y sus videos* (*Peter Capusotto and His Videos*) is an Argentinean satirical television show with a critical angle that focuses on *rock nacional* (national rock), an eclectic cultural movement with a particular sociopolitical history in the country, which has been ingrained in Argentina's urban identity since the 1960s. On the air since 2006 (first on the Rock and Pop network and then from 2007 to 2016 on TV Pública, the state-owned channel), the program is hosted by Diego Capusotto and produced by Pedro Saborido, comedians of the so-called 80s underground generation, which arrived on television during president Menem's neoliberal decade. The program, created and premiered during the kirchnerismo era, was the most viewed show on Argentinean public television and has received a variety of local awards and recognition. At the same time, it is regionally popular due to its successful presence on the Web. In 2016, after the election of right-wing Mauricio Macri as president of Argentina, *Peter Capusotto y sus videos* left the state channel for the cable station TNT (Turner Network Television, Latin America).

Through dozens of characters, *Peter Capusotto y sus videos* parodies *rock nacional* culture and its relation with Argentinean idiosyncrasies. Mimicking the documentary style and various television genres, Capusotto ridicules stereotypes, celebrities, and popular culture's myths while exposing their inconsistencies and absurdities (and also their influence and power). This chapter focuses, first, on an analysis of Bombita Rodriguez, a new wave 70s singer committed to the guerrilla armed struggle and one of the most popular and controversial characters of the program, to show how *Peter Capusotto y sus videos* demystifies Argentinean identities that exist within the framework of the media spectacle, while exposing particular social tensions after the 2001 crisis and during the kirchnerista period (2003–2015). This chapter also shows how the characters Micky Vainilla (a Nazi pop singer) and Violencia Rivas ("the precursor of punk rock in Argentina") are part of a satiric discourse that not only develops a questioning of *rock nacional*'s contradictions (and its distancing from the countercultural and antiauthoritarian ideals that supposedly marked its origins and defined its cultural mythology) but also carries out a structural critique of the entertainment industry and media culture in Argentina.

Pedro Saborido, cocreator and producer of the program, who from his youth wanted to be a journalist and began his career doing comedy based on the political news agenda, explained the program's rock character:

> Diego and I consider ourselves rockers. In a certain stage of life, everyone needs to tie themselves to an identity or a place . . . Rock culture, as Diego and I experienced it during the 70s and 80s, was also a place of refuge from a way of seeing the world that didn't satisfy us. Being in a dictatorship, you didn't have ways to be radical, and rock gave us a way to be different and say: "I don't like *Saturday Night Fever*, I don't like disco music, I don't like television, I don't want to be a hypocrite or to live this way or to spend a lot of money on designer clothing." You are constantly saying "I don't want to be like that," and that attitude and humor many times are related to each other. (Personal interview, 2015)[1]

Connecting with rock's rebelliousness, Capusotto said that the function of his humor is to call into question prevalent beliefs, to "unmask discourses,"

---

1. "Diego y yo nos consideramos rockeros. En determinada etapa de la vida cualquier persona siempre necesita aferrarse a una identidad o a un lugar . . . La cultura rock, vista y vivida como la vivimos Diego y yo en los 70s y 80s, era también un lugar de refugio frente a una manera de ver el mundo que no nos satisfacía. Estando la dictadura no tenías maneras de radicalizarte y el rock daba una manera de diferenciarte y decir: no me gusta *Fiebre de Sábado por la Noche*, no me gusta la música disco, no me gusta la televisión, no me gusta lo que me proponen para ser un careta o vivir de esta manera o tener que gastar mucha plata en ropa de marca. Estás diciéndole todo el tiempo al otro 'no quiero ser así,' y eso y el humor muchas veces se relacionan." (Entrevista personal, 2015)

and "through humor, which supposedly softens viewpoints, [to show] something monstrous" (Garces, 2013, p. 96).[2] This critical humor, however, is also applied to the comedian's own ideological beliefs. "We mock what we affirm that we are . . . At times, from a fatalistic place. Other times, because we need to escape from our own self-importance"[3] (Garces, 2013, p. 96). Saborido explained *Peter Capusotto y sus videos*'s self-critical humor more concretely:

> Humor is like rock. I am a leftist and I can laugh about the left. I can laugh about us. I love rock. If you tell me: Is rock something great? Yes, it is something great and sublime. If it is sublime, could it be stupid? It can also be stupid. Because the world in which we live is like that. Because the people who I love are also like that: They are marvelous and also can be really stupid. I don't believe that someone can be totally stupid or totally sublime. (Personal interview, 2015)[4]

From this double-edged perspective that attacks that which it hates and questions that which it loves, the satire of *Peter Capusotto y sus videos* positions itself in a parodic carnivalesque space of postmodernity: Capusotto's characters actualize the tradition of the court jester from the state's television channel and carry out a social, cultural, and political critique of contemporary Argentina, questioning its principal identities and discourses (whether they are hegemonic or seemingly counter-hegemonic). While the culture of *rock nacional* is the program's angle, its criticism covers a wider ideological spectrum that has taken over a significant part of the country's social life: the spectacle.[5]

2. "A través del humor, que se supone que suaviza la mirada, [mostrar] algo monstruoso."

3. "Hay una burla de aquello que nosotros afirmamos que somos . . . A veces, desde un lugar fatalista. Otras veces porque necesitamos huir de nuestra propia gravedad."

4. "[El humor] es como el rock. Yo soy de izquierda y me puedo reír de la izquierda. Me puedo reír de nosotros. Yo al rock lo amo. Si me decís: ¿El rock es algo buenísimo? Sí, es algo buenísimo y sublime. Si es sublime, ¿puede ser idiota? También puede ser idiota. Porque el mundo en que vivimos es así. Porque la gente a la quiero también es así: es maravillosa y también puede ser muy estúpida. No creo que alguien pueda ser totalmente estúpido o sublime." (Entrevista personal, 2015)

5. See the Introduction for more about the implications and consequences of a society of spectacle for today's democracies.

SOCIETY OF SPECTACLE AND CELEBRITY CULTURE IN MENEM'S ARGENTINA

During the government of Carlos Menem (1989–1999), a society of television spectacle developed in Argentina, which ideologically accompanied the neoliberal changes in the country. After being elected with a populist discourse that promised a *revolución productiva* (productive revolution) and *salariazo* (a substantial growth of salaries) in the middle of an inflationary crisis, Menem betrayed his voters and made a radical political turn toward neoliberalism (Bonnet, 2008; Fair, 2014; Piva, 2010; Wehner, 2004; Weyland, 2003). In the midst of rampant government corruption, his administration implemented a series of structural reforms based on the privatization of state companies, the reduction of public social spending, commercial deregulation, an increase in external debt, and other measures that principally benefited the interests of business and corporate elites. The *Ley de Covertibilidad* (Law of Conversion)—which established parity between the Argentinean peso and the U.S. dollar—created a fictitious economy that minimized inflation and raised the country to an apparent state of well-being. The GNP grew an average of 7.9% annually from 1991 to 1994, salaries increased, and the middle class grew its consumer capacity. Although this economic model led to the collapse of the Argentinean economy in the crisis of 2001, from the middle 1990s the social impact was already clearly manifested in the growth of unemployment and poverty indexes (Rapoport, 2003).

The media was affected by the menemista reforms; in 1990, the Menem administration privatized the main state television channels (Channels 11 and 13) and deregulated the media market (Blanco & Germano, 2005; Druetta, 2011). As a consequence, television and the media were concentrated and centralized under the power of a few national media conglomerates (Grupo Clarín) and multinationals (TELEFE). The new private channels had an aggressive and commercial focus obsessed with ratings. They changed programming and introduced new television formats in order to increase their earnings based on advertising for a consumerist society. It was the era of entertainment (TV stations introduced lots of new talk shows as well as sports and fashion programs), 24-hour news channels, new celebrities, imported technologies, and modern television studios. The new formats also incorporated innovative aesthetics and narrative strategies: more colors, rhythms, and sounds combined with experimental camera movements and dynamic use of images. The entertainment and news programs promoted consumerism and transmitted a "positive" cultural spirit that reproduced the fiction of menemista well-being, its ideology, and values of accumulation. As such, the media played an essential role in installing the neoliberal hegemony: "The media became the main medium for the cultural politics done by President Menem and the main venues for the reproduction of a cultural climate favorable to the capitalist reforms" (Castagno, 2009, p. 130). At the same time, Menem used the media as his main channel to directly communicate with the Argentinean population, evidencing the alliance between the private media and the government. As one of the most representative cases of the connection between neoliberalism and neopopulism in Latin America (Weyland, 2003), Menem appeared on television playing soccer, dancing tango, singing, driving a red Ferrari, and bantering on entertainment programs. In this way, he transmitted the idea that he wanted the same as all Argentineans and that he would take them to prosperity (Castagno, 2009).

In the middle of the menemista party, new celebrities or "cultural mediators" (like the popular program *Videomatch* and its host Marcelo Tinelli) played an important role as authorities of popular culture legitimated to mediate and negotiate "common sense" values between the different social classes (Castagno, 2009). Celebrity culture and entertainment were consolidated and expanded as a political amalgam during a period of economic fiction. Therefore, it is especially relevant that Capusotto's satiric critique aims to ridicule stereotypes related to celebrity and spectacle, suggesting their sociopolitical and cultural implications. The character that most directly ridiculed it was Pomelo, a parody of a national rock star (appearing very much like real musicians such as Juanse from Los Ratones Paranoicos).[6] Pomelo embodies, in an absurd manner, all the vices of the medicated, self-obsessed, and wicked celebrity-artist, suggesting the death of rock's rebelliousness inside today's society of spectacle. Through this character, Capusotto criticizes the process of "commoditization" of countercultural expression, revealing not only the discursive emptiness of celebrity culture but also the responsibility of audiences (converted into acritical consumers) in the death of the rock utopia. One example of this empty discourse is when Pomelo goes to vote in the country's elections.[7] A voice off screen announces: "Here is Pomelo, who in the last elections demonstrated that he is a real transgressor, the type of artist that you like."[8] Later, in front of the voting booth, Pomelo, wearing sunglasses and

---

6. A video of Pomelo can be seen here: https://www.youtube.com/watch?v=zhnbh2blcMI
7. The video can be seen here: https://www.youtube.com/watch?v=fnFaEBG_F5k
8. "Así es Pomelo, que en las últimas elecciones demostró que es un verdadero trasgresor, como a ti te gusta."

apparently drugged, says to the camera: "I am going to express my rebellion against this democratic bourgeois system. I am going to enter the dark room and I am going to put a lot of rock 'n' roll into my vote."[9] He then crashes against the wall. Upon leaving the dark room, he says: "Today is a holiday; and I voted for my genitals."[10] And he shows how he has inserted his sexual member in the ballot envelope. By doing this, Capusotto not only criticizes the superficial transgression of this narcissistic, egomaniacal character but also the influence and the attention that these superficially transgressive celebrities generate in the media and public discourse. Curiously, Pomelo was elected "artist of the year" in the Argentinean version of *Rolling Stone* magazine in 2007, in a meta-textual gesture that exemplifies the adoption of postmodern and self-referential irony within rock culture and the Argentinean media.

Due to their sociopolitical and cultural implications, the analysis of the discourses associated with celebrity offers important cues to interpreting the values and social attitudes of a particular historical moment. Not only is it a space where ideological issues are played out but also where celebrities are crucial elements in the formation of individual and collective identities. Through rejection or identification with celebrities, feelings of belonging to cultural communities are created. From this point of view, Capusotto's carnivalesque satire performs a critical parody of the identities and stereotypes created by the *rock nacional* culture and its celebrities. For its historic place in the evolution of modern Argentina from the 1960s and its current place at the center of the entertainment industry, the culture of *rock nacional* offers the comedian space to extend his criticism to other sociopolitical and cultural spheres of the country, giving it an unexpected novelty. The wide framework of this criticism is the ideological functioning of entertainment and popular culture propagated by the mass media and the consequences of the current society of spectacle, which has filtered into all spheres of contemporary social life.

TELEVISION HUMOR, *ROCK NACIONAL*, AND
THE DECONSTRUCTION OF MYTH

Since Perón introduced television to Argentina in 1951, television humor has evolved significantly. Landi (1992) identified three generations of

9. "Voy a expresar mi rebeldía contra este sistema democrático burgués. Voy a entrar al cuarto oscuro y le voy a poner mucho rock 'n' roll a mi voto."
10. "Hoy es un día de fiesta; y voté por esta."

television humor in Argentina. The first generation, which got into TV be-tween 1960 and 1970, is made up of amateur actors who came from street fairs, circuses, comedy theaters, and the radio. Their humor is costumbrista and is based on the exploitation of social stereotypes.[11] The second gener-ation, which took to the TV screens in the mid 1970s, based its humor on sexual misunderstandings. This generation's era came to an end with the death of the famous comedian Alberto Olmedo in 1988. The third genera-tion, which arose between the return of democracy and the 1990s, included actors of the café-concert,[12] and its humor was acidic and grotesque; its most prominent performer was Antonio Gasalla. Moglia (2013) suggested a fourth generation, which had its origin in the so-called new Argentinean theatre or the 80s underground generation. This generation includes actors like Diego Capusotto, Alfredo Casero, Fabio Alberti, and Mex Urtizberea, who broke into TV on the absurdist and surrealist comedy program *De la Cabeza* (*From the Head*) (1992–1993).

Humor specifically political, as recalled by Fraticelli (2010), appeared early on Argentinean television, beginning as sketches on comedy programs. Pioneering examples are the sketch "Arbolito" ("The Little Tree") on the program *La Tuerca* (*The Nut*) (aired for the first time in 1965 by Channel 9) and "El dictador de Costa Pobre" ("The Dictator of the Poor Coast") on *No Toca Botón* (*Don't Touch the Button*) (a comedy program which aired for the first time in 1981 on Channel 9 and continued until 1987). Later, po-litical humor expanded to encompass the entire program and constituted a genre with the shows of Tato Bores, *Kanal K (Channel K)*, and *La Noticia Rebelde (The Rebel News)*. A particularly successful journalistic satire was CQC (*Caiga quien Caiga [Whoever Falls, Falls]*), which began production in 1995 and continues on the air. CQC offers a weekly summary of news on politics, entertainment, and sports. Its format was exported globally and was adapted in various countries, like Italy (*Le Lene*), Brazil (*Cueste o Que Custar*), France (*Les Hyénes*), Portugal (*Caia quem Caia*), and Holland (*Koste wat he kost*). Brazil's version has been particularly successful.

CQC was also a product of a generation that created the intra-television parody (Colacrai, 2012; Moglia, 2009), or post-television humor (Fraticelli,

---

11. Its most-known examples are Pepe Biondi, José Marrone, Juan Verdaguer, and Juan Carlos Calabró. Starting on TV in 1957, Tato Bores, the mythical host, actor, and political humorist named the "comic actor of the nation," had a sucessful artistic career of about 50 years. He worked on TV until 1993, 3 years before his death.

12. The notion of café-concert or café-chantant, a type of musical establishment where drinks and food are served, comes from the French belle époque. While not as political or controversial as the cabaret tradition, its performances were sometimes risqué.

2013). In a mediatized society, television genres become the target of jokes: Telenovelas, music video clips, journalistic programs, talk shows, and other hybrid and infotainment genres are stripped and deconstructed in order to expose their artificiality. If before television humor picked up social elements and situations to transform them into comedy, "today the tendency of television humor confirms that the television universe offers enough material to make humor. The social stereotypes were progressively replaced by media stereotypes"[13] (Moglia, 2009, p. 5).

As one of the most outstanding comedians of this intra-television humor generation, Capusotto has been a protagonist in some of the most salient programs of this period: *Cha cha cha* (1993–1997), *Todo por 2 pesos* (*Everything for 2 Pesos*) (1999–2002), and, starting in 2006, *Peter Capusotto y sus videos*. The latter intensified its focus on a particular product of media entertainment and spectacle: the culture of *rock nacional*.

Argentina's *rock nacional* is a label used for a variety of musical genres practiced and produced in the country. Since the 1970s, underground and counterculture musicians combined diverse styles of Anglo-Saxon rock 'n' roll with local music traditions (principally, tango and folklore), infusing the movement with its own hybrid identity. In addition, they were pioneers in utilizing the Spanish language in their rock lyrics and in including local themes and references, which narrated a turbulent historical moment and a generational disjuncture in the country. Called "beat," "progressive music," and finally "*rock nacional*," this varied movement has evolved and played diverse sociocultural roles from its inception through the present. Capusotto's characters point out the attitudes and stereotypes associated with the diverse genres of the movement in different historical periods. For example, Bombita Rodríguez, who is analyzed in the following section, parodies the popular singer Palito Ortega, set in a foundational moment of rock during the late 1960s and early 1970s, in the middle of the tensions between socially committed art and commercial art during the exile of Perón.

BOMBITA RODRIGUEZ: ROCK, PERONISM, AND MEDIA SPECTACLE FOR THE WHOLE FAMILY

Bombita Rodríguez, the Palito Ortega Montonero, is a character that satirically contrasts the subversive discourse of the peronista youth of the 1960s

---

13. "Hoy la tendencia del humor televisivo confirma que el universo televisivo es suficiente para hacer humor. Los estereotipos sociales fueron progresivamente reemplazados por estereotipos mediáticos."

and 1970s with the innocuousness of pop music (the so-called Nueva Ola) of that era. On one level, it is a parody of Ramón Bautista Ortega, the famous Tucuman musician known as Palito, an Argentinean popular culture icon and archetype of the artist from a humble background who arrived at the capital city to find massive success with hit songs. Palito Ortega is also a symbol of *El Club del Clan* (*The Clan Club*), a television program that promoted commercial music groups whose songs reinforced conservative values and traditional gender roles. However, the comedic effect of Bombita Rodriguez is created through the juxtaposition of Palito Ortega with the discourse of the Montoneros, a guerilla organization that fought for the return of Perón to Argentina and whose principal objective was to install national socialism in the country.

The first appearance of the Bombita Rodríguez character on May 5, 2008, was preceded, like many of the program's segments, by a presentation from the host.[14] In these presentations, Capusotto appears dressed in a carnivalesque manner, with clashing colors, hats, or wacky outfits. The stage, at the beginning seemingly neutral (with a wall or window in the background), also announces a world turned upside down: The camera moves in unexpected ways, elements appear out of place, and the host moves outside the TV frame, evidencing the artificial construction of TV reality. These introductions become then the first filter of an impossible world that tries to be conceptualized. For example, the introductory presentation of the first documentary segment about Bombita not only offers essential keys in order to understand the sociopolitical context of the character but also reinforces the general focus of a program that defines itself as "rock":

> It is not common for rock 'n' roll to draw on politics. If we are talking about historical moments, especially in the late 60s and the early 70s, very few musicians really drew on the rebellious and revolutionary movement that then sprang forth in the world. . . . But there was one singer who was dismissed by rock because his songs were subnormal, catchy, and commercial. Now that rock makes a lot of songs like this, that nobody thinks of a better world, that the intellectual development of an amoeba is more feasible than that of any human being, we are going to remember this popular revolutionary singer.[15]

14. The video of Bombita's first appearance can be seen here: https://www.youtube.com/watch?v=pPRbBVykn5A

15. "No es habitual que el rock 'n' roll se acerque a la política. Si de momentos históricos hablamos, muy pocos se acercaron realmente, sobre todo a fines de los 60 y comienzos de los 70, a esa corriente rebelde y revolucionaria que entonces brotaba en el mundo. . . . Hubo sí un cantante que fue defenestrado por el rock, ya que sus canciones eran subnormales, pegadizas y comerciales. Ahora que el rock hace muchas

The first element that stands out in the segment is the relation between rock, politics, and rebellion. The character is contextualized in the middle of the tension between the development of the incipient rock movement and the militant politics of the late 1960s, the foundational period of *rock nacional* that coincided with the exile of Perón after a coup d'état removed him from power in 1955 and outlawed peronismo in the country. After a period of "developmental" anxieties and political instability in which civil and military governments succeeded one another, the dictatorship of General Onganía (1966–1970) reinforced political repression and censorship, while intensifying a morality campaign in its attempts to consolidate a "Christian Nation" that would reject communism (O'Donnell, 1988). During this period of conservative values in Argentinean society, *rock nacional* negotiated its identity and its own cultural significance in the middle of commercial tendencies and artistic experiments (Vila, 1989). However, the relevance and mysticism of the counterculture movement were based in an antiauthoritarian sentiment, which offered space for youth to question the hegemonic and patriarchal values of the conservative Argentinean society (Manzano, 2014). *Rock nacional* was one of the many forms of a large antiestablishment youth culture that included student groups, militants, and guerillas. While there were confluences between some *rock nacional* musicians and revolutionary politics, in general it was a distrusting and tense relationship. Manzano (2014) analyzed this relationship and showed how, in an era in which the revolutionary archetype was Che Guevara, the hedonist lifestyle of rockers (in relation to sex, drugs, and other pleasures) was frowned upon from the viewpoint of a strict political militancy, and their practices were considered to be escapism. What really united *rock nacional* with revolutionary politics was a feeling of rebellion against the status quo, and it is in this intersection (more abstract and desired than real) where Capusotto locates Bombita Rodríguez, an impossible character who serves to demystify and parody the ideals of the "committed artist" and also to criticize the genre's present in which it had become just one more form of entertainment. According to Capusotto's introduction, today's rock principally produces commercial products for a predominantly alienated and stupid audience. However, this gaze does not idealize the past; on the contrary, it also demystifies the idea that rock had ever been a homogenous antiestablishment culture, even in its most glorified era. In his introduction to the segments of Bombita, Capusotto often

canciones así, que ya nadie piensa en un mundo mejor, que es más factible el desarrollo intelectual de una ameba que de cualquier ser humano, vamos a recordar a este popular cantante revolucionario."

repeats how commercial temptation frequently co-opted a large part of the rock scene, even from its beginnings.

Bombita is set in a political period that is determinant in order to understand today's Argentinean society and politics: peronism. Bombita is a militant of the rebel youth who advocated for the return of Peron to Argentina from exile through armed struggle. In a 1971 statement, Bombita announced the intentions of his artistic career (launched with the song "Armas para el Pueblo"[16] (Arms for the People), which was later consolidated with the music album *Ritmo, Amor y Materialismo Dialéctico* (*Rhythm, Love, and Dialectic Materialism*): to achieve a national, danceable, and family-friendly socialism. Like many young people of the time, his revolutionary convictions generated frictions with his family, reflecting the era's generational and ideological rupture. The off-camera voice that narrates Bombita's story tells us his contradictory genealogy: "His mother, Evelyn Tacuara, the most famous cabaret dancer of Argentinean Catholic Nationalism, instilled in him a passion for music, but it was his father, Grunkel 'Cacho' Abramov, better known as the Barricada clown, the most renown Trotskyan clown, who bequeathed him a passion for the masses."[17] In another episode, we find out that his father's artistic career also reflected the political ups and downs of the era: "He had split from the leftist trio Tres Tristes Troskos (Three Sad Trotskyites), which had split from the quartet Cuatro Tristes Troskos (Four Sad Troskyites), that had split from Los 5 Troskos del Buen Humor (Five Trotskyites in a Good Mood)."[18,19] After ridiculing the tendency of factionalism inside Argentinean Trotskyism, Capusotto turns to the Right. The surname of Bombita's mother, Evelyn Tacuara, refers to the Movimiento Nacionalista Tacuara (National Tacuara Movement), an organization of the Argentinean ultra-right linked to the most conservative sectors of peronismo, which utilized terrorism between 1955 and 1965 in order to defend nationalistic, Catholic, fascist, anticommunist, anti-Semitic and antidemocratic ideas (Lvovich, 2009). Bombita comes from parents of radical and polarized ideologies, but they have nevertheless coexisted as a

16. The song can be listened to here: https://www.youtube.com/watch?v=KDrLoyE9zoQ

17. "Su madre Evelyn Tacuara, la más famosa vedette del nacionalismo católico argentino, le inculcó la pasión por la música, pero fue su padre, Grunkel 'Cacho' Abramov, más conocido como el Payaso Barricada, el más renombrado clown del trotskismo, quien le legó su pasión por las masas."

18. "Se había escindido del trío de izquierdas Tres Tristes Troskos, que se había escindido del cuarteto Cuatro Tristes Troskos, que a su vez se había escindido de Los 5 Troskos del Buen Humor."

19. The video can be seen here: https://www.youtube.com/watch?v=BQPhnarnxPs&index=2&list=RDpPRbBVykn5A

couple and defined the values of the singer. And, as the narrator reminds us, Bombita's parents are the source of his artistic passion and financed the beginnings of his career. As such, the art of Bombita is only possible due to the convergence of disparate ideologies that created in him an unprecedented hybrid.[20] In spite of his contradictory nature, Bombita's principal personal conflict is the distancing of his mother due to their ideological discrepancies. His maternal void is filled by militant politics. An example is when, for Mother's Day, Bombita interprets the song "La sonrisa de mamá es como la de Perón" ("Mother's smile is like Peron's"):[21]

I always see your smile
And I think with love
My mother's smile
Is like Peron's.
Although you hate the dark-skinned people
Who generate surplus value
And taking up arms
Soon will battle against you,
Although you may be an
Authoritarian and traitor pig,
I love you
Because you are my mother (ER-ERP)[22,23]

20. This might also point out an irony about the Montoneros: a part of the leadership emerged from catholicism and some had even participated in Tacuara.

21. The video of the complete segment can be seen here: https://www.youtube.com/watch?v=HgJ0tKwC0JI Or only the song here: https://www.youtube.com/watch?v=bcJ1ENGee6s

22. These refrains of Bombita ridicule the ERP (Ejército Revolucionario del Pueblo), the armed branch of the Partido Revolucionario de los Trabajadores (PRT; Bombita also uses these initials at the end of some songs).

23. "Siempre veo tu sonrisa
   Y yo pienso con amor
   La sonrisa de mamá
   Es como la de Perón.
   Aunque odies al cabecita
   Que genera plusvalía
   Y que tomando las armas
   Pronto te combatirá.
   Aunque seas una cerda
   Vende patria y gorila
   Yo te quiero
   Porque vos sos mi mamá (ER-ERP)"

In addition to parodying revolutionary terminology and the format of the era's family-oriented melodies, this song satirizes militant politics as a replacement for maternal protection. Bombita compares the socialist utopia to a gesture of tenderness (not of justice). His idealized version of socialism, however, contrasts with the political reality. In a segment called "The magic of General Perón," Bombita, via satellite from Madrid, interviews Perón, who does a magic trick to delight the masses.[24] Perón shows a golf ball that has written on it: "National Socialism." He then hides it under one of two cups, which have written on them the numbers 1 and 2. After moving the cups around, Peron asks Bombita, "In which cup is the ball?" Bombita answers, "In cup number 1." The ball is not there. Bombita says, "In number 2." "Not there either," says Perón, and he laughs. "But, that's incredible," says Bombita. "You showed me National Socialism and it's not anywhere, not even in either cup. Where is it, General?" "Nowhere. And I believe you will never see it," says the General. Bombita makes a gesture of disappointment and murmurs, "Me cagó" ("He fucked me over"). A song announces the closing of the interview while Perón's hands manipulate the Joker's card (or wild card) and other cards with the faces of the politicians who will succeed him in power: "The magic hands of Peron are going to do a trick to stay in power, surprising the Peronist Youth,"[25] says the song. These satiric segments refer to the Argentinean political process after Perón's return from 18 years in exile and the unsustainable polarization between the left and the right factions under peronismo. The Ezeiza massacre in 1974 marked the rupture between the Montoneros and the Justicialista party and an attempt to thoroughly suppress them, even before the military junta's dirty war was set up in 1976. Nevertheless, Capusotto's criticism is not limited to the Peronista Youth's naiveté during the 1970s but also includes the political manipulation that has maintained peronismo as the principal political actor in Argentina (whether it be, for example, through the menemista treason or the polarization promoted by kirchnerismo).

At the same time, Capusotto's historic revisionism implied in the appearance of Bombita Rodríguez in 2008 included an unexpected novelty. The kirchnerista government was going through one of its biggest crises: the "campo-gobierno" conflict (Fair, 2008), an agricultural strike, consisting of a lockout and roadblocks, in which the agricultural production sector protested against the government's decision to increase the

24. The video of the segment can be seen here: https://www.youtube.com/watch?v=oObdHY2T1QE
25. "Las manos mágicas de Perón un truco van a hacer/ para quedarse en el poder/ sorprendiendo a la JP [Juventud Peronista]."

taxes on soybean and sunflower exports. The conflict, which affected the country for more than 3 months, worsened when the protests were coupled with a transportation industry strike and the food supply to the cities was threatened. While Nestor Kirchner reappropriated the terminology and rhetorical strategies of the old peronist discourse during his term (2003–2007) (Muñoz & Retamozo, 2008), the campo-gobierno conflict led the government of Cristina Fernández de Kirchner and the opposition to frame the issue using old social dichotomies. The Kirchner government posed the conflict in terms of "the people versus the oligarchy" and compared the agricultural leaders with the repressive *golpistas* of the past, who aimed to "besmirch the memory of Perón and Evita"[26] ("Conflicto del campo, Néstor Kirchner en la Plaza de los Dos Congresos," 2008). While the government used terms like "oligarchy, gorilas, golpistas," the opposition responded with terms like "lefties, montoneros, and terrorists" (Colacrai, 2012). In this context, the appearance of Bombita Rodríguez on the state TV channel was a controversial subject that generated public debate over the significance of the character. In addition to the sociopolitical tension generated by the campo-gobierno conflict, the debate implied a wider issue: the political use of historical memory in times of crisis and the tendency of fragile Latin American democracies to justify their current contradictions by reinterpreting the past.

BOMBITA AND THE MEDIA

The crisis during the kirchnerismo also connected with one of the fundamental themes of Capusotto's humor: the questioning of the media's sociopolitical and cultural role. The polarization between the ruling party and the opposition reflected a growing tension between the government and the media. It was not a coincidence that during this time, the president promoted a communications law (Ley de Servicio de Comunicación Audiovisual) that sought to limit the power of Grupo Clarín, the country's largest media conglomerate, which had been critical of the government, especially during the campo-gobierno conflict. As part of a debate about the concentration of media ownership versus the freedom of expression, the confrontation underlined the role that the mainstream media has played within the framework of repressive or corrupt power in the country. They were not only subordinated to and acted, in many cases, as accomplices

26. "Enlodar la memoria de Perón y Evita".

of the last military dictatorship, but also were sources of misinformation during the Falkland Islands war. They played a fundamental role during Menem's neopopulist government and its installation of a neoliberal hegemony. Citizens also blamed the media, and their collusion with the powers that be, for the 2001 economic collapse, and the rallying cry "Que se vayan todos" ("Everyone should go") included the media and the press. A satiric reaction to the 2001 crisis was the appearance in 2003 of the magazine *Barcelona*, which criticized the performance and role of the media and targeted the corrupt and inefficient local elites (Alonso, 2007).[27] In a similar vein, one of Capusotto's central satiric criticisms has been the functioning of the media in the reproduction of social values and its responsibility in the spectacle's takeover of public discourse.

In the case of Bombita Rodríguez, the meta-referential criticism toward the media is also a fundamental component: Bombita is essentially a media character whose existence is only possible in the framework of entertainment and mass culture. First, Bombita's story comes to us mediated through the parody of a historical documentary, in black and white, which appeals to nostalgia and memory through narrative codes and aesthetics of the genre. The meta-textual component appears on various levels: For example, the "documentary" includes real segments of old Argentinean entertainment programs (like the popular *Sábados Circulares*) in which Bombita Rodríguez performs. This is a common device of Capusotto: His characters often are framed in a parody of nonfiction audiovisual genres that give them a carnivalesque verisimilitude; he creates a meta-textual universe that transgresses the generic rules, and renegotiates the pact with the spectator in a humorous code.

Second, Bombita is a celebrity who exists in the framework of commercial spectacle. He is not only a popular singer but also (like many artists of the era, including Palito Ortega) a protagonist of diverse strands of media culture[28]. He hosts television programs, appears in advertising campaigns (for the hair spray "La Orga," whose target customer is the modern Montonero), and acts in a variety of movies (such as *Amor y frente de masas* [*Love and a Popular Front*], *Me gustan tus ojos y tu pensamiento leninista* [*I Like Your Eyes and Leninist Thinking*] and *Qué linda es mi familia, lástima que sean*

---

27. The magazine *Barcelona* parodied the format and discourse of the daily newspapers (especially *Clarín*, the daily newspaper owned by the main media monopoly of the country). Its acid and controversial humor is part of an important Argentinean satiric press tradition, which included iconic magazines such as *Tía Vicenta* (1957–1966; 1977–1979) and *Humor* (1978–1999).

28. In this video, the part with Bombita as an entertainment producer can be seen: https://www.youtube.com/watch?v=Raq5uRvGywg

unos burgueses sin consciencia nacional [*How Beautiful Is My Family, It's Sad That They Are Bourgeois and Don't Have a National Conscience*]). In all these spheres, his discourse is explicitly propagandistic, highlighting the media's ideological character. It is not a coincidence that the social and historic framework of Bombita is peronismo: It was precisely General Perón who introduced television to Argentina in 1951, and in 1974, the government of Isabel Martínez de Perón nationalized all television stations, referring to television as "a vital element for the cultural formation of Argentineans and for the maintenance of spiritual values that constitute our nationality"[29] (Sacchetto, 2009).

Capusotto's criticism of the media and the way in which spectacle and infotainment have taken over public discourse connects with the global trend toward television satire exemplified in the other cases in this book. Nevertheless, Capusotto's humor goes further than a parody of the news and journalistic formats and develops a more complex criticism of the entertainment industry and its role in reproducing social prejudices in mass media and in popular culture.[30]

VIOLENCIA RIVAS: PUNK, SATIRE, AND GENDER

Many of the satiric strategies and multidimensional critiques mentioned here with respect to Bombita Rodríguez also appear in other popular Capusotto characters. In a manner similar to Bombita with respect to Palito Ortega, the character of Violencia Rivas, "the precursor of punk in Argentina," parodies Violeta Rivas, a conservative female symbol of El Club del Clan. The Violencia Rivas sketches also use fake documentary material and imitate nonfiction TV: In the present, sitting in a room in her house with a glass of whiskey in her hand, Violencia remembers her artistic trajectory with photographs and archival videos in black and white. While Violeta Rivas was blonde, smiling, and enchanting (Varela, 2005, p. 137), Violencia Rivas is a grotesque, alcoholic, and angry version of her in the present.[31] While Violeta Rivas sang about love subordinated to the masculine gaze,

29. "Un elemento vital para la formación cultural de los argentinos y para el mantenimiento de los valores espirituales que constituyen nuestra nacionalidad."

30. In this way, his work is much like the satire of the Briton Sacha Baron Cohen, in Da Ali G Show (Alonso, 2016). Both create characters that represent the worst social vices, and they take them to an absurd, uncomfortable place that questions and challenges the audience.

31. The sketch introducing Violencia Rivas can be seen on YouTube: https://www.youtube.com/watch?v=NrvPBpL_OUI&list=RDs3D2mhAJ6T8&index=4

the celebration of life, and maternity, Violencia sings against the castrating educational system, against the hypocrisy of the family, against the canons of beauty, and against romantic love, and asks for freedom for her vagina.

Violencia Rivas is part of a tradition of female characters humorously played by male transvestites. Two of the most emblematic are Doña Porota, embodied by the comedian Jorge Luz in the decade of the 1940s, first on the radio and later on TV; and La Abuela (The Grandmother), interpreted by Jorge Gasalla from the 1980s on TV, as part his repertoire of "monstrous women" (Sarlo, 2001). Although Violencia shares a certain grotesque condition with these characters, she transcends her appearance in order to carry out a critique of gender. As noted by Moglia (2013), "This character addresses feminist issues, exploiting them in a way close to misanthropy, but never to misogyny. In this way, the character installs a rupture with the satiric tradition about women's issues"[32] (p. 54). Generally, as Hodgart (1969) emphasizes, "Satire on women is a comedic recording of deviations from the ideal set up by the encomium, and traditionally, it has been centered on the cardinals of docility, chastity, and modesty" (p. 81). Violencia Rivas disobeys all these norms, enabled by her condition as the female precursor of punk rock in Argentina. Through parody, she appropriates the rebellious, nonconformist expressions of this countercultural movement. In this way, Capusotto and Saborido develop a multidimensional critique of the music industry and the mass media and, from there, they expand to target conventional values and the status quo. It is a criticism of the conservative and patriarchal society of the 1960s but also extends up to the present and includes new generations, embodied in the daughters of Violencia Rivas. In the sketches, Violencia frequently explodes furiously against her daughters, who she considers to be functional agents of the system:

> [Her daughter], the psychologist, because she helps to overcome the problems of those who are exploited and to exploit, without blame, those who are the exploiters; the kindergarten teacher, because she indoctrinates children to adapt meekly to the system; the sociologist, because her surveys contribute data to renew social control. And like this, she confronts and attacks each one of her daughters with arguments that, from a fictional and satirical fury, point out their conformist submission to the social establishment: frivolous entertainment, education designed to maintain the status quo, regulated leisure and the

---

32. "Este personaje se sirve de cuestiones feministas explotándolas en un sentido que roza lo misántropo, pero nunca lo misógino. En este sentido, el personaje instala una ruptura con la tradición satírica que ha tenido a las mujeres como tema."

economic productivity sustained through a base of therapies and compensatory medication. (Moglia, 2013, p. 62)[33]

Through Violencia Rivas, Capusotto satirically critiques the country's main social institutions and the domestication of countercultural expressions of rock. About the character, Capusotto has declared: "Violencia Rivas is the one that most represents a certain demystification of our own beliefs. It is more us speaking through the character"[34] (Garces, 2013, p. 97). At the same time, the use of the grotesque in Violencia Rivas serves to develop a gender critique and to reinterpret the place of women in rock culture. She represents not only a criticism of the marginalization and prejudices against women within rock culture but also a ridicule of feminist stereotypes and punk anarchism.

MICKY VAINILLA: POP, FASCISM, AND *PORTEÑO* CITIZENS

The character that criticizes the prejudices of *porteños* (people from the port city of Buenos Aires) most brutally is Micky Vainilla, a pop singer with a Hitleresque mustache and a fascist, xenophobic discourse based on racial supremacy.[35] His catchy songs speak about the dangers that the poor represent and the repulsion that he feels for dark-skinned people, the obese, and the ugly; he talks about the necessity of deporting illegal immigrants and proposes that impoverished towns and slums be hidden away in order to show a nice image of Buenos Aires to tourists coming from the First World. Like Bombita Rodríguez, Micky Vainilla also participates in advertising and public service campaigns. For example, he promotes the dessert "Teresito," a product to help children grow up "healthy and blonde, above the poverty line." He invites his followers to spend time in the amusement

33. [Su hija], la psicóloga, porque ayuda a sobrellevar los problemas a quienes son explotados y a explotar sin culpa a los que son explotadores; la maestra jardinera, porque adoctrina a los niños para que se adapten mansamente al sistema; a la socióloga, porque sus encuestas contribuyen con datos a renovar el control y, así, va presentando y atacando a cada una de sus hijas con argumentos que, desde una furia ficcional y satírica, está señalando la sumisión conformista a lo socialmente dado: el entretenimiento frívolo, la educación funcional al orden vigente, el ocio regulado y la productividad económica sostenida a base de terapias y analgésicos compensatorios. (Moglia, 2013, p. 62)

34. "Violencia Rivas es la que más representa cierta desmitificación de nuestras propias creencias. Ahí estamos hablando más nosotros con la excusa del personaje."

35. The first video of Micky Vainilla can be seen here: https://www.youtube.com/watch?v=RedekhcA6gQ

park "Hitlerama," where, he reminds them, they must take along their corresponding health and racial certificates. From his Vainilla Foundation, he also sells Ku Klux Klan watches, "so that every hour, you remember who is superior." He encourages us to help the poor by giving them a Steve Jobs book (although later they might exchange it for drugs) or to donate paint for their houses in order to "make their poverty more digestible to others." He also carries out a campaign to put a barcode on "suspicious" people in order to be able to discriminate effectively and to distinguish between workers and those who are delinquents.[36]

In the introduction to Micky Vainilla's first sketch, Capusotto presents the character as a "testimony of a singer that from his pop career suffers the problem of not accepting that which is different."[37] The frame shows a close-up of Vainilla's face, and the voice of the character can be heard: "Look me in the eyes. They are trying to tell you something. Does it seem like I am not sufficiently open? I am not accusing anyone. I am only trying to make fun music, nothing more. However, everyone keeps talking and talking about discrimination. I only want to see the kids dancing and having fun."[38] Through this statement, Capusotto announces the main critical angle of the character: the relation between discrimination and entertainment. More specifically, his appeal to pop aims at banishing any problematic aspects of his work and discourse. However, Micky exemplifies several of the worst and most complex social vices in Argentinean society. For him, for example, everything is principally "una cuestión de piel" (a matter of skin).[39] He sings:

> The night shines in the disco
> dancing I give you a bite
> but there is something that worries me
> A morocho is dancing besides me.
> I never make a difference
> But the morocho bothers me.

36. Some of Micky Vainilla's social campaigns can be seen here: https://www.youtube.com/watch?v=AZ2LyS6jFB4
37. "testimonio de un cantante que desde el pop sufre en su carrera el problema de la no aceptación de lo diferente"
38. "Mírame a los ojos. Tratan de transmitirte algo. ¿Te parece que no soy suficientemente abierto? Yo no acuso a nadie. Yo sólo trato de hacer música divertida, nada más. Sin embargo, todos están dele que te dele con el tema de la discriminación. Yo sólo quiero ver a los chicos bailar y divertirse."
39. The video of "Es cuestión de piel" can be seen here: https://www.youtube.com/watch?v=FuFX9uWo7Ac

A morocho isn't strange
If in the disco he is cleaning the bathrooms
oh, if the morocho is an employee, everything is fine
oh, if the morocho is an employee, everything is ok
but don't dance with me
it's a matter of skin.[40]

According to Vainilla, dark-skinned morochos/Latinos are potentially a social danger and have a natural tendency for crime, except when they are employed in the service industry or do society's "dirty work." If they are bricklayers or floor cleaners, everything is fine, but only if they return, after finishing their work, to their houses in the Conurbano, the peripheral area of the city defined by General Paz Avenue. Otherwise, these dark-skinned immigrants from other places (Bolivians, Peruvians, Paraguayans, and also immigrants from rural areas of Argentina), who are poor, and wear sandals, should be "arrested beforehand" or returned to their country so that they don't take work away from the Argentineans. These prejudices also have an aesthetic urban component; for Vainilla, these people make the city ugly and should be hidden away from public view. He proposes, for example, to create a schedule for "the others" to get around town and later to disappear so that the city stays "clean, respectable, and beautiful to look at."[41] This notion of aesthetic well-being is important for Vainilla because he considers Buenos Aires his house and Argentina his home. He summarizes his vision of public space with this sentence: "Our country is a great house and like all great houses, it has house service."[42]

40. "La noche brilla en la disco
    bailando te pego un mordisco
    pero hay algo que me hace el bocho
    tengo al lado bailando a un morocho
    yo nunca hago diferencia
    pero el morocho me molesta
    un morocho no es extraño
    si en la disco es el que limpia el baño
    oh, si el morocho es empleado todo bien
    oh, si el morocho es empleado todo ok
    pero que no baile conmigo
    es una cuestion de piel".
41. "Limpia, respetable y hermosa para ver"
42. "Nuestro país es una gran casa; y como toda gran casa, tiene habitación de servicio."

In between the video clips and commercials, the Micky Vainilla sketches are presented in an interview style—an off-camera voice questions him in the style of certain television genres about celebrities, like MTV. Assuming a critical point of view, the off-camera voice challenges Vainilla about his prejudices and his evident apology for Nazism (his Hitler mustache, his hairstyle, his use of swastikas). Although at first Micky denies or pleads ignorance with respect to the accusations (for example, he contends that he does not know who Hitler is and asks if he is a pop singer), finally he loses his patience, raises his voice, becomes angry and offended, and then defends his position. He justifies his actions that incite hate with the fact that whatever money he collects is going to serve a social good (like a garbage dump for poor children to play with trash on their winter vacations, a trip to the other side of the border in order to visit their relatives and not return, or the construction of a wall so we aren't able to see them). Faced with Vainilla's contemptible utterances, however, the off-camera voice—which until now we have felt as ours—stays silent. That is when, according to Muraca (2011), Capusotto and Saborido construct in Vainilla one possible mirror of post-menemista Argentinean society: a tragic-comedic mirror, uncomfortable and grotesque, that tells us that the people of Buenos Aires accept or share, in the back of their minds, Micky Vainilla's discourse and his xenophobic, fascist, and racist songs. This off-camera voice's silence also tells us that part of Argentinean society, educated enough to identify the Nazi and to reject it, is at the same time incapable of condemning and disarming fascism when it is articulated in social rhetoric. As such, the voice appears to falter and to agree; the voice's silence is also the silence of Argentinean society: "The voice that consents, that enables, that gives in to fascism appeared, not once but various times in the recent history of our past. It is the silent accompaniment to the most aberrant events of our history"[43] (Muraca, 2011, p. 21). This refers, for example, to the festive and cynical complicity of a good part of Argentinean society when faced with the crimes of the last military dictatorship (unsuccessfully disguised with popular media spectacles like the 1978 soccer World Cup in Argentina or the nationalistic framing of the Falkland Islands war) or through its compulsive consumerism and the indolent, celebratory accompaniment of menemist neoliberal politics while the rest of the country drowned in unemployment and misery.

43. "La voz que consiente, que habilita, que claudica ante el fascismo apareció no una sino varias veces en la historia reciente de nuestro país. Son los acompañamientos silenciosos a los sucesos más aberrantes de nuestra historia."

In this way, as Fraticelli (2010) shows, Micky Vainilla incorporates a new way of doing political humor in Argentinean television: "While political television humor has traditionally criticized politicians and portrayed the citizen-spectator as a victim of their actions, Micky Vainilla proposes a new interpretive game: he criticizes the citizens, especially *porteños*, and portrays them as politically active actors, responsible for the country's social transformation" (Fraticelli, 2010, p. 42).[44] Micky Vainilla not only unveils the propagandist and highly charged ideological dimension contained in the apparent innocuousness of pop culture but also targets the moral values of the average *porteño* citizen and unmasks his fragile progressiveness and political correctness. At the same time, he reflects a variety of social tensions in Buenos Aires, a polarized society in which socioeconomic differences and discrimination against immigrants from neighboring countries are increasingly more evident, as well as the society's political shift to the right, manifested clearly in the last elections of 2015 that brought the conservative Mauricio Macri to power.

CONCLUSIONS

The humor of *Peter Capusotto y sus videos* develops sociopolitical and cultural critiques that have multiple layers of interpretation and function on different historical levels of reality/fiction. In the case of Bombita, the comedian carries out a carnavalesque historical revisionism that exhibits an unexpected relation to the present. Bombita not only reflects the intrinsic tensions and ideological contradictions of peronismo of the 1960s and 1970s but also serves to question the functioning of political discourse in Argentina during kirchnerism. The character is also a critique of the "peronismo pop," as a way to show the artificiality and contradiction of identities (whether they are cultural, ideological, or political). Through Violencia Rivas, Capusotto focuses on the country's cultural establishment and social institutions. Mediated by the countercultural spirit of punk, he makes a gender critique from the ambivalent place of a transvestite man and a grotesque fiction. Micky Vainilla, for his part, unmasks the prejudices of the average *porteño* citizen and demonstrates how an increasingly intolerant society shifts to the right. In all these characters (and in others, like

44. "Mientras que el humor político televisivo venía criticando a los políticos y figurando un espectador ciudadano como víctima de sus acciones, Micky Vainilla propone un nuevo juego interpretativo: critica al ciudadano, en especial al porteño, y lo figura como un actor político activo, responsable del devenir social."

Latino Solanas[45]), Capusotto's critiques have constant elements, such as the role of entertainment and the media in the formation of identities and in the reproduction of social prejudices, and through a double-edged satiric self-critical movement, he attacks these vices and our complicity in them.

At the same time, Capusotto demystifies the relation between rock, politics, and rebelliousness in the foundational era of a supposedly countercultural and antiestablishment movement, which ended up being co-opted by the entertainment industry and celebrity culture. In various ways, Capusotto's humor is a structural critique of the society of media spectacle that sustains and reproduces the mythologies of contemporary popular mass culture. Through the parody of audiovisual fiction and non-fiction genres, Capusotto shows the propagandistic, commercial, and ideological character of the media and its role in the construction of cultural, social, and political identities. The satirist deconstructs and ridicules not only the way in which the media and the entertainment industry publicize and make these identities attractive for the public but also the way they are perceived and performed in contemporary Argentinean society.

As such, Capusotto's work can be seen as a reaction to the society of spectacle that developed during the neoliberal decade of the menemista government, the period in which the comedian began his television career. After the collapse of the Argentinean economy in 2001, Capusotto's characters demystified the idealized historic identities that sustained the peronista political elites as well as the fragile identities promoted by the failed neoliberal promises. Developed during the kirchnerismo, a period of economic recovery impregnated with old political rhetoric and new social tensions, *Peter Capusotto y sus videos* has also developed a self-criticism of the rock generation, the militant youth that, at the close of this chapter, stepped down from power after 14 years.

REFERENCES

Alonso, P. (2007). Barcelona: la ácida prensa argentina. *Chasqui: Revista Latinoamericana de Comunicación*, 97, 27–31.

Alonso, P. (2016). Sacha Baron Cohen and *Da Ali G Show*: A critique on identity in times of satiric infotainment. *The Journal of Popular Cultural*, 49(3), 582–603.

45. The character Latino Solanas—a reggaetón/hip-hop singer who tries to pass as a member of marginal society when in reality he is a middle-class youth—evidences the artificiality of the imported identities produced by cultural globalization and transnational entertainment industries. Latino Solanas exemplifies the commercial manufacture of a marginal identity imported from the United States so that the Argentineans "can learn to be Latinos."

Blanco, D., & Germano, C. (2005). *20 años de medios & democracia en la Argentina.* Buenos Aires, Argentina: Konrad Adenauer Stiftung.

Bonnet, A. (2008). *La hegemonía menemista.* Buenos Aires, Argentina: Prometeo.

Castagno, P. (2009). Popular classes and neoliberalism: The practices of television mediators in Argentina. In B. G. Harden & R. Carley (Eds.), *Co-opting culture: Culture and power in sociology and cultural studies.* Lanham, MD: Lexington Books.

Colacrai, P. (2012). Bombita Rodríguez, el cepillo a contrapelo de la memoria. *Trama de la Comunicación, 16,* 57–67.

Conflicto del campo, Néstor Kirchner en la Plaza de los Dos Congresos. (2008). Retrieved from http://cfkargentina.com/conflicto-del-campo-nestor-kirchner-en-la-plaza-de-los-dos-congresos/

Druetta, S. (2011). *La TV que no se ve: relaciones, a menudo imperceptibles, que fueron definiendo nuestra televisión* Córdoba, Argentina: Eduvin.

Fair, H. (2008). El conflicto entre el gobierno y el campo en la Argentina. Lineamientos políticos, estrategias discursivas y discusiones teóricas a partir de un abordaje multidisciplinar. *Iberoforum, 3*(6), 82–106. Retrieved from http://www.redalyc.org/html/2110/211015582006/

Fair, H. (2014). Claves para entender el éxito de la hegemonía menemista en la Argentina neoliberal de los años 90. *Sociologías, 16*(37), 252–277.

Fraticelli, D. (2010). Desenmascarando al ciudadano porteño. El humor político de Micky Vainilla en *Peter Capusotto y sus videos. Revista LIS-Letra Imagen Sonido-Ciudad Mediatizada, III*(5), 41–56.

Fraticelli, D. (2013). Una periodización de los programas cómicos: Paleo, Neo y Humor Post-televisivo. *Imagofagia, 8.* Retrieved from http://www.academia.edu/23300121/Una_periodizaci%C3%B3n_de_los_programas_c%C3%B3micos_Paleo_Neo_y_Humor_Posttelevisivo

Garces, G. (2013). El muerto se ríe del degollado. Una charla con Capusotto y Saborido. *Revista Orsai,* 92–113.

Hodgart, M. (1969). *Satire.* New York, NY: McGraw-Hill.

Landi, O. (1992). *Devórame otra vez: Qué hizo la televisión con la gente, qué hace la gente con la televisión.* Buenos Aires, Argentina: Planeta.

Lvovich, D. (2009). La extrema derecha en la Argentina posperonista entre la sacristía y la revolución: el caso Tacuara. *Diálogos, 13*(1), 45–61.

Manzano, V. (2014). "Rock nacional" and revolutionary politics: The making of a youth culture of contestation in Argentina, 1966–1976. *The Americas, 70*(3), 393–427. http://dx.doi.org/10.1353/tam.2014.0030

Moglia, M. (2009). *Fútbol y rock. Innovación temática del humor televisivo.* Paper presented at the V jornadas de jóvenes investigadores, Buenos Aires.

Moglia, M. (2013). Violencia Rivas. Análisis de un personaje humorístico: una mujer furiosa. *Revista Punto Género, 3,* 47–64.

Muñoz, M. A., & Retamozo, M. (2008). Hegemonía y discurso en la Argentina contemporánea. Efectos políticos de los usos de "pueblo" en la retórica de Néstor Kirchner. *Perfiles Latinoamericanos, 31,* 121–149.

Muraca, M. (2011). Yo sólo hago pop! Micky Vainilla y una crítica a la sociedad pos (?) menemista. In R. Carbone & M. Muraca (Eds.), *La sonrisa de mamá es como la de Perón (Capusotto: realidad política y cultura).* Buenos Aires, Argentina: Imago Mundi.

O'Donnell, G. (1988). *Bureaucratic authoritarianism: Argentina 1966–1973 in comparative perspective.* Berkeley, CA: University of California Press.

Piva, A. (2010). *Acumulación y hegemonía en la Argentina menemista*. Buenos Aires, Argentina: Editorial Biblos.

Rapoport, M. (2003). *Historia económica, política y social de Argentina*. Buenos Aires, Argentina: Ediciones Macchi.

Sacchetto, C. (2009, September 13). Aquel intento de modificar la realidad eliminando programas de televisión. *Clarin*. Retrieved from http://edant.clarin.com/diario/2009/09/13/elpais/p-01997782.htm

Sarlo, B. (2001). Lo cómico y lo inquietante del disfraz sexual. In *Tiempo Presente. Notas sobre el cambio de una cultura* (pp. 76–78). Buenos Aires, Argentina: Siglo XXI.

Varela, M. (2005). *La televisión criolla*. Buenos Aires, Argentina: Edhasa.

Vila, P. (1989). Argentina's "rock nacional": The struggle for meaning. *Latin American Music Review, 10*(1), 1–28.

Wehner, L. (2004). El neopopulismo de Menem y Fujimori: desde la primera campaña electoral hasta la reelección en 1995. *Revista Enfoque, 2*, 25–56.

Weyland, K. (2003). Neopopulism and neoliberalism in Latin America: Unexpected affinities. *Studies in Comparative International Development, 31*(3), 3–31.

CHAPTER 6

Latin American Digital Satire

Critical Humor as Glocal Entertainment in

Times of the Internet

Enchufe.tv, an online comedy series that satirizes Ecuadorian idiosyncrasies and local urban culture, has become the most popular online TV series in the country and a regional phenomenon in Latin America with millions of YouTube views. The online show questions cultural stereotypes and social norms while adapting and parodying transnational audiovisual formats and entertainment genres. The producers—young filmmakers from Quito who also run a commercial production company—have stated that one of their goals is to "reinvent Ecuador's audiovisual culture" while maintaining the Web as their main platform to develop critical entertainment.

Enchufe.tv is a paradigmatic example of a recent trend of independent Latin American digital humor born on the Web, which becomes popular first as alternative entertainment and then negotiates its place in the mainstream media, aspiring to regional or international recognition. While the popularity of these types of digital initiatives probably varies according to the target (or niche) audience, levels of irreverence, format, quality of production, or ideological stand, the new wave of Latin American digital humor has become an increasingly relevant scene to discursively negotiate local and regional identities and to question sociocultural values while developing a postmodern reappropriation of transnational media languages and entertainment formats. This chapter first analyzes *Enchufe.tv* as a hybrid, glocal product successfully received in the region for its cultural proximity. It examines the relation of *Enchufe.tv* with Ecuador's media and political environment, its sociocultural critiques, discursive negotiations, and glocal manufacturing in order to establish a successful connection with national and regional audiences. Second, this chapter describes the case of *El Pulso de la República*, an independent Mexican online satiric news show à la *The Daily Show*, created in 2012 by comedian Chumel Torres, who, after 4 years of producing his show independently on YouTube, transitioned to be the host of a late-night show on HBO with a regional focus; and the case of *Cualca*, an Argentinean satiric sketch show focused on gender issues, created by Malena Pichot, a feminist YouTube star who became famous for *La Loca de Mierda*, a series of homemade online videos about a breakup with her boyfriend that made it onto MTV. These cases not only reveal successful models for the development of Latin American independent digital media but also exemplify how cultural globalization and hybridity operate in today's transnational entertainment and commercial critical humor.

ENCHUFE.TV: HOLLYWOOD AT THE SERVICE OF ECUADORIAN IDIOSYNCRASIES

Enchufe.tv was created in 2011 by a group of young Ecuadorian filmmakers (Leonardo Robalino, Christian Moya, Martín Domínguez, and Jorge Ulloa) who were critical of the country's audiovisual production and were seeking to renovate Ecuadorian audiovisual culture. Produced by Touché Films in Quito, Ecuador, the humorous and satiric skits feature Ecuadorian idiosyncrasies and, according to the creators and producers, are based on personal experiences, popular sayings, Ecuadorian traditions, and family and romantic relationships, among other topics that are relatable to their young audiences.

> The premise was to do something to be criticized and not to criticize from outside. As audiovisual producers, we wanted to do something similar to what we would like to see. . . . One of our premises for renovating the audiovisual culture in Ecuador was to take this to a new level and professionalize all aspects of the media production. Our objective was to be the *College Humor* Latino. . . . A professor of ours said that *Enchufe.tv* is the U.S. audiovisual tradition at the service of Latin American idiosyncrasies.[1] (Jorge Ulloa, personal interview, 2014)

1. "La premisa fue hacer algo para ser criticados y no criticar desde afuera. Como productores de audiovisuales, queríamos hacer algo como lo que nos gustaría

Since the beginning of their project, they had decided that the internet would be the primary medium of *Enchufe.tv*, because they would enjoy fewer restrictions (such as the use of colloquial language, swear words, slang, and controversial topics) than in traditional media outlets. On November 13, 2011, the first sketch (*El peor casting*)[2] was uploaded to their newly created YouTube channel. During their first season, 4- to 5-minute sketches were uploaded every Sunday; shorts lasting less than a minute and known as "microYAPA"[3] were uploaded on Tuesdays. On Thursdays, a preview or "promo" of the upcoming sketch was released. After a few months, their videos went viral, reaching millions of visitors. Some of the most popular videos of this initial period were *Visión carnaval, Me gusta,* and *Compra condones*. The latter remains *Enchufe's* most popular video with 22 million visits. By July 2012, *Enchufe.tv* was ranked as the most popular Ecuadorian YouTube channel on the Web. Viewership at first came primarily from Ecuador, but soon Mexico became its main market, comprising around 30% of viewers and subscribers to its YouTube channel. Colombia, Ecuador, Peru, and the United States are the other principal markets for *Enchufe's* content (Andrés Centeno, personal interview, 2014).

In September 2013, *Enchufe.tv* released a compilation of their first season videos on Ecuavisa, a national television station. In a country where TV penetration is 97% and internet penetration is 57% ("Media Penetration in Latin America," 2013), national TV allowed them to reach a broader national audience. With their massive success, routines of production have evolved, and their processes have been improved. The weekly content demand, however, creates an inevitable tension between constant production and keeping up quality standards. Now the producers try to generate all content (which has increased) during the first half of the year and have the videos ready to be uploaded throughout the rest of the season (Martín Domínguez, personal interview, 2014). Because the Web remains *Enchufe's* main platform, the program's social media routine has become more complex, trying to be active on all relevant platforms, such as Facebook, Twitter, Instagram, and Google Plus.

Enchufe.tv's business model is an interesting example of entrepreneurial efforts to make an independent Web project sustainable: A production

---

ver. . . . Una de nuestras premisas para renovar el audiovisual ecuatoriano fue llevar esto a otro nivel y profesionalizar todos los aspectos del medio. Nuestro objetivo era ser el "College Humor" latino. . . . Un maestro nuestro decía que Enchufe.tv es la tradición audiovisual gringa al servicio de la idiosincrasia de América Latina."

2. The video can be accessed here: https://www.youtube.com/watch?v=TyiMl5doLwU
3. "Yapa" is a slang word that means "something extra given as a bonus."

company (Touché Films) produces a comedy series of high audiovisual quality as a showcase for its talent and potential in order to find new advertising clients. The production company funds the project until it becomes sustainable (through sponsors and advertising), which for *Enchufe.tv* happened in its third year. By 2015, the company employed more than 30 people in diverse areas (creative team, production, postproduction, actors, digital and multimedia operations, and management). Their intention was to shoot their content in international locations, countries in which they not only have large audiences but also new business partners. In 2013, they were ranked globally as the 49th most subscribed-to channel on YouTube. That same year, *Enchufe.tv* received a Golden Play Award, awarded to YouTube channels with over 1 million subscribers. In 2014, *Enchufe.tv* won the "Show of the Year" award at the Streamy Awards (the so-called Oscars of the Web). By February 2015, its YouTube channel reached almost 8 million subscribers. Today, their videos have accumulated more than one and half billion views. The Facebook page has almost 7 million likes, and on Twitter they have around 700,000 followers. With all this local and regional popularity, *Enchufe.tv* has been a breakthrough for audiovisual culture in Ecuador, a country where the media operates in a tense political climate.

Ecuadorian Media and Satire Under Correa's Government

After a period of political instability in which Ecuador had seven presidents in 10 years, Rafael Correa's leftist government was inaugurated in 2007 and reelected to a third term in 2013. A popular president (his approval ratings have remained above 50%), he changed the constitution, increased public spending, defaulted on foreign loans, and clashed with the United States on several issues. According to the World Bank, poverty levels in Ecuador have dropped from 38% in 2006 to 29% in 2013 ("Profile: Ecuador's Rafael Correa," 2013). While many consider him a progressive, Correa, who describes himself as part of a "Christian Left," is opposed to abortion (even in cases of rape) and has called gay marriage "barbarism" (Miroff, 2014).

The relation between the media and Correa's government has been tense. The president has referred to the private media as his "greatest enemy." While protecting WikiLeaks founder Julian Assange in Ecuador's embassy in London, Correa's measures against the private media have been compared to those of Chávez in Venezuela. Both presidents, for example, repeatedly harassed the private media, accusing them of serving the conservative elites, used government advertising and economic incentives to induce positive reporting, imposed legal sanctions and other forms of "soft censorship" to limit press scrutiny, expanded state-run broadcasting, and became media figures through the use of their own airtime on national television (Boas, 2012; Frajman, 2014; Kellam & Stein, 2016). In Ecuador, where media ownership has been described as oligarchic (the media are mostly privately owned by a small number of rich families), Correa's policies have been justified as "state activism" to reduce the traditional privileges that the private media has held in the country and to put the media at the service of citizens (Ramos, 2012, 2013). Nevertheless, Correa has created the "largest media empire in Latin America in the hands of government" (Lara, 2013).[4]

In June 2013, a controversial new Organic Law on Communications was approved in Ecuador. President Correa considered the law an initiative to democratize the media, strengthen freedom of expression, and promote a "good press" in the country (Martinez, 2013). However, several private media outlets in Ecuador and international organizations considered it an attempt to silence the media and punish any criticism against the government. The law created state-mandated ethical guidelines and defined social communication as a "public service," making it susceptible to state regulation. As an ironic result, with 174 documented aggressive acts against media outlets, journalists, and citizens, 2013 became the most hostile year against freedom of expression in Ecuador ("El silencio asfixiante: La libertad de expresión en el Ecuador durante el 2013," 2014).[5]

The government's attacks against freedom of expression in Ecuador have also been aimed at satire and political humor. Political cartoonist Xavier Bonilla (also known as "Bonil"), from the newspaper *El Universo*, has been sanctioned twice for his satirical work ("Gobierno ecuatoriano continúa persecución contra caricaturista," 2015). Similarly, Correa has also targeted digital and social media. In 2013, the Ecuadorian government proposed penalizing individuals who express opinions that could be considered defamatory on social media (Fundamedios, 2013). At the same

4. More than 15 TV and radio stations have been nationalized since Correa took power. The government also controls the dailies *El Telégrafo* and *PP El Verdadero*, the news agency Andes, two television stations seized from former bankers, two radio stations, and a public television station (Lara, 2013).

5. According to the report "The stifling silence," developed by Fundamedios (2014), the year 2013 in Ecuadorian media was characterized by new legal limitations imposed by the country's controversial communications law, an increase in censorship, and public officials' hostilities against the press. The most aggressive acts came from public officials, followed by the government in the form of administrative or legal measures.

time, the president recruited "trolls" among his followers to fight critical and satirical voices against him and his government online (Constante, 2015; Higuera, 2015).

This is the political context in which *Enchufe.tv* appeared and evolved. When it became popular and massively successful, the project not only interested new advertising clients (big companies such as Supermaxi, Movistar, and, later, Claro[6]) but also the government. According to the magazine *Soho*, "There is a presidential document that shows an $11,000 [U.S.] contract for social communication services with Touché Films. It's dated December 2012. This issue brought many problems at the time and accusations that they were sellouts to the government" (Varas, 2014).[7] Andrés Centeno, executive producer of Touché Films, accepted that they had among their clients two governmental ministries (Varas, 2014). According to Centeno, they developed three products for these entities, but it was as Touché Films and not *Enchufe.tv*. Criticism increased in 2012 when a video by *EnchafoTV* (a parody of *Enchufe.tv*) appeared mocking Guillermo Lasso, an opposition leader and presidential candidate. Some former members of Touché Films participated in the production of the video. After these tensions, the creators and producers of *Enchufe.tv* tried to clarify that they do not make political humor.

Enchufe.tv's *Mundo al revés* as Sociocultural Critique

INTERVIEWER: What videos have been controversial?

ULLOA: There are videos that touch sensitivities. In many videos, we have content on sexism and homophobia, topics that are still delicate in our target market. To see a kiss between women or between men is still difficult for our viewers. And of course, we have generated some controversy in one way or another.

INTERVIEWER: Would you say that *Enchufe.tv* could be called satire?

ULLOA: Satire is a very complex concept. We have never used the word satire to describe *Enchufe.tv*.

---

6. Supermaxi is a supermarket chain; Claro and Movistar are two corporations that provide telephone services.

7. "Existe un documento de la Presidencia de la República que evidencia un contrato de 11 mil dólares, por servicios de comunicación social, con Touché Films. Está fechado en diciembre de 2012. Esto trajo muchos problemas en su momento y las acusaciones de haberse vendido al gobierno se multiplicaron por redes sociales."

DOMINGUEZ: Our content is not political per se. We try to distance ourselves the most that we can from the political. Sometimes you hurt sensitivities, but when you get into politics, soccer, and religion . . .

ULLOA: We distance ourselves from those topics, but frequently we do want to develop a criticism about an issue. *Enchufe.tv* creates a social portrait. . . . There is social criticism.

DOMINGUEZ: I'd say that *Mundos al revés* are truly satires.

ULLOA: Yes, that's where we expose homophobia from another perspective . . .

DOMÍNGUEZ: We were thinking about doing a *Mundo al revés* about race.

INTERVIEWER: But, those are political topics.

ULLOA: Of course, you cite political topics, but you don't cite political parties. It's like talking about soccer without saying which one is my team. . . . For example, we do not attack religion. We have had sketches with priests, but we have never taken a position. . . . We protect ourselves at the political and religious level. But we criticize social issues.[8]

(Personal interview, *2014*)

8. "INTERVIEWER: ¿Qué videos han sido controversiales?
   ULLOA: Hay videos que tocan sensibilidades. En muchos videos tenemos contenido sobre el sexismo, la homofobia, temas que todavía son delicados dentro del mercado al que nos dirigimos. Ver un beso entre mujeres o entre hombres todavía le cuesta a nuestro espectador. Y claro, ha generado controversia de una u otra forma.
   INTERVIEWER: ¿Dirían que *Enchufe.tv* se podría llamar sátira?
   ULLOA: La sátira es un concepto súper complejo. Nunca hemos utilizado la palabra sátira para describir a *Enchufe.tv*.
   DOMÍNGUEZ: Nuestro contenido no es político per se. Nos tratamos de alejar lo más que podemos de eso. De herir susceptibilidades vas a herir susceptibilidades. Pero cuando te metes con política, fútbol y religión . . .
   ULLOA: Nos alejamos de esos temas, pero muchas veces sí queremos hacer una crítica acerca de algo. *Enchufe.tv* hace un retrato social. . . . Sí hay cierta crítica social.
   DOMÍNGUEZ: Los que yo diría que son verdaderas sátiras son los *Mundo al revés*.
   ULLOA: Claro, ahí es donde exponemos la homofobia desde otro punto de vista . . .
   DOMÍNGUEZ: Estábamos pensando hacer *Mundo al revés* sobre razas.
   INTERVIEWER: Pero esos son temas políticos.
   ULLOA: Claro, citas temas políticos, pero no citas partidos políticos. Es como citar el fútbol sin decir de qué equipo soy. . . . Por ejemplo, no atacamos la religión. Hemos tenido sketches de curas, pero nunca tomando una postura. . . . Nos cuidamos un montón a nivel político y de religión. Pero en lo social a veces le damos duro.

In this conversation, the ambivalence of the creators and producers about their critical intentions became evident. Their claims about their humor's independence from the political sphere might be explained by Ecuador's sociopolitical tensions, described earlier in this chapter. By distancing themselves from explicit sociopolitical critique and focusing on the esthetic and commercial aspects of their products, *Enchufe.tv*'s producers were able to flourish in a heavily controlled media environment. Nevertheless, in most of their videos, there is a clear carnivalesque component and, in some of them, one of social satire. An example of this is *Mundo al revés, Enchufe. tv*'s series of videos that turn the predominant views about sociocultural stereotypes upside down.[9] It is a carnivalesque world in which inverted values ridicule the social and cultural prejudices embedded in stereotypes, a process with political implications. For example, in the sketch "Gringos y latinos,"[10] working- and middle-class Americans immigrate en masse to Latin America, searching for a better life. Many of them (the poorest ones) cross the border without documents in search of the Latin American dream. A border official shoots them while calling them "malditos ilegales" ("damned illegals") and spitting on the floor with a rifle smoking in his hand. When they arrive, the U.S. immigrants face constant discrimination and challenges in finding work because of their undocumented status and poor language skills. They are stereotyped as ignorant people and potential criminals or terrorists, generating paranoia in the local community. At the same time, immigrant women are exoticized as sensual and good dancers, because "they have the rhythm in their blood."

Like most *Mundo al revés* sketches, the video of 4 minutes and 14 seconds is organized in parallel storylines that are intertwined. The other stories of "Gringos y latinos" change the approach and perspectives on xenophobia and immigration in relation to social class and cultural capital. In one of the stories, a middle-class U.S. family applies for a visa at the Ecuadorian embassy. They dream about earning in Latin American currencies (pesos, bolívares, guaraníes, reales, soles, or sucres) and practice how to adopt the foreign culture (for example, the son practices singing the popular song of "El Chapulín Colorado," an iconic Mexican TV series). When they finally navigate the stressful process and obtain a visa, they celebrate, and

9. The idea of the world upside down is an ancient trope traced to the Middle Ages (Donaldson, 1970) and a central component of carnival culture. Connected to the tradition of Menippean satire, it seeks to offer an inverted (and perhaps clearer) perspective on reality in order to test the "solidity" of our conventional ideological beliefs (Chiang, 2004). The observation of the normal world from this unconventional viewpoint forces us to rethink our most common assumptions.

10. The video can be accessed at: https://www.youtube.com/watch?v=n2ISkJZC6DI

the father comments: "I am going to earn more by cleaning the floor of McChancho there than by being a state agent here." This segment of the sketch not only points at the issue of subemployment of professional and educated immigrants but also to their willingness to acculturate in order to access the opportunities of the receiving society.

The final storyline focuses on the receiving society and how its elites, who travel around the world as tourists, have an ignorant and prejudiced view about "the other." In this segment, a middle-aged, rich Ecuadorian couple tell stories to a friend about their trips around the world. After showing pictures of the Statue of Liberty in New York, they complain about how dangerous these foreign countries can be. Exhibiting her ignorance, the friend asks if the United States is an island, because "she really doesn't know anything about whatever is north of Mexico." The conversation is interrupted by the arrival of the couple's son and a blonde girl, who is introduced as his new girlfriend. The parents are shocked and astonished, looking with contempt at the American girl who speaks with a strong foreign accent. "He screwed up our race" ("nos cagó la raza"), comments the father finally with disappointment. The last seconds of the sketch show photos of the young couple's wedding and the American bride proudly exhibiting her new legal residence card. Ignorance, entitlement, racism, and utilitarianism are exposed as prevalent characteristics of the dynamics between local elites and working-class immigrants. While racial "whiteness" is challenged (the American girlfriend is white), class "whiteness" is still displayed as the root of prejudiced views. The fact that the wedding is framed in relation to the "residence card" also highlights the suspicion that immigrant/local marriages have more to do with utilitarian arrangements than love.

The satiric strategy is similar in the sketch "Gays y heteros,"[11] which criticizes homophobia. In this sketch, heteronormative values are inverted, and being heterosexual is presented as a marginal deviance. By positioning homosexuality as hegemonic and heterosexuality as marginal, the reversed scenario presented in the sketch emphasizes the absurdity of misconceptions and prejudices based on sexual orientation. At the same time, it not only satirizes the arguments against same-sex marriage (a controversial topic in the country) but also, with the final scene, suggests the decadence of marriage as an institution in a prevalent Catholic society where the president, a declared Christian Leftist, opposes same-sex marriage.

11. https://www.youtube.com/watch?v=3at_j5JtDik

Other videos of *Mundo al revés* are "Hombres y mujeres,"[12] "Sexismo,"[13] "Belleza,"[14] and "Hombres y mujeres de fiesta."[15] From the opposite perspective of the dominant ideology, these videos ridicule stereotypes and sociocultural prejudices (such as xenophobia, sexism, homophobia, and canonical notions of beauty, among others). It's a carnivalesque space in which the spectator identifies himself as marginal to an absurd system of values, which, nevertheless, replicates inversely hegemonic values, exposing their arbitrariness. In this sense, *Mundo al revés* questions static identities and promotes understanding of difference, of "the other." In the line of satire that seeks to ridicule social vices in order to transform them, *Mundo al revés* includes an optimistic spirit that reveals a desire for a better world. This critical humor has transgressed certain norms of the country's television and media culture (such as the use of profanity and new framing and treatment of controversial topics in Ecuador); however, its critical and transgressive spirit seems restricted by the sociopolitical context of the country and its own commercial nature. In other words, *Enchufe.tv*'s satire criticizes homophobia, xenophobia, sexism, and other social vices without risking its commercial development, because these topics resonate positively with their young target audience and their treatment does not exceed the limits set by the government's policing.

Hybridity, Parody, and *El Chavo del Ocho*

Enchufe.tv is an essentially hybrid or glocal product.[16] In many interviews, the producers have defined their creative work as "Hollywood (or the American audiovisual tradition) at the service of Ecuadorian (or Latin American) idiosyncrasies." They adapt transnational formats, styles, and genres and combine them with local themes, stereotypes, and popular culture. The resulting intertextual dialogue is made evident by the producers: "We cite these references in our videos: 'Mother's Day' is treated as Indiana Jones; 'Four Heroes in Space' is treated as Armageddon"[17] (Jorge Ulloa, personal interview). The ethnic diversity of

12. https://www.youtube.com/watch?v=ZU8zS-l45ZA
13. https://www.youtube.com/watch?v=kgQNGwJ-xlg
14. https://www.youtube.com/watch?v=h7aSEuxaRjo
15. https://www.youtube.com/watch?v=4HlN4FPdi2w
16. For the theoretical framework on hybridity and cultural globalization, see the Introduction of this book.
17. "Citamos estos referentes en nuestros videos: 'Día de la madre' está cubierto por un tratamiento de Indiana Jones; 'Cuatro héroes en el espacio' está cubierto por un tratamiento de Armageddon."

their actors also highlights *Enchufe*'s hybrid aspect. In a Latin American television and advertising system where white actors and models are still prevalent in the media, *Enchufe.tv*'s casting of multiethnic, *mestizo* Ecuadorian actors offers local verisimilitude to the narratives. At the same time, their physical or racial attributes rarely define their roles, which avoids the reinforcement of discriminatory stereotypes. From another angle, the use of local expressions and colloquialisms[18] is a recurrent mark of *Enchufe*'s process of glocalization by manufacturing national identity.

One of *Enchufe*'s most controversial videos reveals its hybrid and multidimensional manufacturing more clearly. On July 6, 2014, *Enchufe.tv* uploaded a parody trailer of a fake movie spinoff based on *El Chavo del Ocho*,[19] a Mexican television sitcom widely broadcast since 1971 in Latin America as well as in Spain, the United States, and other countries. Created by famous Mexican comedian Roberto Gomez Bolaños, also known as Chespirito (a diminutive hispanization of "Shakespeare"), *El Chavo del Ocho* chronicles the adventures and misfortunes of a poor orphan (nicknamed "el Chavo") and other inhabitants of "la vecindad" (the neighborhood), a fictional low-income housing complex in Mexico. At the peak of its popularity during the mid-1970s, *El Chavo del Ocho* was the most watched show on Mexican television and had a Latin American audience of 350 million viewers. The show continues to be immensely popular as an emblematic comedy of "clean" humor for the entire family. Very different from *El Chavo del Ocho*, *Enchufe.tv*'s parody (titled *El Chico del Barril*) has a similar plot to *The Da Vinci Code* and copies the style of Christopher Nolan's action movies. It features two agents, one American and the other Middle Eastern, who are searching for the real name of "el Chavo." The trailer shows a dark, violent, and sexual configuration of the beloved sitcom characters. Parodies of the most famous characters of *El Chavo del Ocho* appear in *El Chico del Barril*, making references to their popular catchphrases and configurations from a twisted perspective. The trailer ends with the U.S. agent discovering the classic squeaky hammer of the "Chapulín Colorado" (another character created by Chespirito) in the desert. A few hours after uploading the YouTube video, the controversy began. Mexican radio and TV (and later diverse Latin American media) disseminated the news. Actors from the original Mexican series, *El Chavo del Ocho*, publicly accused *Enchufe*'s parody of distorting

18. Local expressions such as "quién dice'" (Who says that?) or "chuta" (exclamatory expression) are recurrent in the show.
19. https://www.youtube.com/watch?v=pQFzVr2YUGM

and twisting their creations ("La parodia del Chavo de Enchufe TV bajo los ojos de la prensa internacional," 2014). Roberto Gómez Fernández, the son of Chespirito, initially accused *Enchufe*'s producers of profiting from his father's work and criticized the trailer for its shocking images. Televisa, the Mexican TV station that owns the rights to *El Chavo del Ocho*, asked YouTube to take the video down. While the video was taken down for a few hours, *Enchufe*'s producers defended their product as an original tribute to the iconic show. The video became public again, and the controversy ended when Roberto Gomez Bolaño's son praised *Enchufe*'s work, accepting the tribute to his father ("'Los de EnchufeTV son talentosos,' afirma el hijo de 'Chespirito,'" 2014). By then, the video had millions of views in a few days, and *Enchufe*'s audience had grown 700% in Mexico (Varas, 2014).

Enchufe's parody of *El Chavo del Ocho* is an interesting and representative textual object for understanding the show's hybrid or glocal dimension. As a parody, it already implies a combination, dialogue, and juxtaposition of different texts in order to create a new one. In the case of "El Chico del Barril," it is a double parody: of the local/regional tradition and of the global one. It is a tribute to one of the most important referents of Latin American popular humor, developed through the trailer format of a Hollywood action movie. The objects of parody are also revealing. On the one hand, *El Chavo del Ocho*, a symbol of noncontroversial and innocuous comedy, is not only a Mexican referent but also a popular icon for most Latin American countries, where several generations watched daily reruns of the show on national TV for decades. On the other hand, the movie *The Da Vinci Code* and filmmaker Christopher Nolan's style are representative of the most effect-driven and commercial Hollywood action films. Both objects of parody are connected by their huge regional/global commercial successes.

The parody of both audiovisual products is based on the transgression of codes and themes of their respective genres. In the case of *El Chavo del Ocho*, *Enchufe*'s parody distorts the configuration of the original naive characters (children played by adults): They carry guns, have blood on their clothes, and have erotic encounters while maintaining traits and dress codes of their original models. In relation to "*The Da Vinci Code* and Nolan's movies, the focus is on the formal aspect: The parody adopts the narrative visual strategies of Hollywood action movie trailers, while evidencing the artificial and spectacular techniques employed to catch the audience's attention in the service of an absurd plot. In this sense, the parody works at the content and formal level. From another perspective, "*The Da Vinci Code* is in itself an interpretation of a previous mass culture product: the bestselling novel by Dan Brown, which has the same title and has motivated the creation of a variety of literary and audiovisual parodies itself. At the same time, Nolan's style also has an intertextual dimension, which is manifested in his reboot of the *Batman* film franchise, a successful trilogy. Chespirito's work also has a parody aspect, especially in relation to his character "El Chapulin Colorado" (which is also referenced in *Enchufe*'s trailer). Embodying many aspects of Latin American and Mexican culture, "El Chapulín Colorado" is a critique on the unrealistic image of American superheroes. In contrast to Superman or Captain America, the "Chapulin" is imperfect, clumsy, and timid, but he is good hearted and succeeds at the end of his adventures (most of the time by good luck). The final text involved in the parody is a nonexistent one: the movie that the trailer promotes. In this sense, *Enchufe*'s trailer parody becomes an intertexual and metatextual object with several layers of parody that reflect its hybrid discursive universe. Combining diverse cultural traditions, audiovisual genres, and levels of re- ality, *Enchufe*'s discourse appeals to different audiences that could relate to any (or many) of the different layers at the local, regional, and/or global level. Consequently, it also reveals the manufactured condition of its car- nivalesque hybridity as a commercially successful strategy for independent digital media that seeks a transnational audience. While the parody of *El Chavo del Ocho* became popular in many Latin American countries, it targeted Mexico, where *Enchufe.tv* has its biggest audience. The producers' plans for shooting new episodes in different Latin American countries with local talent highlight a similar strategy for increasingly glocalizing their au- diovisual production in the region.

EL PULSO DE LA REPÚBLICA: ONLINE POLITICAL NEWS SATIRE IN MEXICO

In 2012, Chumel Torres, a mechanical engineer in his early 30s from the northern city of Chihuahua, moved to Mexico City and created *El Pulso de la República (EPR) (The Pulse of the Republic)*, a weekly online satiric po- litical news show on YouTube that soon became very popular. Torres has frequently referred to *EPR* as his take on the satirical work of his American heroes—Jon Stewart and Stephen Colbert—and has declared that he wanted to be "the Mexican Seth MacFarlane" (Ramos, 2014). In fact, using Mexican slang and references to local popular culture, *EPR* follows closely the format of *The Daily Show, The Colbert Report,* and *Saturday Night Live*'s Weekend Update: A comedian host dressed in a dark, serious suit delivers satirical monologues about political news accompanied with images and videos that ironically illustrate his critical points. By 2016, *EPR* had more than 1,600,000 subscribers to its YouTube channel, 400,000 followers on Facebook, and applications for a variety of platforms. Due to this success, Torres was hired by HBO to write and host a show for Latin American audiences.

Before becoming a media celebrity, Torres worked for 7 years in a *maquila*, a border factory that assembles goods for sale in the United States, and made a name as a *tuitstar* (a star from Twitter) due to his satirical tweets in the lead-up to the 2012 presidential elections, especially a controversial one about candidate Andrés Manuel Lopez Obrador's declarations. Because of his influence on social media, Torres was offered a weekly column in a political blog and then was hired as editor of a digital newspaper in Mexico City, where the idea of creating a satirical news show took shape:

> I wrote columns that basically were scripts of *EPR* but without a camera. It occurred to me that we could convert them into videos. I began recording myself with an iPhone. I did different takes, because I didn't know if it'd be better to do a left-wing or right-wing character, or muppets, or a woman. I decided that later. Then I met Durden (cowriter of *EPR*), we talked, and we began to write.[20] (Torres cited in *El País*, 2016)

Torres had already written several pilots in Chihuahua before he met José Alberto Sánchez Montiel (his cowriter, known as "Durden," a social media specialist and a Mexican "tuitstar" himself), and then together they wrote a "super-pilot" for CNN. However, the news company took too long to edit it, and Torres decided to do it by himself and release it on YouTube ("Entrevistamos a @ChumelTorres, creador de 'El Pulso de la República,'" 2015). He described the early stages of the project before it became a success:

> We did it with a webcam and edited it in iMovie, very low quality. But the script was good, and we already had our followers on Twitter, so we did not begin from zero. Then Yayo [a famous YouTuber who had more than 1,700,000 subscribers] published our shows in his space. We had 18,000 views, but after he published our show on his channel, we reached 250,000. Then we took off.[21] (Torres cited in *El País*, 2016)

20. "Escribía columnas que básicamente eran guiones de El pulso pero sin cámara. Se me ocurrió que podíamos convertirlos en videos y ya. Empecé a grabarme con el iPhone y hacía diferentes takes (tomas) porque no sabía si era mejor hacer un personaje de izquierda o de derecha, o muppets o una mujer, eso lo decidí después. Luego conocí a Durden (co-escritor de *El Pulso de la República*), platicamos y comenzamos a escribir."
21. "Lo hacíamos con una webcam y editábamos con iMovie, todo chafa [ríe]. Pero el guión estaba padre y ya teníamos nuestros followers en Twitter, entonces no

For the next 4 years, *EPR* videos, of which there are almost 300, were consistently uploaded once or twice a week, consolidating its style. While Torres has not disclosed revenue numbers, he said he makes money from advertising and sponsorship on his social media (YouTube and Twitter) accounts. The production of the show has remained low budget. Developed by a small crew, Torres has described *EPR*'s production routines as *Wayne's World*: "We are three dudes in a small room doing a good show" (Mulato, 2016).[22] Nevertheless, the main work is still done by Torres and his co-writer Durden and focuses on developing a solid script that balances entertainment and sociopolitical critique:

> At the beginning, we argued a lot because, for example, I am more pop in my criteria to choose stories, and Durden is more serious. I could choose the story of Justin Bieber taking his dick out at the beach, and he would choose a story about the community self-defense groups in Michoacán. But in three years we learned to balance comedy and journalism.[23] (Torres cited in *El País*, 2016)

In Mexico, some of the biggest challenges to freedom of expression have been the endemic corruption of politics and institutions (including journalism), the concentration of the media and telecommunications in the hands of a few rich people, the generalized violence generated by drug trafficking, and the attacks against journalists from public officials and organized crime.[24] *EPR* has covered the most prominent issues of the news agenda from a critical perspective rarely seen in the mainstream media. In fact, *EPR*'s most popular video (with more than 2 million visits) has been the political scandal of President Enrique Peña Nieto's White House ("Angélica Rivera responde: La Casa Blanca," November 19, 2014),[25] which involved corruption accusations and raised questions about conflicts of interest in relation to the contractors that built the president's house, allegedly bought by his wife, the actress Angelica Rivera. In the video, Torres

empezamos de cero. Luego Yayo, creador de 'No me revientes' (canal de YouTube que nació en 2010 y que cuenta con más de 1.700.000 suscriptores) publicó en su espacio nuestros programas. Teníamos 18.000 vistas, pero después de que publicó en su canal ya teníamos 250.000, ahí despegamos."

22. "Somos tres güeyes en un pinche cuartito haciendo un buen show."

23. "Antes nos peleábamos mucho porque, por ejemplo, yo soy más pop en mi manera de escoger notas y Durden, más serio. Yo podía escoger la nota de Justin Bieber sacándose el pito en la playa y él la de las autodefensas de Michoacán. Está cabrón, pero en tres años aprendimos a hacer un balance entre comicidad y periodismo."

24. For more detailed context on Mexican media and challenges to journalism in the country, see chapter 4.

25. https://www.youtube.com/watch?v=z74G7AuCVKc

satirically reframed the first lady's explanations about her acquisition of the property and the accusations surrounding it while mocking her affected, solemn soap-opera-actress tone. The second most popular *EPR* episode is about the Mexican businessman Carlos Slim, the second richest man in the world, and Telmex, his telecommunications monopoly ("Carlos Slim Shady," April 21, 2014).[26] After contextualizing Slim's power in Mexico, Torres explains the abusive practices of Telmex. He informs viewers about the company's bad customer service, its economic role in the country, and its impact on the average Mexican family's budget, and compares its practices with the telephone companies in other countries. Through jokes, Torres explains the history of Telmex and its questionable privatization in order to highlight the implications that the telecommunications monopoly has had for freedom of expression and citizens' lives.

While Torres has declared that he does not do stories about organized crime because he "loves the fact that he has his head attached to his shoulders" (Tuckman, 2015), he has covered the responsibility of the government and its inability to pacify the country. One of his most popular videos is about the capture of the world-famous Mexican drug lord Joaquín "El Chapo" Guzmán Loera in 2014 ("Se escapó el Chapo! (Anteriormente)," February 24, 2014).[27] After questioning the competence of the Mexican intelligence system, Torres mocks how Peña Nieto's government used the military accomplishment politically. But he also warns that El Chapo has escaped before and that he could do it again. Torres even satirically creates a game for viewers to place bets on how long El Chapo would stay in jail before becoming a fugitive again. Months later, in 2015, El Chapo scandalously escaped from a high-security prison, creating one of the biggest political crises of Peña Nieto's administration.[28] Other *EPR* videos about important sociopolitical issues in Mexico have included inequality in the country ("México: Los más ricos y los más tontos," March 24, 2014),[29] the political links between the Institutional Revolutionary Party (PRI) and networks of prostitution ("PRIstitución," April 7, 2014),[30] the public protests and deaths in Oaxaca stemming from educational reforms ("Qué pasó en Oaxaca," June 23, 2016),[31] the case of censorship against journalist

26. https://www.youtube.com/watch?v=BoP9q-j5FhQ
27. https://www.youtube.com/watch?v=CIsosUPetwU
28. EPR also covered the escape of El Chapo and its implications: https://www.youtube.com/watch?v=ZVyWV5Gc7Fc; https://www.youtube.com/watch?v=uFTN0XVpB7Y
29. https://www.youtube.com/watch?v=xZEN8LhUXaU
30. https://www.youtube.com/watch?v=mogkSr1v8UU
31. https://www.youtube.com/watch?v=RQLGDNrafbE

Carmen Aristegui ("Carmen Aristegui y el Pulso de los 70," March 16, 2015),[32] the impact of drug trafficking on the lives of Guerrero's peasants ("Narcopulco," May 5, 2016),[33] and, of course, the investigation of the disappearance of 43 students in Ayotzinapa ("Ayotzinapa: Capítulo final?," May 2, 2016).[34] *EPR* has also covered international issues, offering context or creating connections to national issues so that Mexican viewers could understand their impact: Donald Trump's presidential campaign ("Y Trump mamá también," June 25, 2015),[35] Britain's exit from the European Union ("Brexítame," June 27, 2016),[36] the massacre in Orlando gay nightclub Pulse ("El Pulse de Orlando,"June 16, 2016),[37] and the scandal about fiscal havens known as the Panama Papers ("Panama Pay-Per-View," April 7, 2016).[38]

For Torres, the function of his show is to translate news into an appealing format and to inform people about news stories that have already been covered but that the audience might not have read or understood. Despite its news coverage, he has described his show as political entertainment and distinguished his satirical take from journalism:

> We are not a news channel; we analyze what has already happened with journalistic rigor because I don't lie. In other words, *EPR* has never been a show about current news . . . I do not want to have breaking stories, because we are not protected by any huge network or TV station. We try to do a show that responds to what you have already seen.[39] (Torres cited in *Hora Cero*, 2014)

While the show is critical of how power works in Mexico, Torres rejects taking any type of partisan political stand, having activist intentions, or being a militant of any social movement (Ramos, 2014). In order to maintain this ideological independence, Torres considers YouTube the most democratic platform to develop digital projects and treasures the freedom of expression the online medium offers: "On *El Pulso de la Republica* I can

32. https://www.youtube.com/watch?v=DF9febPq0Xo
33. https://www.youtube.com/watch?v=z0KapGuJ1a0
34. https://www.youtube.com/watch?v=64ajZUssYQI
35. https://www.youtube.com/watch?v=MQ3WWj5h59A
36. https://www.youtube.com/watch?v=724hvmhnYIA
37. https://www.youtube.com/watch?v=xrUgURj-vFk
38. https://www.youtube.com/watch?v=URR4FB72FRs
39. "No somos un canal de noticias, somos un canal de análisis de lo que ya pasó con rigor periodístico porque no digo mentiras. Es decir, *El Pulso de la República* nunca ha sido un noticiero coyuntural, no maneja noticias nuevas . . . No quiero tener exclusivas de nada porque no nos protege ningún tipo de aparato de noticias, canal o un network gigante. Tratamos de hacer un programa que sea como réplica de lo que ya viste."

say whatever the fuck I want without anybody wagging a finger at me," he said to *The Guardian*. The internet is also the perfect medium to reach his target audience, which is 14 to 34 years old and "either don't watch the news or are sick of watching the news" (Tuckman, 2015). He believes that the internet has much better content than mainstream television and is the ideal platform for the dissemination of relevant public information. For Torres, television has become obsolete: "Television treated us like idiots and we just got sick of it, so we started making something we would watch. They are paying for their sins," he said to *The Guardian*. The comedian has repeated his perspectives on media in several interviews and conferences, taking a do-it-yourself message to young people who are frustrated with the coverage of politics by the major media:

> If the newspaper doesn't like you, doesn't listen to you, doesn't give you any money, doesn't offer any opportunities, well then, create your own project. Anybody can shoot a video or record a radio program and upload it to the Web. The only limitation is what you have in your head. (Torres cited in *News Entrepreneurs*, 2014)

In many ways, *EPR* is a reaction to mainstream media and its coverage of news—particularly to Televisa, the country's biggest network, which has traditionally aligned with the political ruling class and has become a "de facto" power in the country. "For 50 years they have been censoring the news and stomping on the truth. It's a news source that nobody believes. My target audience doesn't watch it. It's on the point of dying, if not economically, then because of its content," said Torres to *News Entrepreneurs* (Breiner, 2014). In spite of his critical attitude toward mainstream TV, *EPR*'s growing audience brought Torres offers to migrate his show to major channels, including Televisa. He rejected the offers, and his response to the media giant was: "You're the enemy, man" (Breiner, 2014). He explained that he would not have the editorial control he wants even if the media conglomerate offers it. "On national television nobody mucks with the president," he said to *The Guardian*. Nevertheless, he agreed to do a series of "cápsulas" [short videos] during the World Cup in Brazil for Televisa, which prompted a major backlash. "It was a really dark time for us. I had around 1,000 tweets a day saying you fucking sold out, how could you do this. I will never ever ever ever ever do it again," he said to *The Guardian*. This episode evidences one of the prevalent tensions between independent satirists and mainstream media: how to deal with attempts at co-optation while also developing a sustainable career and media project when its legitimacy is built on being an alternative to corrupt or biased commercial TV. In the case of Torres, the answer has been in regional cable. In 2016, HBO hired him to write and host *Chumel con Chumel Torres*, a weekly late-night show a la *Last Week Tonight With John Oliver,* targeting Latin American audiences. The comedian explained his decision to his viewers in an internet promo: "I feel HBO focuses more on the content instead of pleasing sponsors and people."[40] The show began in July 2016, and it remains to be seen if its format and Torres's humor will work for a regional audience. Interestingly, *EPR* continues as a local satiric infotainment show that deals primarily with Mexico's national news agenda. The glocalization process of this case is also noteworthy and aligns with others included in this book: *EPR* adapted a global format, creating a unique hybrid product primarily targeting a national audience, and then, after significant success, the satiric show was re-elaborated for a regional audience.

CUALCA: THE FEMINIST HUMOR OF MALENA PICHOT IN ARGENTINA

In 2008, Malena Pichot, a liberal arts student in her early 20s from Buenos Aires who worked as a proofreader in a publishing house, broke up with her boyfriend. Her way of dealing with the separation was to upload a series of humorous videos to YouTube under the title *La Loca de Mierda*.[41] The series was based on monologues of a hysterical, depressed woman going through heartbreak while questioning several clichés about women and their relationships with men. She explained her motivations to *El País*: "The problem that women have is that we get defined by the guy we are with. I felt so embarrassed that it happened to me; it was so humiliating for me that I took it to the extreme doing the videos" (Suaréz, 2015).[42] "I felt like the typical 'concheta' (upper-class girl) without problems who gets depressed because a guy does not love her; and it wasn't that terrible; I was just an unsatisfied bougie girl," she added to *La Nación* (Pizarro, 2011).[43] *La Loca de Mierda* became an online success and was acquired by MTV for a second season of 29 episodes in 2009. From then on, Pichot's media career

40. The promo can be accessed at https://www.youtube.com/watch?v=oKbgBY-l4hA
41. The first video of *La Loca de Mierda* was uploaded on August 30, 2008, and can be seen here: https://www.youtube.com/watch?v=yK5fhmOsnx8
42. "El problema que tenemos las mujeres es que nos define el tipo con el que estamos. A mí me dio tanta vergüenza que me pasara eso, para mí fue tan humillante y tan vergonzoso, que lo llevé al extremo haciendo los videos."
43. "Me sentía la clásica concheta sin problemas que se deprime porque un pibe no la quiere, y no era tan terrible, sólo una burguesa insatisfecha."

took off and has included collaborations in radio, TV, and film.[44] While she has established a name as a stand-up comedian, the internet has remained her most constant platform to showcase her work. Pichot was not only a pioneer in Argentina in using social media to launch her comedy career but also soon became a public feminist figure in the country.

While she has described herself as a "cheta" from Belgrano, a middle-upper-class neighborhood in Buenos Aires, her satiric humor frequently targets the prejudices of this social sector (Garófalo, 2012). In 2012, Pichot created *Cualca*, a series of satiric television sketches that criticized sexism, racism, homophobia, and other social prejudices through surreal, absurd, and visceral humor. The name "cualca" comes from a colloquialism that loosely means "whatever" (Zavaley, 2012). While *Cualca* was initially included as a segment of the TV show *Duro de Domar* (Channel 9), its viral videos (of around 5 minutes) became especially successful online through its Vimeo and YouTube accounts. *Cualca* was written and acted by Pichot and other comedians (Julián Kartun, Julián Lucero, Julián Doregger, and Charo López) who she brought together, describing them to the *Rolling Stone* as "the most talented young actors from Argentina" (Zavaley, 2012).

"Piropos"[45] has been one of the most popular of *Cualca*'s videos. In this sketch, Pichot satirically criticizes street harassment against women. She enumerates the types of this sexist practice and then presents the experience from the point of view of a woman who reacts violently, killing the men that harass her on the streets. She ends the sketch by saying: "We want to be clear that we are against murdering people. But society does not seem to care that you show me your dick or that you tell me that you want to fuck me in the ass. So, keep doing it. Maybe one day you might even rape me."[46] Other *Cualca* videos that deal explicitly with issues of gender are "Negación" (Negation),[47] about women who live in a state of denial as a strategy to cope with gender norms, beauty canons, sexual harassment,

44. She worked with famous filmmaker Juan José Campanella in the film *El hombre de tu vida*, for which she was nominated for the prestigious Martín Fierro Award.

45. "Piropos" can be viewed here: https://www.youtube.com/watch?v=nXsEVOar6TA&index=33&list=PL0phEjHCeBGuxCDv1OtZnGy0jOB3j2Zt1

Similar ideas to "Piropos" have also been developed by the Spaniard Alicia Murillo in her video series "El cazador cazado" (The Hunted Hunter), and other recent social experiments such as "10 Hours of Walking in NYC as a Woman."

46. "Queremos dejar en claro que nosotros estamos absolutamente en contra del asesinato. La sociedad no está de acuerdo con matar gente. Pero a la sociedad no parece importarle que me muestres la pija o que me digas que me quieres romper el orto. Así que seguí haciéndolo, por ahí que un día te animás y me violas."

47. "Negación" can be viewed here: https://www.youtube.com/watch?v=gOk7IsFziK4

and domestic violence; and "Chicas inseguras" (Insecurity Girls),[48] in which she satirizes young women's behaviors to get attention from stupid men while at the same time mocking the industry of teen entertainment and rock TV shows. In "Entrevistando al enemigo II" (Interviewing the Enemy II),[49] Pichot parodies a TV talk-show host who interviews an antiabortion activist and a rugby player (characters played by other actors), who are presented as examples of the Argentinean Right. She confronts the conservatism of these characters, revealing some of their most despicable moral values and prejudices, especially in relation to gender. In a "teaser"[50] for the second season of the show, Pichot plays herself receiving instructions from a TV producer who announces some changes for the new season: For example, the new theme will deal with "three girls over 30 that still can." Malena asks: "Can what?" The producer responds: "Have children, be happy, have a purpose in life." Other requests for the new season are that she needs to show more skin, "taking advantage of the fact that she still has a few years of physical validity left." And finally, the producer asks her not to do scatological jokes—those should be left to the male actors. The sketch ends with Malena farting on the producer's face. This satirical video connects with a constant preoccupation of Pichot's humor: the way women are portrayed in the media. "It upsets me that society educates women to be dumbasses, to show their ass, and appear in Big Brother,"[51] she said to *La Nación*.

At the beginning of her media exposure with *La Loca de Mierda*, Pichot did not define herself as a feminist and playfully answered questions about her militancy: "I shave, I want to have brand clothes, I'm within the system . . . I don't hate men, I don't say that they are all sons of bitches; I just say that my ex is a son of a bitch," she said to *La Nación*.[52] Pichot has also rejected the label "female humor" for her work:

The category of "female humor" only exists because men cannot identify with a woman. Female humor does not exist because there is not a male humor. There

48. "Chicas inseguras" can be viewed here: https://www.youtube.com/watch?v=xS0DVNPJivg

49. "Entrevistando al enemigo II" can be viewed here: https://www.youtube.com/watch?v=vxFv3Vf4JlQ&list=PL0phEjHCeBGuxCDv1OtZnGy0jOB3j2Zt1&index=43

50. The teaser can be viewed here: https://www.youtube.com/watch?v=HsCnWiB_37A

51. "Me angustia que la sociedad eduque a las mujeres para que sean pelotudas. La media es mostrar el culo y salir en Gran Hermano."

52. "Me depilo, quiero tener la ropa de moda: estoy adentro del sistema . . . No odio a los hombres, no digo que son todos unos hijos de puta, digo que mi ex es un hijo de puta."

is only humor; sometimes it's done by men and sometimes by women. But because the hegemonic discourse is male, women have to identify with men, but it's hard for men to identify with a woman. Men need the category of "female humor" because women are always the otherness, the distinct, the different.[53] (Pichot cited in *La Capital*, 2013)

Pichot's rise to fame happened at a time when sexism and violence against women was being highly discussed in Argentina as part of a movement that had its highest point with #NiUnaMenos ("Not one less"), a public protest against femicides in the country that took place at the Congressional Plaza in Buenos Aires on June 3, 2015. The demonstration, publicly supported by several television personalities through media campaigns, was attended by nearly 300,000 people and backed by women's rights groups, unions, political organizations, and even the Catholic Church. As part of this movement, Pichot has frequently participated in public debates about feminism in Argentina and has strongly reacted to sexist remarks by public figures. When Argentina's President Mauricio Macri said that "women like to be catcalled, even if you tell them 'What a nice ass you have,'"[54] Pichot reacted in a column:

No woman is going to die because someone says "What a nice ass you have to fuck into pieces," but neither the president nor 90% of society understands that it is wrong. And it has to do with all those who were killed because they were black, fat, homosexual, or Jewish, and many women were killed and treated with violence because they were women.[55] (Pichot, 2014)

When rock star Gustavo Cordera, former front man of the legendary Argentinean band Bersuit Vergarabat, defended the rape of underage women by saying on a public show "there are women who need to be raped," Pichot was clear in her accusation: "A person who says that women need to

---

53. "La categoría 'humor femenino' existe porque los hombres no pueden identificarse con una mujer. No existe un humor femenino porque no existe un humor masculino. Existe el humor, a veces lo hacen hombres y a veces lo hacen mujeres. Como el discurso hegemónico es masculino, la mujer puede identificarse con el hombre pero al hombre le cuesta identificarse con una mujer. El hombre necesita crear la categoría de 'humor femenino' porque la mujer es siempre la otredad, lo distinto, lo diferente."

54. "A las mujeres les gustan los piropos, aunque les digan qué lindo culo tenés."

55. "Ninguna mujer se va a morir porque le digan "que hermoso culo que tenés para rompertelo todo" pero ni el jefe de gobierno ni el 90% de la sociedad entiende que está mal. Y aquello que todos sabemos que está mal tiene que ver con que es real que muchos se murieron cagados a palos por ser negros, gorditos, putos o judíos y a muchas mujeres las violentaron realmente y las mataron por ser mujeres."

be raped does so because he himself has raped" ("Malena Pichot: 'una persona que dice que a las minas hay que violarlas es porque violó,'" 2016). Similarly, she has publicly questioned the way the media portrays cases of violence against women and has confronted conservative voices, such as a journalist and political scientist who linked feminism with pedophilia ("La increíble discusión entre Malena Pichot y un periodista que vinculó al feminismo con la pedofilia," 2016).

With the same critical tone, Pichot, who doesn't like to be labeled as an actress and considers herself primarily a scriptwriter, has frequently reflected on the state of comedy in Latin America:

> In Latin America, comedy is very underdeveloped, because the trajectory of humor is misogynistic and simplistic. I'm not saying that everything is shit; there are exceptions, but at the popular level, it is all shit. There is not a social consciousness in any sense, and I think that is the main problem of Latin American stand-up comedy and humor in general.[56] (Pichot cited in *El País*, 2015)

Pichot described the humor that she enjoys as uncomfortable, politically incorrect, and visceral (Sobrero, 2011). She has frequently revealed that most of her comedic referents are American—she has mentioned names such as Jerry Seinfeld, Sarah Silverman, Amy Schumer, Kristen Schaal, Maria Bamford, Dave Chappelle, and Louis C.K.; and series such as *Will & Grace*, *Friends*, *Arrested Development*, *Cheers*, *Curb Your Enthusiasm*, and more recently, *Girls*. As for comedy in Spanish, she included shows such as *Muchachada nui* (from Spain) and the Argentinean *Cha cha cha* and Juana Molina. Nevertheless, the comedian has stated that she considers most Argentinean humor of the 1990s "deplorable" ("Malena Pichot: 'Hago humor para molestar un poco,'" 2013), and many of her critiques about the sexist component of the entertainment industry in Argentina deal with the type of commercial TV produced during that decade and still prevalent in the country. This is why Pichot has rejected offers to work in mainstream media: She wants to keep control of her creative work and does not want to be restricted in the type of content she is allowed to produce. For this reason, the internet has remained her preferred platform.

---

56. "En América, la comedia está muy atrasada porque tenemos una trayectoria misógina y simplista del humor. No quiero que parezca que digo que todo es una mierda, hay excepciones, pero sí creo que a nivel popular es una mierda. No hay conciencia de nada, no hay conciencia social en ningún sentido y creo que ese es el problema mayor del stand up y del humor en general en Latinoamérica."

When *Cualca*'s TV season in *Duro de Domar* ended in December 2013 after 46 episodes, Pichot took her comedy back to the Web. *Cualca*'s acting group developed an online crowd-funding campaign (#ojalavuelvaCualca) to independently fund the show's second season. They had a goal of $22,995 USD that was exceeded by more than $5,000 through fans' donations. The second (and last) season had 10 episodes, and the last video was posted on January 16, 2015. Pichot explained the reasons for the end of the show: "*Cualca* was a very expensive product; it had a lot of production costs. It looked very cute and was very well done. But the truth is that there is no money for that. We worked almost for free for a year, but we cannot do it anymore" (López, 2014).[57] In fact, *Cualca*'s videos have been described as "unprecedented in Argentina" (Garófalo, 2012) because of their high production quality. This slick quality has also marked Pichot's other comedic projects, such as *Por ahora*, a comedy series for Cosmopolitan TV that was described as *Cualca*'s spin-off,[58] and *Mundillo*. In 2015, Pichot took her stand-up show to Spain, where she has been intensively promoting her work and participating in comedy festivals with a focus on gender. It's symptomatic that the internationalization of her work is aimed at Spain, one of the main destinations for Argentinean immigrants of her generation after the 2001 economic crisis. While the cases from Mexico and Ecuador looked at the U.S. market for their regionalization (*Enchufe.tv* has tried to target the U.S. Latino audience, and Torres took his humor to HBO), Argentina's cultural connection with Europe still seems to be a strong one.

CONCLUSIONS

In times when traditional media intensely seek new formulas to make their online operations profitable, the cases of *Enchufe.tv, El Pulso de la República*, and *Cualca* reveal successful models for independent digital media and online TV to develop, consolidate, and negotiate their place in relation to mainstream media and public debate. Their formula involved producing innovative, risqué, and high-quality audiovisual humor that filled gaps left

---

57. "*Cualca* era un producto muy caro, tenía mucha producción. Se veía muy lindo y estaba muy bien realizado. Pero la verdad es que no hay guita para eso. Nosotros trabajamos un año casi por amor al arte, pero ya no podemos hacerlo más."

58. *Por ahora* involved the same group of actors from *Cualca*. It was ironic that Cosmopolitan TV in Latin America broadcast the series, since it's one of those media outlets that reinforce female stereotypes. In contrast to *Cualca*, the episodes of *Por ahora* were around 30 minutes, and focused more on the problems of a group of friends in their 30s (relationships, immaturity, insecurities) than on social issues.

by national mainstream TV. These online TV shows dealt critically with sociocultural and political issues and became especially appealing for young urban audiences eager for new content aligned with international (usually U.S.) media production, but with a local flavor. While heavily influenced by the U.S. comedy tradition (*College Humor* and Hollywood formats in the case of *Enchufe.tv*; political satire such as *The Daily Show* and *The Colbert Report* for *El Pulso de la República*; and, in the case of *Cualca*, contemporary stand-up comedy—Sarah Silverman, Amy Schumer, Louis C.K.—and series such as *Seinfield*), all the cases successfully digested their foreign influences and adapted them to the local culture, creating a unique glocal voice that tapped into particular national tensions (the conflictive relation between the private media and Correa's government that results in limiting freedom of expression in Ecuador; the audience's frustration with the political news coverage from Televisa in Mexico and its historic relation with the PRI; and the role of entertainment and advertising in reproducing sexist values in Argentina, a country with high rates of femicides and growing social movements for women's rights).

As part of their core critiques, all these cases have been openly critical of national television. After becoming popular on the Web with millions of subscribers, followers, and viewers on their social media platforms, they negotiated their relationship with national mainstream TV (*Enchufe* released their videos on Ecuavisa, reaching new national audiences; Chumel Torres rejected the offer to take *El Pulso de la República* to Televisa, but agreed to do a series of videos during the World Cup for the media giant; and Malena Pichot's *La Loca de Mierda* made its second season on MTV, while *Cualca* was originally developed as a segment for a TV show). Nevertheless, all these cases maintained the Web as their main platform, frequently naming as their main reasons the creative freedom that the medium offers and the possibility of reaching loyal audiences at any moment.

As part of their evolution, all these online satirists finally had a regional or international reach. As an independent and commercial producing company, Touché Films has developed strategies to reach Latin American audiences with *Enchufe.tv* by developing content that dialogues with different national popular culture traditions or works with local talent from those countries. Chumel Torres expanded the political satire of *EPR*, focusing on Mexican and Latin American issues with his recent late-night show on HBO that reaches a regional audience, while Malena Pichot, whose feminist videos are already famous in diverse Latin American cities, has intensively promoted her humorous work and stand-up show in Spain. This internationalization becomes an interesting stage of their relation with cultural globalization: All the cases first adapt international referents and create a distinctive unique voice at the local/national level, and then adapt this voice to reach wider regional or geolinguistic audiences, creating a new layer in their hybrid process.

The success of these online satiric cases reveals their potential as critical voices in cultural, social, and political topics at the local, regional, and transnational level, while the national context remains relevant in order to understand the role of satire in negotiating the limits of dissent in media culture. The existence of other independent cases of audiovisual critical humor and digital satire in the region—such as *La Isla Presidencial* (Venezuela), *Porta dos Fundos* (Brazil), *La Pulla* (Colombia), or *Flama* (Latinos in the United States), among others—confirms the increasing visibility of the genre in times of the internet and its complex condition as a hybrid media text within the framework of cultural globalization.

REFERENCES

Boas, T. C. (2012). Mass media and politics in Latin America. In J. I. Dominguez & M. Shifter (Eds.), *Constructing democratic governance in Latin America* (4th ed.). Baltimore, MD: John Hopkins University Press.

Breiner, J. (2014). Mexican blogger builds a business out of political satire. *News Entrepreneurs*. Retrieved from http://newsentrepreneurs.blogspot.mx/2014/03/mexican-blogger-builds-business-out-of.html

Chiang, H.-C. (2004). The trope of an upside-down world: Carnival and Menippean satire in Richard Brome's *The Antipodes*. *Concentric: Literary and Cultural Studies*, *30*(2), 55–72.

Constante, S. (2015, February 4). Correa recibe de su propia medicina en las redes sociales. *El Pais*. Retrieved from http://internacional.elpais.com/internacional/2015/02/04/actualidad/1423076927_196128.html

Donaldson, I. (1970). *The world upside down*. London, U.K.: Oxford University Press.

El silencio asfixiante: La libertad de expresión en el Ecuador durante el 2013. (2014). *Fundamedios*. Retrieved from http://www.fundamedios.org/el-silencio-asfixiante-la-libertad-de-expresion-en-el-ecuador-durante-el-2013/

Entrevistamos a @ChumelTorres, creador de 'El Pulso de la República' (2015). *Hello DF*. Retrieved from http://hellodf.com/entrevista-con-chumel-torres-creador-de-el-pulso-de-la-republica/

Frajman, E. (2014). Broadcasting populist leadership: Hugo Chávez and Aló Presidente. *Journal of Latin American Studies*, *46*(3), 501–526.

Fundamedios. (2013). Gobierno ecuatoriano pide que se penalice la opinión en redes sociales. *IFEX*. Retrieved from http://www.ifex.org/ecuador/2013/09/03/penalice_opinion/es/

Garófalo, L. (2012). Malena Pichot, no cualquiera. *Los Inrockuptibles*. Retrieved from https://losinrocks.com/malena-pichot-no-cualquiera-9cc55c846623

Gobierno ecuatoriano continúa persecución contra caricaturista. (2015). *Freedom House*. Retrieved from https://freedomhouse.org/article/gobierno-ecuatoriano-contin-persecuci-n-contra-caricaturista#.VQhKJhY8r5l

Higuera, S. (2015, February 27). Críticas del presidente de Ecuador y amenazas de muerte llevan al cierre de cuenta satírica de Facebook. *Knight Center for Journalism in the Americas*. Retrieved from https://knightcenter.utexas.edu/es/blog/00-15945-amenazas-de-muerte-y-criticas-del-presidente-de-ecuador-llevan-al-cierre-de-cuenta-sat

Kellam, M., & Stein, E. (2016). Silencing critics: Why and how presidents restrict media freedom in democracies. *Comparative Political Studies, 49*(1), 36–77.

La increíble discusión entre Malena Pichot y un periodista que vinculó al feminismo con la pedofilia. (2016). *El Destape*. Retrieved from http://www.eldestapeweb.com/la-increible-discusion-malena-pichot-y-un-periodista-que-vinculo-al-feminismo-la-pedofilia-n19867

La parodia del Chavo de Enchufe TV bajo los ojos de la prensa internacional. (2014, July 11). *El Comercio*. Retrieved from http://www.elcomercio.com/tendencias/parodia-chavo-enchufe-tv-ojos.html

Lara, T. (2013, June 13). Ecuadorian legislators approve new communications law. *Knight Center for Journalism in the Americas*. Retrieved from https://knightcenter.utexas.edu/blog/00-14044-ecuadorian-legislators-close-approving-new-communications-law

López, C. (2014). Fenómeno Cualca: la youtuber que reinventó nuestra manera de entender las series. *Playground Noticias*. Retrieved from http://www.playgroundmag.net/noticias/historias/fenomeno-Cualca-manera-entender-series_0_1445855411.html

'Los de EnchufeTV son talentosos', afirma el hijo de 'Chespirito'. (2014, July 11). *El Comercio*. Retrieved from http://www.elcomercio.com/tendencias/youtube-enchufetv-televisa-trailer-derechos.html

Malena Pichot: "Hago humor para molestar un poco". (2013). *La Capital*. Retrieved from http://www.lacapital.com.ar/malena-pichot-hago-humor-molestar-un-poco-n437053.html

Malena Pichot: "una persona que dice que a las minas hay que violarlas es porque violó". (2016). *El Patagonico*. Retrieved from http://www.elpatagonico.com/malena-pichot-una-persona-que-dice-que-las-minas-hay-que-violarlas-es-porque-violo-n1503739

Martinez, A. (2013). Ecuador's controversial Communications Law in 8 points. *Knight Center for Journalism in the Americas*. Retrieved from https://knightcenter.utexas.edu/blog/00-14071-8-highlights-understand-ecuador%E2%80%99s-controversial-communications-law

Media penetration in Latin America. (2013). [Press release]. Retrieved from http://latinlink.usmediaconsulting.com/2013/08/media-penetration-in-latin-america/

Miroff, N. (2014, March 15). Ecuador's popular, powerful president Rafael Correa is a study in contradictions. *The Washington Post*. Retrieved from http://www.washingtonpost.com/world/ecuadors-popular-powerful-president-rafael-correa-is-a-study-in-contradictions/2014/03/15/452111fc-3eaa-401b-b2c8-cc4e85fccb40_story.html

Mulato, A. (2016, February 6). Chumel Torres: *"El pulso de la república* no es un noticiario. Somos pizza, chelas y muchas risas". *El País*. Retrieved from http://verne.elpais.com/verne/2015/12/28/articulo/1451341987_641339.html

Pichot, M. (2014). Mauricio y la violencia de todos los días. *Telam*. Retrieved from http://www.telam.com.ar/notas/201404/60768-malena-pichot-macri-piropos.html

Pizarro, E. (2011, February 20). Loca pero no tanto. *La Nación*. Retrieved from http://www.lanacion.com.ar/1351193-loca-pero-no-tanto

Profile: Ecuador's Rafael Correa. (2013, February 27). *BBC*. Retrieved from http://www.bbc.com/news/world-latin-america-11449110

Ramos, I. (2012). La contienda política entre los medios privados y el gobierno de Rafael Correa. *Utopia y Praxis Latinoamericana*, *17*(58), 65–76.

Ramos, I. (2013). Trayectorias de democratización y desdemocratización de la comunicación en Ecuador. *Iconos. Revista de Ciencias Sociales*, *45*, 67–82.

Ramos, A. (2014, November 12). 'Me gustaría convertirme en el Seth MacFarlane mexicano'. *Hora Cero*. Retrieved from http://horacerotam.com/espectaculos/gustaria-convertirme-en-el-seth-macfarlane-mexicano/

Sobrero, N. (2011). Entrevista a Malena Pichot. *BK*. Retrieved from http://www.bkmag.com.ar/bkmag.php?seccion=3&contenido=453

Suaréz, R. (2015, October 23). Malena Pichot: la loca de mierda quiere conquistar España. *El País*. Retrieved from http://elpais.com/elpais/2015/10/21/tentaciones/1445424424_962719.html

Tuckman, J. (2015, August 28). *El Pulso de la Republica*: Meet Chumel Torres, Mexico's answer to Jon Stewart. *The Guardian*. Retrieved from https://www.theguardian.com/world/2015/aug/28/el-pulso-de-la-republica-chumel-torres-mexico-youtube-show

Varas, E. (2014). Enchufe TV, fenómeno ecuatoriano en internet. *Revista Soho*.

Zavaley, E. (2012). Cualquierismo en TV abierta. *Rolling Stone*. Retrieved from http://www.rollingstone.com.ar/1497143-cualquierismo-en-tv-abierta

CHAPTER 7

Conclusions

TV Satire as Critical Metatainment and

Negotiated Dissent

When institutions fail, satire flourishes. That seems to be the case not only in the United States, where political TV satire had a renaissance after 9/11 and during the Bush administration (and has more recently taken a firm position after the election of Donald Trump as president), but also in Latin American defective democracies. After the brutal effects of military dictatorships, autocratic governments, and the application of neoliberal policies, there has been a period of sustained macroeconomic growth based on the exportation of natural resources and political volatility between the Left and the Right. This period has been the framework of growing inequality, corruption scandals, drug trafficking violence, social protests, and increasing awareness and public debate about social vices such as sexism, homophobia, racism, and other despicable prejudices, which might have produced a superficial veil of political correctness. Media culture has been a key actor and mediator in all these processes, and this book positions satire as a unique type of media text that condenses the prevalent sociopolitical and cultural tensions of Latin American democracies in the 21st century.

Contemporary TV satire has been a reaction against the role that the traditional news and entertainment media have played as accomplices of antidemocratic forces, power elites, and the discriminatory discourse, while at the same time satire has become a barometer of the limits of dissent within a particular national media culture and its commercial systems. This particular spaceof satire highlights its metadiscursive nature, which is at the core of the concept that I suggest to describe the satiric audiovisual trend in the region: critical metatainment, a postmodern, carnivalesque result of and a transgressive, self-referential reaction to the process of tabloidization and the cult of celebrity in the media spectacle era. Satiric media as critical metatainment are multilayered and complex discursive objects that use humor to develop a sociocultural or political critique, while at the same time questioning the role of media in society and deconstructing news and entertainment genres through parody in order to challenge their claims of authority and/or moral consistency.

As the cases in this book show, the national sociopolitical and media contexts are essential to understand the dimensions of satire in the Americas. The satiric programs analyzed here are not only products of their national contexts, they are reactions to them. In the same way that the recent U.S. satiric infotainment trend (Stewart, Colbert, and, later, Oliver) developed as a reaction to the Bush administration, the invasion of Iraq in the aftermath of 9/11, and the "Foxification" of news, the role that Bayly played in Peruvian politics can only be understood in connection with how Fujimori's authoritarian government co-opted and corrupted the media during the 1990s and stimulated the growth of tabloid and celebrity culture. In Mexico, Brozo represented the opening of the country's media after 71 years of the PRI's government and its symbiotic relation with the media monopolies. Years later, *El Pulso de la República* also became a reaction to the role that Televisa played in the return of the PRI to power through the controversial election of Enrique Peña Nieto. Capusotto's satire primarily criticizes the historic role that media spectacle has played in framing power, culture, and dissent, and particularly in mediating the neoliberal mentality installed during Menem's governments in the 1990s, which led to the collapse of Argentina's economy in 2001. In the midst of the subsequent ideological polarization of Argentinean society during the Kirchner era, Capussotto's satire highlighted (and even prefigured) the right-wing turn that the society was experiencing, while Malena Pichot evidenced the sociopolitical implications of sexism as part of this conservative and discriminatory discourse. In Ecuador, *Enchufe.tv* developed progressive, sociocultural critiques within the limits imposed by Correa's policing of the media and his attempts to limit freedom of expression by repeatedly targeting satire and online dissent.

As part of the dialogue that satire as critical metatainment establishes with the TV journalism and popular entertainment genres, it subversively adapts or parodies their languages and formats in order to question their reactionary politics and negative effects on society. Satire deconstructs the media's claims of authority, exposes their limitations and contradictions, and suggests new forms to communicate about relevant political and sociocultural issues. As a consequence, satiric programs tend to have an ambivalent relationship with national TV and/or the oligarchic media conglomerates of which they are a part. Bayly, for example, several times threatened on air to quit if the TV station interfered with the contents of his show and viciously attacked the owner of the station. Before going to Televisa, Brozo publicly criticized the role that the media conglomerate played in the country and, after becoming a Televisa personality, was pushed repeatedly to clarify that he was not censored on Foro TV. On the other hand, Chumel Torres has rejected Televisa's attempts at co-optation and clearly stated that the media giant "is the enemy." In Argentina, Capusotto's satire existed within the parameters of the public national TV station, being accused both of being a Kirchner partisan and also of ridiculing the peronista legacy. Regarding the pressures within the public TV station, Capusotto's producer, Pedro Saborido, stated that he preferred the various restrictions on public media to the ratings demands of commercial TV. Malena Pichot's case is similar. While participating in certain progressive media outlets, Pichot has repeatedly rejected offers to work in commercial media projects because they do not align with her feminist discourse and has insistently accused the media of being an essential factor in the reproduction of sexist values in the country. In Ecuador, *Enchufe. tv*'s producers developed their project with the intention of renovating the conservative audiovisual culture of the country. While they have broadcast their content on national TV, reaching new audiences, their critical vision of Ecuadorian TV's restrictions prevails, and that's one of the reasons why they maintain the Web as their main platform. All these critical perspectives and satiric attacks on national media culture are possible because of these shows' main leverage: They are all successful (in commercial terms, influence, and/or audience reach). This is also what allows them to negotiate their space for dissent and transgression within the media culture that they criticize and that they are also, paradoxically, part of. The satirists' relation with celebrity culture is similar: They use their own celebrity to navigate the media world and get attention for their satire while also tending to attack and dismiss the values of the celebrity world. Partly due to this critical self-reflective condition, satire is able to position itself morally above the commercial media spectacle and the vacuous celebrity- and entertainment-driven culture that they criticize.

Another essential layer of the complexity of today's satire is the critical dialogue that it establishes with prevalent sociocultural and political tensions in its country. The satiric shows target issues such as inequality, social injustice, corruption, homophobia, racism, sexism, or violence against vulnerable populations, among others that generate social tension. Bayly combated homophobia in one of the most homophobic countries of the region; Pichot attacked the different ways in which sexism is carried out in Argentina, a country with high rates of violence against women and the center of the regional social movement #NiUnaMenos; Capusotto tackled the ideological polarization during the Kirchner era and the right-wing turn in Argentinean society that led to the election of conservative President Macri; Brozo took the side of the common citizen against the dishonest and inefficient Mexican political elites in a country with a history of institutionalized corruption and violence; and *Enchufe.tv* targeted the conservatism in Ecuadorian society, where even the president called gay marriage a "barbarism." As can be seen, the satiric cases analyzed in this book critically and creatively reframed and attacked social vices with a liberal, progressive approach, making their points accessible and appealing through humor, therefore fulfilling an informative and/or analytical role. Nevertheless, it is also interesting to note not only the social vices that satire criticizes but also the ones that it reproduces. For example, Bayly took a progressive stand about issues such as same-sex marriage, legalization of marijuana, and abortion but was conservative about the economic model of the country, and his discourse reproduced class and race prejudices in Peru. In Mexico, Brozo targeted the powerful political elites and criticized social injustice, but his performance also reproduced the prevalent sexist culture in the media. In relation to this last point, gender in Latin American satire remains a problematic issue. It is not only a male-dominated environment, in which male comedians host most of the satiric shows (except in the case of Malena Pichot, whose comedy actually focuses on gender issues from a feminist perspective); satire also still struggles to leave behind traditional gender roles or overacted political correctness. At the same time, satire reproduces social and geocultural privileges. In societies that have historically marginalized their indigenous and rural people, most of the satirists analyzed here are middle class, urban personalities based in the capital cities, evidencing the centralization of mass culture in Latin American countries.

In spite of its own biases, satire remains a subversive form that pushes the limits of what can be criticized in the public discourse while at the same time revealing the parameters of transgression and dissent. In a similar way that the performance of the news media and journalism has traditionally been an indicator of the level of freedom of the press and the state of democracy in a country, sociopolitical satire serves also as a marker of these issues in Latin American societies. For example, Brozo and *El Pulso de la República* became symbols of iconoclastic resistance against the political power elites in Mexico, but they were unable to elaborate on their concerns about the drug trafficking cartels, highlighting the fear that communicators and civil society in general have about these criminal groups' violence. Similarly, *Enchufe.tv* criticized social issues in Ecuadorian society but never crossed the limits established by Correa's media policing. In Peru, Bayly has been a pioneer in introducing LGBT issues on national TV since the 1990s but wasn't able to overcome the pressures of the TV station where he worked when he intended to become a legitimate presidential candidate. A particular type of case is when the satire's subversiveness aligns with the TV station's interests (for example, some have interpreted Brozo's satiric attacks against the government, from his show on Televisa, as a tool that the media giant uses [or tolerates] as a response to electoral legislation approved by the government related to advertising that reduces its profits). Nevertheless, the limits of dissent are not only established by the government's censorship, criminal groups' violence, or the media companies' policing and conflicting interests; the boundaries are also established by the commercial pressures experienced by the producers of satire and their ambitions to reach wider audiences. It's important to highlight, then, satire's condition as a site of negotiated dissent. The satiric cases negotiate their transgression within the framework of national TV media conglomerates owned by oligarchic families or transnational corporations and the sociopolitical and commercial pressures applied on them. In the case of online satire, the commercial demands to reach broader audiences tend to place some boundaries on their humor in order to refrain from alienating their audiences. Even this book is testimony to this point—by focusing only on the most resonant or "successful" cases of satire in different countries, other forms of satire that don't transcend social or geographical boundaries are sidelined, probably due to their cultlike or overly transgressive nature. In this sense, this silence also speaks volumes in terms of what could be said and what remains as an inaudible whisper in the countercultural satiric sphere.

As part of this negotiated dissent, satire also engages in discursive struggles about "truth" and moral authority. In this sense, it is not only a unique type of media text that negotiates the limits of transgression within the prevalent national media culture and sociopolitical environments, but is also a discourse that seeks constant legitimization. While modern news, for example, became a unique media form that based its authority in being an "accurate" or "objective" reflection of reality, satire has arisen as a distinctive media form that purports to be a carnivalesque mirror that illuminates or evidences certain hidden, unspoken, and socially uncomfortable aspects of reality and calls out the status quo's "bullshit." In this sense, both cultural constructs have claims of "truth" and embody a constant struggle for power, meaning, and representation. Nevertheless, satire as critical metatainment deconstructs and parodies media formats of news and entertainment, exhibiting their artificiality and questioning their claims of "truth," and as a consequence, validating its own authority. In other words, satire exposes the artificiality of other media discourses in order to legitimize its own artificiality as, at least, more honest. Similar to U.S. satiric infotainment, Latin American news satirists, for example, reject being labeled as journalists and refuse to accept any official affiliation with political or activist groups, projecting an image of independence and transparency and protecting themselves against legal or professional repercussions. Another common trait is, as evident in many interviews with satirists in the media, to avoid taking themselves too seriously by resorting to self-deprecation or self-mockery. From this ambivalent space, they reflect on their country's media practices, develop sociopolitical critique, and construct their authority in public discourse.

At another level, satire as critical metainment is a product of cultural globalization. As suggested by Baym and Jones (2013), the story of political satire is also a story of global programming flows. As they note about news parody, the power of the genre lies in its portability and ability to cross national, cultural, and linguistic boundaries: "In each instance of global format transfer, the original is reinterpreted within older national-cultural artistic and performative traditions" (Baym & Jones, 2013, p. 7). In Latin America, satire's hybrid nature connects with the *mestizo* condition of these societies. The satiric cases analyzed here are glocal products that combine local popular cultures, national media history, and regional referents with international satiric infotainment and global entertainment formats. Bayly adapted the late-night show tradition in the early 1990s—especially David Letterman's show—but has frequently mentioned local TV personalities as his main influences. Brozo adopted the news parody format but built upon the Mexican tradition of the *teatro de carpas* and the figure of the *pelado* as a marginal underdog able to mock power. Chumel Torres copies the latest U.S. news parody satirists (Stewart, Colbert, and Oliver) but infuses his parody with his version of Mexican-ness with local slang and a combination of references to global and national popular culture. Malena Pichot frequently cites the U.S. comedy and stand-up traditions as her main comedy influences (from Seinfield to Louis C.K. and Amy Schumer), while *Enchufe. tv* might be the clearest example of an attempt to use "Hollywood at the service of Ecuadorian idiosyncrasies." As can be noted, while satiric shows that broadcast on national television rely more heavily on national popular culture and local context, online TV shows are more clearly influenced by international comedy, especially from the United States.

As a cultural product of postcolonial societies, Latin American satire exists within cosmopolitan anxieties that accommodate and condense different cultures existing within and beyond national borders, including a dominant U.S. cultural influence. It is within this tension that Latin American satire negotiates its local, regional, and global identity. In this sense, it follows hybridity as the cultural logic that legitimizes globalization (Kraidy, 2005)[1] but also becomes a particular type of syncretic popular culture that both adopts and resists dominant culture with a subversive objective.

As part of this tension between the local and the global, it is also interesting to observe how satirists negotiate regional celebrity. Bayly, for example, has hosted shows not only in Peru but also in other Latin American countries and in the United States, and his literary work and media scandals have made him famous in Spain. He is definitely the biggest regional TV celebrity of all the satirists analyzed here. Contrastingly, Victor Trujillo or Capusotto are less known outside their countries. This might be because Bayly has adapted his discourse and language to conform to more international audiences and aligned with the Latin American Right from his show in Miami, where, for example, he mocks leftist leaders of the region, capitalizing on the antisocialist sentiment of powerful Cuban exiles in the United States. On the other hand, Trujillo and Capusotto kept focusing on their national realities and connecting primarily with local, progressive audiences. The coverage of these satirists on prestigious international/global media outlets—such as *The Guardian*, *The New York Times*, and *El País*—also becomes a factor in positioning them in the global scope and in legitimizing their domestic influence, one that is exerted in a variety of platforms. As part of today's multimedia world, the satirists not only create content for their TV shows but also tend to write for print media, have other radio or TV shows, or deliver live presentations, with most of this content available online.

While the TV shows analyzed here are representative of the Latin American trend toward satiric metatainment in sociopolitical communication, they are not by any means the only ones. While writing this book, I learned about another influential case in Chile. The satiric character Yerko Puchento is a flamboyant celebrity pundit who humorously analyzes and

1. "Hybridity entails that traces of other cultures exist in every culture, thus offering foreign media and marketers transcultural wedges for forging affective links between their commodities and local communities" (Kraidy, 2005).

rants about sociopolitical issues in the country. Wearing flashy outfits and using his own exaggerated idiolect, Yerko has a popular segment on Vertigo, a national celebrity contest TV show on Canal 13 (Channel 13), in which he develops lengthy humorous routines based on the news agenda, mocking politicians, celebrities, and powerful Chilean and foreign personalities. For example, in a segment posted online on April 7, 2016, Yerko's 43-minute routine criticized corruption in Chilean politics (from the Right and the Left), scorned Bolivian president Evo Morales, and ridiculed different social elites ranging from celebrities to the business class.[2] The introduction of this segment featured a recurrent element of Yerko's routines: He irreverently addressed the TV executives of his own station, saying that neither they nor any other powerful figure would be able to silence or censor him. Similarly, in a controversial skit, he parodied Andrónico Luksic, the powerful owner of Canal 13, generating national controversy and extended media coverage. Yerko's provocations also include other powerful sectors of Chile, such as the military. In a segment posted online on May 6, 2016, Yerko performed his routine dressed in a military uniform and satirically explained corruption scandals within the armed services, constantly referring to Chile's dictatorship past and its repressive practices.[3]

Created by actor Daniel Alcaíno and scriptwriter Jorge López, Yerko Puchento debuted on Chilean television in 2001, 12 years after the restoration of democracy in the country and 3 years after former dictator Augusto Pinochet was arrested in London in 1998 for crimes against humanity. Yerko also appeared at a moment when satire was playing an essential role in Chilean political communication through the rise of *The Clinic*, a satiric magazine that began as a pamphlet and in a few years became one of the country's most influential media outlets (Alonso, 2005). A self-declared leftist of Mapuche descent who openly votes for the communist party, Alcaíno has sustained a vocal discourse about inequality and the fascist aspects of Chilean society inherited from the dictatorship (Sharpe, 2004). For him, Pinochet's dictatorship persists through the national economic model and an unjust social system (Retamal Muñoz, 2013). In public appearances and interviews out of character, Alcaíno has also maintained a critical and provocative political discourse; he has mentioned, for example, that he supports the controversial idea of giving Bolivia access to the ocean, recognizing the Mapuche Nation, approving adoption rights for gay couples, and legalizing marijuana, among others ("Daniel Alcaíno

2. https://www.youtube.com/watch?v=cyG2Ofpqb7Y
3. https://www.youtube.com/watch?v=SVvwgiVO_mw

se saca el disfraz de 'Yerko Puchento' e incendia la pradera con quemante entrevista," 2016).

According to the creators of the character, Yerko's role is to remind the country about its past and connect it with the current sociopolitical tensions, and to expose the moral double standards of the political elites (Bisama, 2016). In fact, Yerko mocks and attacks political leaders from different ideological strands, addressing them by name directly on camera and calling them out through ridicule. While his routines have become very popular and influential in Chilean political communication, generating debate and frequently making national headlines, Alcaíno rejects accountability as a political analyst, journalist, or activist by saying that he is "only an actor, a simple clown" (Retamal Muñoz, 2013). As can easily be seen, the case of Yerko Puchento shares many similarities with the other satiric cases analyzed here, reinforcing the notion of critical metatainment suggested in this book. Through his parody of a media celebrity pundit, Yerko mocks the banality of media spectacle's discourse. He infuses the emptiness of celebrity culture with a subversive political voice broadcast in a commercially successful entertainment show on one of the country's main TV stations. His commercial success allows him to satirically criticize power, reframe the news agenda, and target media culture at large. In contrast to the traditional media and the conflicting interests that they respond to, Yerko says what otherwise could not be said, voicing the people's concerns about their elites and Chilean sociopolitical tensions. Yerko's transgressive role in the public discourse is augmented by the critical and politically committed voices of his locally famous creators outside the comedy box.

As part of an ancient philosophical tradition that seeks to question hegemonic discourses and illuminate some sort of "truth" through humor, satire as critical metatainment in the Americas ranges on a dynamic spectrum between the cynical and the kynical. As noted in the introduction of this book, while cynicism is a nihilistic form that questions and doubts that which it finds hypocritical or untrustworthy and sees no hope for change (Chaloupka, 1999), kynicism is a subversive form that also questions and doubts but maintains that there is a better way of doing things, serving a morally regulatory purpose (Sloterdijk, 1988). In contrast to the cynical nihilistic claim that the only truth is that all claims to truth are distorted, kynicism assumes "a basically serious and upright posture towards truth and maintains a thoroughly solemn relation, satirically disguised, to it" (Sloterdijk, 1988, p. 296). However, kynical morality "is not about what is right or wrong, but rather what is true, and frequently the moral struggle towards the truth involves challenging another morality" (Higgie, 2014). In this sense, kynical morality connects with contemporary satire's critical approach toward traditional news media and entertainment as well as the moral implications of their relation to power and their representations of "truth." However, this commitment should not be confused with idealistic hope. Connecting with kynic tradition, contemporary satirists tend to maintain that there are better ways of doing things but do not offer advice about how this might be attained. Instead of providing hope, solutions to sociopolitical problems, or a moral code, they struggle to establish their version of truth.

While the contemporary satirists analyzed in this book can be considered modern-day kynics, there is probably no satire that is purely kynical or cynical (Higgie, 2014). In this sense, contemporary satire as a predominantly hybrid form encompasses the cultural contradictions of our time: "it is postmodern in its irony, self-awareness, and suspicion of grand narratives, yet simultaneously exhibiting an ethical impulse that is ultimately modern" (Higgie, 2014, p. 192). Within this condition, today's satire tends to stand against, rather than for, something. In the case of the Americas, satiric TV tends to stand, principally, against the media and its practices as the central target from which to expand to other sociopolitical and cultural issues. Nevertheless, it is important to note that the characteristics of contemporary satire also call attention to the rise of modern cynics in power and their attempts to adopt satiric discourse. Modern cynics know we exist in a world of empty constructions, but instead of subverting and exposing them or simply mocking them, they benefit from playing within these constructs (Higgie, 2014). Neopopulists from the Left (e.g., Chávez) or the Right (e.g., Trump) have used modern cynicism to advance their political agendas through the construction of powerful, dangerous, and often hilarious media personalities. The co-option of cynical satiric discourse by these types of political and media celebrities with concrete participation in democratic institutions might also be a symptom of satire's need to move further outside of the comedy box in order to exercise its ancient role of speaking truth to power. In this sense, the future of the genre, as some cases in this book suggest, might be in satiric activism or more concrete interventions in reality.

Nevertheless, a question remains: How are the multicultural audiences in Latin American societies really interpreting today's satire? A limitation of this book is the lack of audience research about the region. While this study analyzed representative satiric shows in terms of their content, their production conditions and sociopolitical contexts, their critical intentions, and their influence on public debate, there is a lack of knowledge about how these programs are received by their audiences. Are diverse social groups similarly reading these satiric shows? How do the different social classes, ethnic groups, genders, and regional populations perceive characters like Bayly, Brozo, and Capusotto? What's the difference between how *Enchufe.tv, Cualca*, and *El Pulso de la República* are perceived in their own countries in contrast to their reception abroad? Can we talk about levels of satiric literacy? How would that be defined? These are important questions for further research on audiences in order to fill a gap not only in the area of sociopolitical communication, but also in Latin American media studies in general.

In spite of this gap, this book has not only been able to map satiric TV in the region but also to suggest some of its main challenges for the near future. While TV remains the most popular mass medium in Latin America, the diversity of experimental online entertainment media suggests that new paths for the most provocative TV satire will be digital, at least in their initial stages. As Chumel Torres had to negotiate the reframing of his satiric product on HBO after rejecting offers from Televisa and Malena Pichot also had to navigate the waters of Argentinean commercial TV, the subversive capacity of new independent satire seems to lie in its ability to maintain independence by resisting attempts at co-optation or to uphold its transgression and broaden its influence when transitioning to national TV or regional platforms.

Finally, it is important to highlight again that the political context and changing sociocultural tensions remain essential in the development and evolution of the genre. After the election of Donald Trump as president of the United States, the role of satire in political communication will probably adjust to deal with new realities and social conflicts. Just a week after the election, the reappearance of comedian Dave Chapelle as a host of *SNL* addressing racial issues or Jon Oliver's "serious" call to support traditional journalism media outlets and to be aware of potential limitations to freedom of expression in the Trump era are symptomatic of the years to come. When reality resembles more than ever a global absurdist spectacle hosted by a reality TV celebrity who seems to be mocking the system, critical metatainment might need to rethink its position to fulfill satire's ancient function. As Diogenes of Sinope, the founding father of kynical satire, once did in the public spaces of Athens, it might be time for satirists to more outrageously defecate and masturbate in front of today's audiences in order to bring about uncivil enlightenment.

REFERENCES

Alonso, P. (2005). *The Clinic*: La nueva prensa satírica de Chile. *Chasqui: Revista Latinoamericana de Comunicación, 92*, 26–31.

Baym, G., & Jones, J. (Eds.). (2013). *News parody and political satire across the globe*. New York, NY: Routledge.

Bisama, Á. (2016, July 28). Daniel Alcaíno y Jorge López: "Es el mejor momento de la historia para hacer lo que nos ha tocado hacer." *La Tercera*. Retrieved from http://www.latercera.com/noticia/daniel-alcaino-y-jorge-lopez-es-el-mejor-momento-de-la-historia-para-hacer-lo-que-nos-ha-tocado-hacer/

Chaloupka, W. (1999). *Everybody knows: Cynicism in America*. Minneapolis, MN: University of Minneapolis Press.

Daniel Alcaíno se saca el disfraz de "Yerko Puchento" e incendia la pradera con quemante entrevista. (2016, April 21). *The Clinic*. Retrieved from http://www.theclinic.cl/2016/04/21/531424/

Higgie, R. (2014). Kynical dogs and cynical masters: Contemporary satire, politics, and truth-telling. *Humor: International Journal of Humor Research*, 27(2), 183–201.

Kraidy, M. (2005). *Hybridity or the cultural logic of globalization*. Philadelphia, PA: Temple University Press.

Retamal Muñoz, L. (2013, March 28). Daniel Alcaíno: "El poder todavía está en el pueblo." *El Ciudadano*. Retrieved from http://www.elciudadano.cl/2013/03/28/65087/daniel-alcaino-el-poder-todavia-esta-en-el-pueblo/

Sharpe, J. (2004, June 20). "Todos somos maricones." *La Nación*. Retrieved from http://www.lanacion.cl/todos-somos-maricones/noticias/2004-06-19/184906.html

Sloterdijk, P. (1988). *Critique of cynical reason* (M. Eldred, Trans.). London, U.K.: Verso.

INDEX

Carlson, Tucker, 27–28
carnivalesque culture
    Bakhtin's conceptualizations of, 13
    of Brozo and *El Mañanero*, 16, 76–77,
        84–87, 92–93
    of *The Colbert Report*, 34
    critical metatainment and, 10–15
    definition and characteristics of,
        13–14
    of *Enchufe.tv*, 129–131
    in parody of *El Chavo del Ocho*, 134
    of *Peter Capusotto y sus videos*, 99,
        101–102, 105
    potential lack of political importance
        of, 14
Carr, David, 32
CC Studios, 44
celebrity culture
    contemporary society's obsession
        with, 2
    critical metatainment as reaction
        to, 151
    definition and characteristics of
        celebrities, 6–7
    and identity, 6–8
    Jaime Bayly as participant in, 65–67
    in Menem's Argentina, 100–102
    political involvement of celebrities, 1–2
    of politicians, 1–2
    ridiculed by Diego Capusotto, 16
    tabloid media's criticism of, 14
Centeno, Andrés, 127
ChaChaCha (Argentinean comedy show),
    6, 104
Chapelle, Dave, 160
Charlie Hebdo attacks, 1
Chávez, Hugo, 5, 125–127
Chespirito, 132, 134
"Chicas inseguras," 142
chicha, 53, 72–73
Chile, Yerko Puchento character,
    156–158
cholo, 56, 72–73
*Citizens United v. Federal Election
    Commission* (FEC) 2010 ruling, 32–33
civic disengagement, 2, 24, 31–32
Clinic, The (satiric magazine), 157
Clinton administration, 28
Clinton, Hillary, 45
CNN (Cable News Network), 27, 30, 41

Colbert Report, The (TCR)
    criticisms of, 36
    impact of satiric TV on U.S. political
        communication, 22–45
    influence on Chumel Torres, 134
    vs. *Last Week Tonight With John Oliver*,
        15, 23, 39–40
    news reporting function of, 3
    political influence of, 11
    satiric activism as a reaction to
        spectacle's truthiness, 32–36
    satirization of right-wing pundits
        by, 24
    as source of news, 24
    success of, 22–25
    as tool for education, 33
Colbert, Steven
    appearance at 2006 White House
        Correspondents' Dinner, 27
    concept of truthiness introduced by,
        34–36
    focus of, 43
    goals of fictional character, 33–34
    as host of *The Tonight Show*, 36
    influence of, 1
    influence on Chumel Torres, 134–135
    as modernist, 35
    news parody format adopted by, 155
    as reaction to the Bush
        administration, 151
    satirization of Bill O'Reilly by, 24, 34–35
    success of, 22–25
    super PAC organized by, 24, 32–33, 43
    testifies on behalf of migrant farm
        workers, 33
    work on *The Daily Show With Jon
        Stewart*, 23, 28
Colleta, L., 31
Combe, K., 35, 36
Comedy Central
    effect of multiplatform
        communication on, 44–45
    political humor and satire branding
        of, 26
conservatism
    in Ecuadorian society, 153
    satirized by Malena Pichot, 142
convergence culture, 11
Conway, M., 29, 34–35
Cordera, Gustavo, 143–144

media spectacle
    Bombita Rodríguez and, 111–112
    culture of narcissism and, 7
    family-oriented rock, Peronism, and,
        104–110
    and global infotainment, 4–6
    negotiation of political power
        through, 16, 52
    relation to tabloidization, 8–11
    role in postmodern culture, 7–8
    use of by Fujimori government,
        54–55
    See also spectacle
Menem government
    neoliberal mentality of, 151
    satiric media under, 97
    society of spectacle and celebrity
        culture in, 100–102
    use of spectacle and infotainment, 5
    voter betrayal by, 100
mestizaje, 10, 53n3, 72–73
mestizo condition, 55, 132, 155
Mexico
    challenges to freedom of expression
        in, 136
    corruption and media concentration
        in, 77–79
    influence of satiric TV in, 2–3
    opening of county's media post-PRI
        government, 151
    tradition of clowns and satiric
        underdogs, 16
    violence against journalists in, 16,
        77–79
    *See also El Mañanero; El Pulso de la
        República*
Micky Vainilla (Argentinean TV
        character)
    pop, fascism, and *porteño* citizens,
        114–118
    role of in Argentinean society,
        118–119
    satiric approach of, 16, 98
Moglia, M., 102–104, 113
Monos y Monadas (Peruvian magazine),
        53–54
Moore, Michael, 44
Morgan, Piers, 41
Morris, J., 31, 36
Moya, Christian, 123

Moyers, Bill, 30
multiplatform communication, effect on
        TV viewing trends, 44
Muraca, M., 117

negotiated dissent
    role of postmodern satire in, 3
    satire as site of, 154
neoliberalism
    effect on Latin America, 77
    in Menem's Argentina, 100–101
    relation to neopopulism and mass
        media, 53, 101
    role of tabloidization and
        infotainment in, 9
neo-modern journalism, 11, 35–36
neopopulism
    El Francotirador (Peruvian TV show)
        and, 71
    relation to neoliberalism and mass
        media, 53, 101
net neutrality, 22–23, 38–39
Nightly Show With Larry Wilmore, The
        (U.S. TV show), 44
Noah, Trevor, 44
Nolan, Christopher, 132–134
Not Necessarily the News (U.S. TV show),
        26
Not the Nine O'Clock News (English TV
        show), 26
NOW with Bill Moyers (U.S. TV show), 30
Nugent, J. G., 56
Nussbaum, E., 44

Obama, Barack, 41–42, 45
Oliver, John
    apology for election of Donald
        Trump, 43
    beginning of, 6
    call to action on internet neutrality,
        22–23
    call to support traditional journalism
        outlets, 160
    coverage of intricate topics, 39
    as driving force behind *Last Week
        Tonight*, 39, 42
    exposes corruption in FIFA, 36–39
    focus of, 43
    vs. Jon Stewart, 40–42
    news reporting function by, 2–3

uncivil enlightenment, sought by
    Diogenes of Sinoe, 12, 160
United States
    diminishing credibility of press in, 2
    Donald Trump, 5
    influence of satiric TV in, 2–3, 22–45
    Project for Excellence in Journalism
        1997 study, 6
    satiric media influencers in, 1
    self-referential tradition of satire in
        U.S. television, 25–27
Utero.pe (Peruvian news portal), 73

Vargas Llosa, Mario, 59, 77
Vásquez Mota, Josefina, 87
Viacom, 44
Violencia Rivas (Argentinean TV
    character)
    punk, satire, and gender, 112–114
    role of in Argentinean society,
        118–119
    satiric approach of, 16, 98

war against drugs, 78
Warner, Jack, 38

Web-based programming. *see* digital
    satire; online media
"Weekend Update" segment, 26, 134
Weiner, J., 44
Wheeler, Tom, 23
WikiLeaks, 125
Williams, B. A., 9
Winstead, Lizz, 25
World Cup Soccer, 36–39

xenophobia, satirized by *Enchufe.tv*,
    129–130

Yerko Puchento (Chilean satiric
    character), 156–158
Yerovi, Leonidas, 53n4
YoSoy132, 79
Young, Dannagal, 39
YouTube
    as chosen platform for *El Pulso de la
        República*, 138–139
    search for more, all chapters
    videos by Malena Pichot, 140–141

Žižek, S., 5